Message in a Matchbox

Memories of a Childhood in Tehran

Sara Fashandi

Message in a Matchbox: Memories of a Childhood in Tehran
By Sara Fashandi

Published by: Nicasio Press,
                 Sebastopol, California
                 www.nicasiopress.com
Cover Art: Samira Sarif
                 samira.sharif.1369@gmail.com

ISBN: 978-1-7375814-6-8
Printed in the U.S.A.

در کلبه ما رونق اگر نیست صفا هست

انجا که صفا هست در ان نور خدا هست

DEDICATION

I am dedicating this book to Momman —
the rock of our family!
1930–2018

TABLE OF CONTENTS

PROLOGUE

I began to speak with my brother. "Mohsen, you're up too," I half-whispered as I sat next to him. He turned to look at me. The surprise on his face turned into a smile, and he nodded. The whisper of my voice echoing in the large kitchen yanked him out of his memories. I pointed to the paper that was receiving an immensely satisfied look from my brother. "Was this really a true story or did you make it up?" I asked.

He smiled, and the proud look on his face suggested he was flattered. I thought the entertaining childhood story he'd written was either exaggerated or made up completely.

"It was true, all of it. Nobody believes the things I did during my childhood!" he responded.

I raised my eyebrows. "Like what?"

Before he answered, he put his glasses down, leaned back in his chair, and stretched his legs under the table; then he folded his arms behind his head. It was a gesture of his that I was familiar with.

"When I was growing up, our lives—Etty's, Motty's, and mine—were different from when you and the other siblings were born. We were extremely poor; had truly little to eat; and lived in a tiny room where we had to cook, eat, and sleep. I was always hungry, even after finishing a meal. Our portions were so small." He made a circle about the size of a softball with his hands to illustrate. "I was bored all the time too, since we couldn't afford to buy any toys or books to keep us entertained the way our own kids are now with all these computer and video games." He paused for a moment, as if remembering something interesting. "We had no libraries in our neighborhood. I was dying to know about the news."

He went on. "There was a guy who used to stand at the corner of Khosh Street, a block away from our father's shop, with a copy of *Etelaat*, one of the most popular newspapers back then. He opened it in front of his face. I would position myself behind the paper, out of his sight, and read the front page while he read the inside. One day, he lowered the newspaper as he turned the page, and our eyes met. He jumped, scared. He didn't expect to see a human being standing right behind his paper!"

Mohsen and I laughed at full volume, briefly forgetting about the rest of the sleeping household. We tried to muffle our laughter, with only minimal success. "Poor guy," I said, still giggling.

"Poor guy?! Poor me! The guy never showed up again! I got mad because I couldn't read the news, and I lost my only source of information!"

After wiping away tears of laughter and catching my breath, I stared intently at my brother. "Mohsen, what got you to become so creative, so innovative?"

He only had to think about his answer for a split second. "I had no choice," he said matter-of-factly. "While I was growing up, I was always looking for ways to make money to buy junk food to fill my hungry stomach or gadgets to entertain my curious mind."

"But when you talk about those days, you always have such a cheerful look. You seem to have enjoyed your life back then even though you didn't have much."

"You know, when I think of my childhood, I wonder how I survived it all—no clean drinking water; not enough food to eat; dirty, cracked hands; shabby, torn clothes; and shoes with holes in the wintertime . . ." He stopped for a minute, his voice cracked, and his eyes filled with tears.

Is my brother going to cry? I wondered as my heart began to race. I couldn't even remember the last time I had seen my older brother cry. In fact, I was certain I had ever seen him cry.

"I wouldn't have done it any other way. I cherish my childhood memories—the painful experiences and the fun ones. They made me who I am today."

Something inside me stirred, and I wanted to know more about my brother and his childhood memories. I brewed some fresh coffee. Its rejuvenating and pleasant aroma filled the kitchen. I poured two cups and grabbed a notepad and a pencil. I put a cup of coffee in front of him. "Okay, Mohsen, tell me your stories, and I'll write them."

Later, I realized these stories—his memories and experiences—which I am positive are constantly rattling around in Mohsen's brain, really did make him the interesting, jovial, yet hardworking man I know. By the time he was fourteen, he had been through so much and lived a fuller life than most people can recount on their deathbeds.

Now, when our family gets together and washes the dishes after an abundant Persian meal, I sometimes notice Mohsen pause, if only for a second, dishtowel still in hand, with a half-smile on his face and a slight vacancy behind his eyes. He has traveled the eight thousand miles due East and sixty years back in time to his childhood in Tehran.

The stories he told brought me closer to my brother, and simply by retelling this mix of short stories, I began to understand him little by little. More importantly, I began to learn from him. Gradually, through each of our "story times," the things I value most in life—and the type of person I most want to be—became clearer.

Abigail Van Buren, author of the famous advice column Dear Abby, once said that if we could sell our experiences for what they cost us, we would all be millionaires. Mohsen could have sold his for billions.

TASTE OF A RICH LIFE

AGE SIX

When your stomach is empty, you become more observant of your surroundings, you notice things you would not have normally, and you produce inventive ways to put some food in your body. I was only six years old when I first experienced the feeling of being rich—which for me, at that time, meant having a full stomach.

Our parents, Momman and Aghajoon, as we called them, were young. Momman was just twenty-four and Aghajoon was twenty-eight. By then, they already had three children, including two daughters: Etty was four; Motty was two; and I, the eldest, Mohsen, was six. We lived in a tiny room we rented from Ost Gholam Reza and his wife Belquees Khanoom, who lived upstairs. They had two daughters, Banu, who was the same age as me, and her sister, Zahra, who was Etty's age.

We did everything in that one tiny room—cooked, ate, and slept. In one corner, Momman stacked a couple of copper pots and pans on the floor, along with dry food, such as rice, beans, tea leaves, flour, and a cooking-oil tin can. Next to the cookware, we had a kerosene heater, which we used to warm up the place during the cold winter days as well as cook our food—mostly *abgoosht* (a type of savory stew).

When Momman cooked abgoosht, our tiny room filled with the pleasant aroma of sautéed onions, tomatoes, and meat. It was one of my favorite scents because it made me feel safe and certain that my tummy would not rumble with hunger that day.

At the other corner of our small abode were our bed rolls, pillows, and blankets. A small window overlooked the backyard. Momman had nailed a white square cotton cloth to cover it for privacy; it was from there that I used to see Ost Gholam Reza go to the bathroom, which was located in the corner of the backyard. When he was done with his business, he yelled, "Belquees Khanoom, fill up the *aftabeh*!" He was referring to a container with a spout and a handle, similar to a watering can. Sometimes, if his wife didn't hear him calling, he would call me instead: "Mohsen, Mohsen, fill the aftabeh and bring it here."

I'd immerse the aftabeh in the six-foot *hooz* (still pond) located in the middle of the backyard and fill it with water. I'd knock at the door, before cracking it open to see him squatting down on the hole in the ground. This is how Iranian bathrooms were designed at that time—a small room with a simple hole in the ground where one squatted, one foot on each side of the hole.

During the freezing wintertime, I had to break the ice from the surface of the water before filling the aftabeh. I remember thinking the icy water must really wake him up once it hits his bottom. I always thought Ost Gholam Reza seemed to be so proud of himself, walking with his chin up all the time. I think he felt superior to others, and that is why he thought it was beyond him to fill a device to wash his private parts when he wanted to use the facility. My father would never have asked Momman or me to do this sort of thing for him.

The city hadn't brought electricity to the poorer areas, such as ours, so the entire neighborhood was pitch black in the wintertime by five or six in the evening. The only light was a lantern placed in the middle of our room.

At night, my two little sisters slept next to me on the floor—one on my right and the other on my left. We shared a blanket and two pillows. Aghajoon and Momman were in another corner of the room, snoring. Sometimes I would wake up in the middle of the night and Momman would not be next to him. I would look around, wondering where she was, and find her in a corner, dimly lit by our lantern, her neck bent, her eyes focused, stitching away. She would insert a needle into a piece of fabric and pull it through to the other end. She had to stitch the fabric tightly enough that it would look as if it were sewn together by a machine.

This took more effort, and so she often worked into the late hours of the night.

Momman sewed clothing for our neighbors, to help Aghajoon with the expenses. It wasn't customary back then for women to work—they were mostly homemakers—but Momman was wise, and she realized that with Aghajoon's forty *tomans* a month, we wouldn't be able to do much in life. She had her own goals and dreams, and she was determined to make them realities.

Her customers were always satisfied with her work. Almost as soon as she finished one item, there would be someone lined up, holding a big piece of colorful, vibrant fabric, ready to place the next order.

Sometimes, as I watched my mother sew late at night, she would look up at me as if she could feel my gaze. With a loving sparkle in her eyes, she whispered, "Mohsen Jon, go back to sleep," as she gestured for me to put my head down.

I knew why she worked so hard. Some nights, I heard her whisper to Aghajoon, "Agha, we have three children, and this place is so small. We can't keep renting for the rest of our lives; it's a waste of our money, and we'll never be able to save anything for our kids' education."

My father's response was always the same: "I know, Khanoom, but how can we afford to buy? Houses are expensive, and we don't make enough money."

These conversations went on for some time, but I knew Momman would get her wish in the end. She wasn't the type of person to take a simple no for an answer.

In the early mornings, Momman was the first one up, despite having little sleep herself. She'd light the samovar to boil some water for tea, and within an hour or so, everyone woke up. Most of the time, I was responsible for getting the fresh bread from the *nanvaii* (bakery).

Before heading there, I washed my face outside by the hooz. Not having a toothbrush, I wetted my index finger to scrub my teeth, then took some water from the hooz and swished it from side to side in my mouth, before spitting. Sometimes I saw white worms wiggling in the water, but I would shrug and still rinse my mouth with it. It's not that I didn't mind them, because truthfully, I did. I mean, who would really want to gargle worm water? But back then, there was no city plumbing in our area, so to bring home drinking or cooking water, I had to take the *koozeh* (a clay vessel) and head to Lulagar Street. It was blocks from our place, and the city had installed a water faucet in a basement there, for public use. In the summertime, climbing down was easy, but in the winter, we had to be very careful not to slip and fall on the icy stairs. Sometimes, if there were older people ahead or in back of me, I helped them fill their containers. I didn't want them to get injured.

"*Khayr bebinii*" (God bless you), they said, while taking back their filled vessel from me. On certain days, the city distributed non-drinking water via a *joob* (trench). We used this water to wash our clothes, dishes, private parts, face, and mouth.

Every household had a ten-foot-deep reservoir in the corner of its backyard, connected by a wide pipe to a nearby joob. We never knew when the city was planning to open the main valve to fill the joobs that filled the reservoir via the pipe. Sometimes, late in the evenings, I woke up with the sound of neighbors outside and knew the water must have been turned on. A few of our greedier neighbors put a rock or sandbag in the stream to direct the water into their water pipe, causing the adjacent houses to receive less water. As you can imagine, that caused havoc. Fights often broke out; they punched or hit each other with wooden sticks, and blood flowed everywhere. Then, the following day, I saw the same people with bruised faces, missing teeth, or broken noses. Even as a six-year-old boy, I knew these were selfish acts, and I couldn't understand how or why adults could act like this. There was enough water for everyone if people would just be a little patient.

Some days, when I pumped the water out for washing, I smelled a foul odor and saw those small white worms wiggling around in it again. Momman didn't allow us to drink it, but sometimes, out of laziness, we did, because we didn't want to walk back into the room to get the drinking water stored in the koozeh. Whenever I suffered from stomach cramps, diarrhea, or other digestive problems due to the contaminated water, I wished I had listened to Momman because, as usual, she had been right.

At the nanvaii, very few people were usually in the line—just a couple of shop owners and some older women who had covered their bodies from head to toe with black *chadors* (a large piece of fabric). I watched, slightly mesmerized, as the baker pulled the naan out of the *tanoor* (a cylindrical open oven), amazed at how fast he worked. He stuck the round dough he had on a cushion onto the hot surface of the oven and then removed the steaming hot bread using a long stick.

I thought he must never feel cold, working next to the fire all the time. No wonder he only wore a thin undershirt and constantly wiped his sweaty face with a handkerchief hung from his back pants pocket. I held the hot bread with the corner of my sleeve to avoid getting burned, but still felt its warmth in my fingertips. Its pleasant aroma woke up my stomach, sometimes even making it growl.

By the time I returned to our house, Momman had spread the *sofreh* (a cloth) on the floor next to the samovar. Then she placed the feta cheese on a plate and the empty teacups on the saucers. I placed the bread in the middle of the sofreh. Everyone sat around it, eager to eat. Momman filled our teacups with freshly brewed tea and put two sugar cubes on the saucer. She then divided the cheese into four equal parts, for Aghajoon, Etty, me, and herself. She shared hers with Motty, who was sitting on her lap. Momman made small bites for Motty while eating her own breakfast. We filled our stomachs mostly with bread and sweet tea, since there was very little cheese to eat.

Aghajoon always left for work as soon as he finished his breakfast. He was a *kafash* (cobbler) and had rented a small place from Momman's maternal uncle, Hassan Agha. According to Momman, he was so handsome that people called him Hassan *ghashang* (beautiful). Unlike his outsides, however, he had an ugly inside, and the longer you knew him, the faster it showed. As soon as he realized Aghajoon had established a good rapport with his clients and his work had picked up, he doubled the rent. Of course, Aghajoon couldn't afford it.

I will never forget the day my father returned home as quickly as he had left that morning. Most of the time, he came home around noon for lunch, but not that day.

Momman was sewing a blue flowery skirt for one of her customers, while my sisters and I were playing in the corner of our small room. We only had one toy, a plastic rabbit one of Momman's customers had gifted us. We always included the rabbit in our imaginary adventures—it became a horse, a baby, a cat, or anything we desired, but oddly enough, never a rabbit. Occasionally, Momman would stop stitching, look up, listen to our conversation, and smile. Then she would sigh softly, before gazing down to continue her work. I think it made her happy to see her children having an enjoyable time, but perhaps she was also imagining along with us— imagining what she wanted for our lives and who we would become.

But on that dreadful day, we were all surprised to see Aghajoon come home so early. He had a frown on his face and looked very angry. It was common to see him get angry, but there was something different on that day. Even as a child, I could tell he was furious.

"Khanoom, your uncle raised my rent! I can't afford it, so I picked up my things and left the shop," he said, his voice angry. He had brought home all the items he used to repair and polish shoes.

Momman glanced at us, then whispered lovingly and serenely to him to calm down so we wouldn't get worried.

The next day, Aghajoon tried to reason with Momman's uncle, but that terrible man slapped my father's face and pulled his hair so hard that a handful came out! Aghajoon came home with a swollen red face, and part of his head was bald. We were shocked to see him like that. Etty started crying and held onto Momman's leg. Momman patted the top of Etty's head and kept saying, "Don't cry, don't cry. Nothing is wrong. Nothing is wrong." I stared, puzzled, at Aghajoon, trying to figure out what had happened.

With fire in his eyes, as well as a mixture of pain and frustration, he looked at my mother and said, "Your uncle told me to feed this to my kids." He opened his palm to show a handful of hair.

The sparkle in Momman's eyes dimmed as she quieted Aghajoon, saying, "Agha, we'll talk about it later. You are scaring the kids."

He looked at our concerned faces, forced a smile, and went outside to cool down.

That was part of Momman's beauty. She had a way of calming my father like no one else. That night, while Etty and Motty were sleeping, I overheard Momman and Aghajoon whisper to each other, and the name Hassan Agha came up many times. I lay in bed, doing my best to eavesdrop, while pretending to be asleep.

In the end, nobody could change Hassan's mind. He was a rich, heartless man. He didn't care that Aghajoon was married to his niece. All he cared about was adding to his wealth. To prove he didn't really need Hassan, my father worked under a tree near the old shop so his customers could see his new location and continue to bring him their shoes to be repaired or polished.

The day Aghajoon set up shop under the tree, Momman gave me a pitcher of water to take to him. The image of my father sitting on a flimsy wooden stool that wiggled every time he brushed the shoes in a side-to-side motion, with part of his head bald and his face bruised and swollen, will forever be in my memory. Despite the circumstances, he kept on working with his head held high, because the most important thing to him was to provide for his family.

That night, while we sat around the sofreh, Momman encouraged Aghajoon to keep working under the tree. She told him that something good would come out of all this eventually. She never stopped reassuring him. Momman was always optimistic and always goal oriented.

Luckily, it was summertime, so Aghajoon was able to continue working without a shop, using the shade of the large tree to keep himself cool. He wouldn't have been able to do that in the cold and snowy winter season or stormy, rainy fall or springtime. His work went on like this for weeks, until one day Ost Gholam Reza passed by Aghajoon's outside shop and inquired about it.

Aghajoon explained the entire story. After listening in disbelief at how cruel Hassan had been, Ost Gholam Reza patted Aghajoon's shoulder and told him that he would have a place for him shortly. We didn't know what to think of this. Ost Gholam Reza had never been so kind before, but he kept his promise. He found Aghajoon a place with very little rent on Khosh Street, which turned into his permanent place until he retired.

During the summer, to pass the time, I often went to my father's cobbler shop on Khosh Street. It was a small place, with one chair in the corner for customers to use while they waited to have their shoes repaired or polished. Aghajoon sat behind a counter, doing his work and conversing with his clients—going on about politics, the country's economy, and what the shah of Iran was doing to improve things. He was a cheerful man when talking to his customers, but with me, he was never very friendly. He frowned when he spoke to me; his black eyebrows furrowed together, and his black eyes narrowed. My father was always displeased with me somehow. I often found myself wishing I could be one of his customers, so that Aghajoon would speak to me too with kindness.

Inside the shop, he had a low counter, and behind it, a small stool where he sat to polish or repair people's shoes. There was a foot-operated shoe repair machine on his right, and on the floor next to his foot was a kerosene heater he used to warm up the place during the freezing winter seasons. Above the shoe repair machine was a small shelf where he kept a tiny battery-operated radio. In front of his shop was a sidewalk, and next to it was a joob with running water that ran for kilometers.

The first thing Aghajoon did every morning after opening his shop was fiddle with the radio knob to hear either the news or Iranian classical singers: Marzieh, Golpa, or Iraj. Meanwhile, I took Aghajoon's sharpening stone outside where the joob was. I knelt in front of the joob and picked up a handful of mud with my bare hand, scrubbed it on the sharpening stone to remove any grease or residue, then washed it in the running water in the joob. I carefully checked the stone at different angles to make sure it was clean before taking it inside to Aghajoon. If he wasn't satisfied with my work, he angrily told me I'd done a "crappy job" and ordered me to redo it. If I had cuts on my fingers, the mud would sting as if I had scraped it on a piece of hot coal. On chilly winter days, I had to break the ice with my bare hands and dip them in the icy water. I hated doing this job regardless of the season.

While Aghajoon worked, he often gave me things to do around his store. I would sweep, dust the counter, or hang the polished shoes on the high-up panels, using a long stick with a hook on its end. I enjoyed seeing rows of shiny, high-heeled, red, black, and white women's shoes; men's black and brown leather shoes; and children's shoes in all styles, colors, and sizes. Sometimes I even delivered them to his customers. The kinder ones gave me a tip, enough to buy a small piece of candy, which I often shared with Etty or with my best friend Ramazoon, who worked for Mamad Agha, the butcher next door.

I met Ramazoon for the first time that same summer. Aghajoon had asked me to watch his shop until he returned. This was the first time I'd been alone there. I walked toward the door, peering out to see Aghajoon's silhouette getting smaller and smaller in the distance. The smaller it became, the more nervous I got. I examined my surroundings. What would I do if a customer came in? What should I say to them? That was when I noticed a dark-skinned boy with short black hair and big sad brown eyes.

He was leaning against Mamad Agha's shop next door. I had never seen him there before. He looked to be about my age, but shorter and thinner, and his clothes were much dirtier—torn and patched with different colored fabrics at the knees, elbows, and several other places. He finally raised his eyes to meet mine.

"Is this your father's place?" He spoke Farsi with a funny accent. I had to listen very carefully to understand him. I thought he must be a *daahatii* (villager), because of how he spoke.

I nodded and asked, "What are you doing here? You work for him?" I gestured to Mamad Agha's shop.

"Yes, Agha."

I was astonished. He was talking to me as if I were an adult. "I'm Mohsen, not Agha." I chuckled. My lighthearted response made him smile.

"My name is Ramazoon," he informed me, with a newfound joy in his eyes.

I quickly discovered that Ramazoon was extraordinarily kind, possessing a generous heart, despite the extreme poverty in which he lived. Sometimes, when he received his wages from Mamad Agha, he bought a kabab sandwich. The grilled ground meat wrapped in fresh naan, topped with basil, tomatoes, and onions, was a rare and mouthwatering treat.

Ramazoon could have easily eaten the entire sandwich by himself, but instead he shared half of it with me.

One day, on a lunch break much like any other, we sat by my father's shop, in our torn shabby clothes, with our dirty cracked hands, biting into our delicious and succulent sandwich, and talked about our families and what we wanted to be when we grew up.

"Do you go to school, Ramazoon?" I asked.

"No, my father says education doesn't bring money, skills do. All of us work: my brother works for a carpenter making picture frames, and my sisters are maids at rich people's households." He pointed into the distance, as if to indicate that the rich people existed far away from this place.

I glanced at Ramazoon, surprised at his response. Not attending school was an option in my family. Momman always said education was necessary in order to be successful and live a better life. I knew that as soon as I was eligible to enroll in school, at seven years old, Aghajoon would sign me up in the first grade at a nearby elementary school.

I was intrigued by this new kind of lifestyle lived by Ramazoon and his family. I didn't want to argue with him or hurt his feelings. I just wanted to know more about him. "What does your father do for work?" I asked.

"He sells ice blocks and cold *doogh* (a watered-down yogurt drinks) in the summer. During the wintry weather, he sells cooked beets and fava beans on the streets." He wiped his mouth with his sleeves as he swallowed the last bite of his kabab sandwich. "You should try the doogh sometime," he offered as he smiled at me.

Often, when Ramazoon and I took a break from our daily chores, we crumbled up pieces of paper that we found on the street into little balls and kick them back and forth while we talked about life and how nice it would be to have lots of money to be able to buy things like *lavashak* (an Iranian treat with a thin layer of dried fruit extract and a sour and salty taste), *bastanii* (ice cream), or any other food the street vendors were selling.

"Don't worry," I told him once. "When I am rich, I'll buy one big container of *bastanii Akbar Mashtii* (a yellow creamy ice cream with crushed pistachios and saffron) and bring it over to share with you."

He smiled widely and wiped his mouth, salivating at the thought of the rich vanilla-flavored bastanii.

The loud, angry voice of Mamad Agha interrupted our conversation, yelling at Ramazoon for not working. He came out in his bloody apron, flailing the sharp knife at Ramazoon as he scolded him. "Get back here! I'm going to complain to your father about your laziness! I'll hire somebody else if you don't shape up and get organized!"

It made me sad to see him upset or embarrassed in any way. Plus, it just didn't seem fair. Ramazoon worked constantly, sharpening the bloody knives, sweeping the floor, wiping the walls, and cleaning the windows. He rarely rested.

"You'd better go back in there before you get into trouble," I said, pushing Ramazoon toward Mamad Agha's shop. It was too late. Mamad Agha spanked him extremely hard on the butt three times. Ramazoon turned around and looked at me with teary eyes. I pretended that I didn't see him being beaten. I didn't want him to feel embarrassed, as I felt when my father hit me. I could never understand why the grownups hit young kids. Was it just to get rid of their own frustration?

After Ramazoon went into Mamad Agha's shop with those sad eyes, I sat by Aghajoon's place, knees to my chest, feeling sorry for him. In an attempt to distract myself, I picked up pieces of rock and threw them into the joob, listening for the plop sound as they hit the water. Sometimes the muddy water splashed if I threw a stone hard.

Whenever the city opened the water source, several kilometers away from our area, a stream of water flowed through the joob. The forceful torrent carried all kinds of things with it: paper, tree leaves, branches, pieces of clothing, feces, and small pieces of garbage that people had thrown in there.

One day, when I accompanied Aghajoon to his shop, I jumped over the joob and noticed that the water had stopped, and a pile of items had collected at the bottom. I didn't have the time to examine the joob and didn't want to make Aghajoon upset, so I hurried along to work.

However, as soon as I had finished, I ran back to the joob to look. I took the long wooden stick with the hook along with me—the one I used to hang the shoes on the panels in Aghajoon's place. I pushed the heavy items around inside the joob. Suddenly, a shiny round metal object caught my eye.

"Money?" I asked myself aloud.

I bent down to pick it up, my head all the way inside the joob. It was a one rial coin. I wiped it on my pants and put it inside my pocket. Happily, I went up and down the joob, always staying close to my father's shop so I could hear him if he called my name. I began pushing aside the rest of the garbage, trying desperately to spot more coins. *There must be more in here,* I thought.

I found nothing else that day but couldn't wait to tell Ramazoon about my small success. The day seemed to drag on endlessly. I sat outside Aghajoon's shop after finishing my chores. I shoved my hands into my pockets and shuffled my feet impatiently as I waited for Ramazoon to come outside on one of his breaks.

Finally, I heard Ramazoon's feet dragging his old, worn-out, ugly shoes. He always walked as if he was physically carrying a heavy load on his shoulders, the front part of his shoes dragging slowly against the ground, before he picked his foot up to take a step. He approached me inquisitively, noticing the glimmer of excitement in my eyes.

"Guess what I have in my pocket," I said with an uncontrollable smile.

"Candy?" he stretched out his worn-down hand to get some.

"No. Better!" I reached into my pocket and pulled out the little silver coin. "I found it in the joob." I motioned to the lengthy joob, only a few steps away from us.

Ramazoon's eyebrows rose, and the sadness in his eyes vanished, if only for a moment. "What are you going to do with it?" he inquired excitedly.

"Should we get ice cream or candy tomorrow? I can share with you this time," I said proudly.

"How about ice cream? It'll cool us down in this hot weather," he replied, wiping a bead of sweat from his face.

I nodded. "All right then. Tomorrow, when my father goes home to have lunch and a nap, I'll get ice cream. I don't want him to know I found money, or he'll make me hand it to him and give me a big lecture about saving it for later."

We conducted our endeavor just as planned. Ice cream had never tasted so delicious.

The next afternoon, as I continued searching for coins at the bottom of the joob, an idea came to me. I looked around to find anything I could use to dig the bottom of the joob. I found a long nail and started working away at the joob.

Shortly afterward, I heard Ramazoon's slow dragging footsteps near me; I could always hear the scraping sound of his shoes against the pavement, getting louder as he got closer. He stopped only a few centimeters away. Placing his hands on his knees, he bent over and peered into the joob.

"Mohsen, what are you doing?"

"Making money," I replied.

He came even closer and chuckled. "I see you're making a big hole. Do you think people have hidden a treasure down there?"

My hands were tired and muddy. I stood up and rubbed my knees. They ached from kneeling down by the concrete joob. "Find something to dig with, and I'll tell you how it works," I said proudly.

We both got down on our knees, our heads all the way in the joob, and began removing the dirt to make the hole bigger. I used the nail, while Ramazoon used a piece of wood. Our hands and faces became very dirty from all the mud splashing around our faces. People stopped periodically and looked at us curiously, but nobody bothered to ask any questions. They probably thought we were searching for bugs or something down there.

"You see, Ramazoon, when people drop their money and jewelry in this joob, the water will carry them along and deposit them right into this hole we're digging here."

"I like your idea. We'll get rich sooner than we thought!"

We were two extremely poor and hungry six-year-old boys with simple minds. Being rich to us just meant the ability to buy all the candy, cookies, and ice cream our hearts desired.

The next day, as Ramazoon and I went to work, we listened keenly for the sound of water flowing in the joob. When we did finally hear the initial swoosh from the joob, as the water began its journey from one side of our neighborhood to the next, it brought us hope and joy.

After finishing our work for the day, Ramazoon and I sat by the joob, knees to our chest, looking at the muddy water in the joob carrying all kinds of junk. As more debris flowed in, I imagined coins being deposited one by one into the hole we had made. We waited impatiently for the stream of water to finally stop so we could examine our small treasure. Of course, the amount of money we collected mattered, but more importantly, I wanted to see if my idea had worked. That day, the water only taunted me, showing me just a few glimpses of the contents of the hole, because its tiny waves and the trash it carried blocked my view.

The following day, however, on my way to the shop early in the morning, I noticed that the stream of water had begun to decrease. I saw Ramazoon sweeping Mamad Agha's shop.   As soon as he saw me, we exchanged anxious looks.

On our break, we ran to the approximate location of the hole and used the same long stick I had used previously to remove the things accumulated at the bottom of the joob. After only a few moments of searching, we found the hole, and there they were: coins of all sizes— several one rial, a few two rials, and even a five-rial coin—filling the small crevice. It took an enormous amount of self-control for two six-year-old boys not to scream and jump up and down. We knew that if Mamad Agha and Aghajoon saw us, they would make us hand over the money to them, so we smiled but acted nonchalantly, an extremely tricky thing to do when discovering riches.

We removed our newfound wealth and cleaned the coins in the surrounding water. We had accumulated over one toman, equivalent to two kabab sandwiches. We were beyond astonished. I had just discovered a grownup's wage by means of a plan I had thought of all on my own.

But I didn't want to bask in the success all on my own. "Here, you take half." I handed half of the coins to Ramazoon.

He didn't know what to say as I dropped a full day's wages into his tiny, muddy hands. All he could do was give me a big smile. Ramazoon thought I wouldn't divide the money equally with him, but he was my best friend, and I wanted to be as generous as he had been to me, sharing his kabab sandwiches whenever he bought one.

For some weeks, the joob brought us money—not as much as the first time but enough to continually afford us snacks, toys, candy, and ice cream. I thought, *what a fantastic life wealthy people must have, buying whatever they want whenever they want it.* I wished I could live this way all the time.

That dream sadly ended when the kids in our neighborhood eventually discovered our money-making technique, copied us, and defaced the joob with their own holes from one end to the other.

Sometimes fights broke out among us, and we argued over which hole belonged to whom. By the end of the summer, Ramazoon and I were no longer making any money, and we were forced to go back to living poorly, our bellies constantly rumbling and our mouths once again watering at the thought of ice cream. Nevertheless, for that one delightful summer, it felt good to have a small taste of the "rich" life—a feeling neither of us would ever forget.

First Love

Age Seven

I think of Banu even after many years have gone by. Sometimes I see a lady who resembles her and is smiling at me. I am tempted to walk to her. Then I realize that can't be Banu, so I turn around.

Over time, Momman's sewing business grew. Some of her clients, who appreciated the value of our mother's trade, began to approach her. They asked her to teach their daughters how to sew. After a quick and easy consultation with Aghajoon, she agreed to do it. She would charge about a hundred toman a month to each of her clients. That was no petty amount of money for our family at the time. We were malnourished to the point that Etty, my poor younger sister, sometimes chipped the paint off the hallway walls to eat it. The landlord could never figure out what caused the big patches of peeled paint on the walls, but Etty and I knew.

Momman held her sewing classes in the mornings, just after we finished breakfast. By this time of day, our father had left for work at the little shop on Khosh Street. Momman sat on the floor, chopping and cleaning vegetables for lunch, while Etty and I helped clean up our tiny room before her students showed up.

Motty, my younger sister, was only two at the time and far too small to do much of anything, sat in the corner until we finished our chores, patiently waiting for us to play with her.

As soon as Momman's students arrived, she brought them into the center of our room and immediately turned to me and said, "Mohsen Jon, take your sisters' hands and go outside to play."

Technically, my sisters could stay in the room, but since I was a boy, I wasn't supposed to be around the conservative religious students, as some of them believed men and women should always be separate. I still don't understand what they thought a little boy would do to them. The worst thing I could think of doing at the time was to interrupt their lessons and invite them to come outside with me and Etty to play hopscotch, hide and seek, or jump rope.

If Banu, our landlord's daughter, saw us, she would run out in one of her colorful outfits to join us, with her sister, Zahra, following close behind. Banu and I were only a few months apart in age, and both the firstborn in our families.

The four of us spent time together often, but I felt a lot closer to Banu than I did to Zahra, who was very selfish and wanted everything for herself. Banu, on the other hand, was kind, beautiful, and playful. I loved Banu as much as I loved my own sister, Etty.

Around noon, we heard Belquees Khanoom, Banu's mother, shout, "Banu, Zahra, get back here, it's lunchtime!" By that point, our mother's students had left, so we headed back as well, hungry and tired. Motty had usually fallen asleep in my arms by then. The delicious aroma of food coming out of each of the neighboring houses made my stomach rumble with hunger.

As we entered the front door of our place, we said our goodbyes. Then Banu and Zahra ran upstairs to join their mother. Etty and I smiled back at them just before going into our room on the first floor. The pleasant smell of cooked meat and tomatoes made our stomachs groan for a taste of the delicious meal, but we had to wait a bit longer for the food to be completely ready.

After putting Motty down on the floor, careful not to wake her, Etty and I peeled the potatoes to put in the abgoosht, while Momman picked up the fabric remnants from the floor.

During the cold winter days, instead of going outside to play when Momman's students arrived, we sometimes went upstairs to be with Banu and Zahra, safe from the harsh chill of Tehran's winter.

Their place had two rooms and a lot more things in them than ours did—more dishes, more pots and pans, more toys, and two kerosene heaters! Their pantry was filled with rice, beans, and cooking oil. The curtains were nicely hung on a rod, not like ours, which were nailed on the wall by two rusty nails. Their rugs were thicker, and when we sat down on the floor, it felt soft and comfortable, not bumpy the way it did in our room. It felt like a palace, with Banu and Zahra as its princesses.

Unlike life in our household, they always had some delicious snacks for us to munch on: almonds; pistachios; hazelnuts; dried mulberries; or *klooche* (a sweetbread), which Banu's grandparents brought especially for her every time they visited from their village, Damghan, about 340 kilometers away from Tehran. They knew klooche was one of her favorite snacks, and they enjoyed spoiling her a little.

Even after we'd had a nice snack of nuts and dried fruits or some sweet bread, Banu would ask her mother if she could give us more to eat. She knew I was hungry most of the time, and in return for her kindness to me, I fixed her toys.

One time, the eyeball of her doll popped out, and I was able to put it back in. Another time, I noticed her staring with admiration at a cloth doll I had made for Etty, using fabric remnants from Momman's sewing classes. I could tell that Banu wanted one too, so every time Momman sewed, I sat next to her and collected whatever extra piece she cut and threw on the floor. I stitched a beautiful little doll for Banu from those many pieces.

Each hand and leg was made from a different fabric: one hand was yellow with red polka dots, and the other had pink flowers. One leg was adorned with bright blue stripes, while the other was solid red. The mismatched patterns didn't matter to Banu; she loved it and was happy when I gave it to her. She hugged it and jumped up and down. "Momman, look what Mohsen made me," she exclaimed with joy as she proudly showed the doll to her mother.

Belquees Khanoom smiled and gave her daughter a kiss. Everyone could tell how precious Banu was to her entire family, especially to her mother.

According to Momman, Belquees Khanoom had given birth to seven children, but they all died after a day or two. She made a *nazr* (an offering to God) to make *ash-e reshteh* (a thick noodle soup) for seven years at the shrine of Shahrbanu, who was the daughter of one of the great Islamic leaders, Imam Hussein. She vowed to name the child Shahrbanu if it were a girl and Hussein if it were a boy. God must have been pleased with her offering because it didn't take long for her wish to be granted. Banu, short for Shahrbanu, was born a year later.

Momman told me how all the neighbors came up to Belquees Khanoom holding Banu in her arms and said, "What a beautiful daughter you have. Look at those big brown eyes, those cute lips, and button nose. She looks like an angel. You know, she is going to be my son's bride someday." And they kissed Banu's cheeks.

Every year, on the night before Banu's birthday, her mother put the ingredients for the soup—beans, lentils, noodles, onions, garlic, and a variety of greens—in a *bowghcheh* (square-shaped cotton cloth) and brought the four corners together and tied them in the middle. She had everything ready by the door for the next day to take to the shrine to make the soup.

I remember the year Banu turned six. Early in the morning, Belquees Khanoom gathered some of the women in the neighborhood and their children to hike up the hills to Shahrbanu's shrine, a few kilometers away from the house, to execute her promise to God. Everyone, including the children, was carrying something. They had bowls, spoons, a ladle, and anything needed to make and serve the soup—except for the big pot, which the shrine keeper would lend to us. The women took the heavier items wrapped in a bowghcheh, while the children carried the various utensils. We had to catch two buses and walk up the hill for about an hour to get there. It was a lot of work for Belquees Khanoom, but it was a small effort for the big reward she had received from God: a perfectly beautiful, healthy, and sweet little girl.

As I climbed the hill toward the shrine, I looked back to see women trudging along determinedly. Momman was holding onto Motty with one hand and a bowghcheh with the other. The four of us—Etty, Banu, Zahra, and I—reached the top first. We put down what we were carrying on the ground and ran around on the green lawn. Beautiful colorful wildflowers were everywhere, and the air was fresh and pleasant; the view from the top gave even the smoggy, cluttered landscape below a hint of intrigue and beauty.

Children couldn't go inside the shrine without an adult, which was perfectly fine with us because all we really wanted to do was play. We knew the reason for our journey to the shrine, but we couldn't comprehend the seriousness of the ceremony. To us, it was just an excuse to have another adventure together.

Several minutes later, the women arrived, panting and sweating. They put their things down, spread a blanket on the ground away from the entrance of the shrine, and relaxed a bit before they started making the soup. Belquees Khanoom gave us biscuits to eat until lunch was ready.

The keeper of the shrine knew immediately why we were there when he saw Belquees Khanoom. He came out with a large copper pot. He then helped the women start a fire on the ground outside, at a corner away from the wind. He stacked two or three bricks on each side, high enough so the big pot could easily rest on them. Then he put dried-up branches in between the bricks and lit a match. The smell of burned wood filled the air. The women started chopping the onions, garlic, and other vegetables, while we played imaginary games in the field. Over time, more people arrived at the shrine. They went in to pray and then stood around outside to partake of some soup. They knew it was nazri food and would be distributed among everyone.

By noon, the aroma of sautéed onions and garlic filled the area, and we knew that the soup was ready. "Mohsen! Banu! Etty! Come here and help us distribute the ash to people," Belquees Khanoom ordered as she ladled the thick soup into bowls and put a spoon in each one."

After the small meal, everyone handed their empty bowls and spoons back to a woman who was sitting by the hooz, as they solemnly said, "*Ghabool basheh*" (May God accept your offering).

The woman washed the utensils and dishes so they could be used again. This process continued until Belquees Khanoom had fed everyone —thirty or forty people. Then she gave soup to the women and children who had helped her. The taste was exceptionally delicious because the food had been cooked over an open fire, and the substantial portion filled my empty stomach.

In the afternoon, after all the dishes and utensils had been washed, we gathered everything to head back home. We walked down the hill and then caught the two buses back to our neighborhood. Motty fell asleep in Momman's arms on the way down, and the other women took turns holding her to give my mother a break.

As we were walking, Banu showed me a glittering headband given to her by one of the ladies, the only birthday gift she received that year.

Birthdays were not celebrated or acknowledged in our families because everyone had a tough time meeting their everyday needs, let alone the expense of baking a cake and giving presents.

"Look what Pari Khnoom gave me for my birthday. Isn't it pretty?" she asked with a smile.

I took it from her and jokingly put it on my head, then ran down the hill laughing.

"Give it back! Momman! Mohsen took my present," she whined. Her mother didn't say anything, so Banu ran after me. "Mohsen! give my headband back or I won't speak to you until judgment day! *Ghahram ta roozeh gheyamat!*"

I halted my fast downward sprint so she could reach me. "Here's your headband, Banu."

She grabbed it from me.

"Are you mad at me?" I asked a bit nervously.

"Until judgment day," she said with a big, teasing smile.

A couple of weeks after Banu's sixth birthday, her mother enrolled her in a private kindergarten. My family couldn't afford that, so I had to wait till I turned seven to attend elementary school.

Very soon after the school year began, Banu was suddenly able to read simple words. I didn't like it when she brought her books into the backyard. Her new talents made me jealous.

"Mohsen, do you want me to write your name?" she asked, waving her notebook at me, or she said, "Mohsen, do you want me to read you this book," as she placed her book in between the two of us so we could both see the words and pictures.

Although I didn't like it when she showed off like that, I didn't want to hurt her feelings, so I sat next to her and listened patiently.

"*Baba aab daad*" (Dad gave water). She pointed to the words with her tiny, chubby fingers.

"Okay. That's enough. Let's play!" I stood up energetically.

She sighed and closed her book. "What shall we play?"

"I don't know. Whatever you say."

"Let's play hide and seek. I hide, and you find me!" she squealed.

I couldn't help but smile as I tried to follow her big brown eyes, darting back and forth, searching for a place to hide.

On Friday afternoons, during the hot and long summer days, I swept the yard and then used a hose to cool it off. I liked the musty smell it gave out. When the sun went down, my family would spread a blanket and sit outside to enjoy the late evening breeze. Sometimes my maternal uncle and his family showed up. We didn't have a ball or any other conventional toys, so my cousins and I used a sandal or crumpled pieces of paper we had found on the streets to kick around. Sometimes Banu and her sister, Zahra, joined us.

"Guys, do you want to play house?" Banu would ask excitedly. "Mohsen, you're my husband, and these are our children." She pointed to Etty, Zahra, and my cousins. "Pretend you are a doctor, and our children are sick, so I bring them to you to be examined." With that, she touched everyone's forehead and said, "My children, you don't look so good. You have a fever. Let's see your father. He can treat you."

I ran to the other corner of the yard, where I waited for Banu and the other children. On the way there, I picked up a few broom bristles that were scattered on the ground to use as pretend needles to give injections to all the kids. It was always fun to play these games with Banu.

During our play, Momman called, "Kids, come over and have some fruit!" She held out a round metal tray filled with slices of watermelon to entice us over to where the adults had gathered in the yard.

The watermelon juice ran down my chin and onto my white pajama shirts and pants. My hands felt sticky afterward. I jokingly told Banu, "Did you know that if you eat a seed, a watermelon will grow in your stomach?"

"I don't believe you." She rolled her big brown eyes.

"Okay." I smiled and dared her: "Just eat one and you'll see. Your stomach will grow so big, and one day, a long stem will come out of your mouth with a huge, round watermelon on it."

She looked very scared, her brow furrowed, and her lower lip puckered in a manner that told me she was about to cry.

"I was joking! Look. I'm going to eat some myself." I put a handful of seeds in my mouth and swallowed. She smiled, relieved she wasn't going to have a watermelon growing in her.

Whenever the group of us—my family, Banu, and Zahra—were together, our yard was filled with laughter. That same afternoon, Asghar, my cousin, showed us a game to play with watermelon seeds. "You keep the seeds in your mouth and then spit them as far as you can. The winner gets a piggyback ride from everyone else," he said.

Banu and Etty tried to beat the boys, but Asghar and I won most of the time. The rest of our summer passed in a delightful fashion—full of innocence, imaginary games, and turning random pieces of trash into objects of entertainment.

FIRST DAY OF SCHOOL

I don't think anyone remembers their first day of school as vividly as I do.

Gradually, the days got shorter, and instead of playing outside, we entertained ourselves indoors. It felt good to be inside with the windows closed, soaking in warmth from the kerosene heater. The school year was about to begin, and the neighborhood mothers, including Banu's mother, brought several types of fabric to Momman to make uniforms for their daughters. The time for both Banu and me to attend the first grade was approaching fast.

One day, during breakfast, Momman told Aghajoon that I needed to get my *shenasnameh* (birth certificate) to be able to sign up for elementary school. I was beyond excited when I heard that, because I knew Banu wouldn't be able to show off to me anymore; I would learn just as many words as she knew, or even more. After eating, Aghajoon and I headed to the Edareh Sabt va Amar (Office of Registry).

In 1948, when I was born, most babies, like me, were born at home, with the help of a midwife who had no professional training. They learned by watching other midwives deliver babies. Nobody had a birth certificate issued until later in life, when they needed it to sign up for school.

Sometimes parents held onto their dead child's birth certificate to hand it down to their next newborn. They either didn't want to go through the hassle of applying for a new one or could not afford to pay for another. For this reason, some children appeared older on paper than they were. Although I didn't receive my birth certificate until much later in life, my birth date had been scribbled on the back of the Holy Book, the Qur'an, so my parents remembered my birth date.

On the morning of our trip to the registry, I scarfed down my breakfast much faster than usual. Aghajoon appeared to be in a rush as well, but it seemed to be for a completely different reason. His demeanor was gruff, almost frustrated, as if he were mentally preparing himself to do something he really dreaded. I decided it would be best to stay out of his way and do nothing to add to his bad mood. As soon as I finished my breakfast, I opened the door and sat outside, waiting for Aghajoon. I watched men and women carry fresh naan back to their homes from the nanvaii. I could see rows and rows of shops next to one another, including Aghajoon's, with their black metal roll-up doors pulled down. To the left of Aghajoon's cobbler shop, I noticed Mamad Agha carrying a lamb carcass on his shoulder, while Abas Sabzi Fooroosh, the fresh produce vendor, pulled out his carts filled with red apples and grapes.

Rahim, the kababii, whose shop was on the other side of Aghajoon's, was cleaning his grill—getting it ready to grill kababs for his customers when they arrived at lunchtime. He stopped and waved as soon as he saw Mamad Agha pass by.

Further down the street was an old man with a hunched back, guiding a donkey carrying two loads of dried bread and salt. He hollered, "*Namakii* (salt)! Namakii!"

The cool, sharp autumn breeze felt refreshing and made some of the red, yellow, and orange leaves dance playfully on the ground. Aghajoon finally walked out the front door, after finishing breakfast, and rushed past me, without even glancing back to see if I was following.

I stood up and went after him, practically jogging just to keep up with his fast pace. Thank God for the shop owners nearby, who made him stop when they greeted him. This meant I could relax and catch my breath.

We passed Mamad Agha's shop. He had hung the carcass and was sharpening his knife, getting it ready to cut the meat for his customers. He looked out through the door of his shop, and came outside as soon as he saw Aghajoon. The nauseating smell of raw meat surrounded the immediate area. I looked for Ramazoon but didn't see him nearby.

Aghajoon waved his hand. "Salam Mamad Agha," he said. "Where are you going with Mohsen? How come you're not at the shop?"

"We are getting his birth certificate. If any of my customers show up, tell them I will be back soon."

Aghajoon picked up his pace, but in less than a minute, Abas Sabzi Fooroosh stopped him to ask the same question: "Where are you going with Mohsen? How come you're not at the shop?"

Aghajoon gave him the same answer.

We passed the nanvaii, where people were standing in a line that ran all the way outside and down the sidewalk, everyone waiting for their turn to get bread. I saw the man at the tanoor sticking dough into it. I was still lacking a full belly, and the smell of fresh bread only made me hungrier.

At last, after a thirty-minute walk, the old, two-story, brick building came into sight. We crossed a dirt road, maneuvering between bicycles and donkeys, careful not to step on the animal droppings lying on the roadway. As we got closer, I could see two small windows overlooking the street. One was so dirty you could barely see inside, and the other was cracked and broken. We entered the worn-down front door and walked quickly through a narrow, dimly lit hallway, the smell of mold filling our nostrils. On the first floor, there was a fabric store with colorful yarns; fabric with polka dots, and beautiful striped, green, pink, and white material—all organized on different shelves.

Across from the fabric store was a shop stocked with miscellaneous items; school supplies; and a variety of bags, books, and sewing accessories. At the end of the hallway, to our right, we climbed up a set of cement stairs and arrived at another narrow, dimly lit hallway, at the end of which was a small office filled with three wooden desks, each covered with a mess of files.

We stood in a short line, behind a man who was holding his little daughter's hand. I stepped a bit out of line to glance behind the counter and saw four men in worn shirts and black pants. They had big bellies and were drinking tea and laughing. None of them paid any attention to anyone waiting in line. Based on the way everyone in line was dressed, I could tell they had similar jobs to Aghajoon—all were working-class people, mostly shop owners, who needed to get back to their business to make money. I'm sure Aghajoon was worried he might lose a few customers if he stood there too long.

I dreaded that thought, fearing my father might blame me for the loss of customers and the desperately needed income.

People started mumbling and complaining to one another about the efficiency of the government workers.

"Looks like they're having a good time back there, having tea and chatting while we wait in line," the man in front of us whispered to Aghajoon.

"They don't care. They're getting paid either way," Aghajoon grumbled.

One official finally began working, and the line started moving at a snail's pace. My feet were starting to hurt, and I was getting bored. I just wanted to go back to talk to Ramazoon, who must be at Mamad Agha's shop by now.

Finally, the man in front of us reached the desk, and I knew it would be our turn soon. "Salam. I want to get a birth certificate for her." He pointed to his daughter.

"How old is she?" the clerk behind the counter asked.

"She is six years old."

The clerk glanced at the little girl and raised his eyebrows. "Why are you lying? She looks four to me."

"*Ghorban* (sir), Why would I lie? Look at me. We're all short." The man was right. He was a head shorter than Aghajoon.

"Okay, Okay. What's her name?"

"Homa."

"What kind of name is that for a Muslim girl? *Homa* is the name of an Iranian airline. Why did you name her after an airline?" He chuckled and continued, "You should name her something Islamic, like Zahra, Fatima, or Sakeeneh, something with a decent meaning, not after an airline."

Aghajoon whispered to me, "This idiot doesn't know that Homa also means happy and joyous." My father had never learned to read or write, but his knowledge and street smarts could rival that of an educated person.

The clerk looked at the little girl. "She looks like a Fatima to me. We are calling her that officially."

The girl looked at her father with a puzzled expression. He almost opened his mouth to say something but quickly decided against it. The poor man couldn't say anything for fear the officials might not issue a birth certificate for his daughter, and what would he do then? She needed the certificate to go to school. As they passed us, I heard him whisper, "Don't worry. At home we'll still call you Homa. Fatima is only on your birth certificate."

Aghajoon and I stepped toward the desk. My heart was pounding as I wondered what might happen if the narrow-minded man didn't like my name. I knew my name originated from the Arabic word *hassan*, meaning someone who does good deeds. I was glad at least it had a good meaning and met some of this clerk's criteria. But what if he wasn't satisfied with Mohsen and wanted to call me something I didn't really care for, like Taghii, Naghii, or Rajab—very old and traditional names.

We stood there waiting. One of the clerks approached the counter, and suddenly a big smile appeared on Aghajoon's face. He was one of his customers. "Salam," he said to Aghajoon.

Aghajoon called him Masht Ali when he responded to him and shook his hand. "We're here to get a birth certificate for my son, Mohsen." He gestured toward me.

"How old is he?" Masht Ali questioned.

"He is seven years old."

He shot a quick glance down at me and nodded. "Yeah, he looks like a healthy seven-year-old . . . You said his name is Mohsen, yes? That's a nice name."

I was so happy that I got to keep my name and age, with his approval. He opened his desk drawer, took out a piece of paper, and jotted down the relevant information about me—my first name, last name, date of birth, city of birth, parents' first and last names, birth dates, and place of birth. Then he signed it, and since Aghajoon was illiterate and didn't know how to sign, my father placed his thumb in black ink and rolled it onto the piece of paper.

Aghajoon paid about one toman, and Masht Ali told him to come back in a couple of weeks to pick up the certificate.

Two weeks passed, and once again, we left early in the morning, right after breakfast, to try to be the first ones in line.

The man in front of us, who looked the same age as Aghajoon, wanted a copy of his birth certificate. There were no copy machines back then, so the authorities had to write the information on an official paper and stamp it. "When will my birth certificate copy be ready?" he asked politely.

"In two days," the clerk behind the counter replied.

"But I need it today, sir," the man pleaded.

"I can't do anything about it." He shrugged. "That's how long it takes."

The man in line then took out his original certificate from his pants pocket and placed a two-toman bill inside it, before handing it over to the clerk.

The clerk noticed the money right away and smiled. He looked around the room and said, "Have a seat, there are not too many people in line today. I'll have it ready in fifteen minutes."

That moment was one of the first times, and certainly not the last, that I realized wealthy people lived in a different world than the rest of us. They could make anything happen with their money.

We walked up to the counter and received my birth certificate without any issues. It was a three-page booklet, the size of a small wallet, with a green cardboard cover. On the front page was the black image of a lion with a sword in his right front leg and the sun in the background—the same image as on the Iranian national flag. It had a very professional and clean look. I was proud to own something so official looking. I flipped through the pages, curious about the information on them.

A couple of days later, Momman took the certificate from under the Qur'an, which had been placed high up on a shelf. She sat on the floor with Motty on her lap, Etty on one side of her, and me on the other. "Here is your first and last name and the date and place of your birth. This is my name and that's your father's name, and here is all the information about our birth dates, birthplaces, and names of our parents." She pointed to each word, then turned the page. "Here is where they will add information later on."

"Like what, Momman?" I asked.

"It's not important for you to know now." She turned to the last page. "This is for future use too." She put Motty down on the floor and put my certificate back where she had stored it. Later, when I was able to read, I found out that the second page was for the names of my spouse and children, and the last page indicated my death date.

Now that everything was in order, Aghajoon signed me up for first grade at Daryush, an all-boys elementary school. He announced it during lunch one day. I was officially enrolled in school, and my first day was approaching fast.

The same afternoon that I heard this news from Aghajoon, I went upstairs to tell Banu about it. She was going to Sareh, an all-girls school only a couple of blocks away from Daryush.

"Do you want to walk to school together?" she asked.

I wholeheartedly agreed. It would be nice to start off the morning of my first day of school in the company of a dear friend. This was the first time I would be away from my family and under the authority of some unfamiliar adult.

The closer the first day of school came, the more rambunctious the butterflies in my stomach became. My mind was riddled with questions: *What if my teacher is mean? What if they give me so much homework I don't have time to play? What if I don't like school?*

There were so many "what ifs" buzzing around in my young, imaginative brain that I was beginning to scare myself. Luckily, Banu's birthday was a couple of days before school started, and that helped keep my mind off the start of school. As in previous years, Belquees Khanoom started preparing for her daughter's birthday the night before. She placed all the ingredients for the soup in a bowghcheh and left them by the door, just like clockwork.

The next morning, we woke up early to catch the two buses and begin our journey toward the shrine. My sister Motty was three years old now and didn't need to be held as much as the previous year, so she joined the rest of the children. Occasionally, she slowed down to give a break to her tiny legs, but she never let Momman carry her. She wanted to be a grown-up girl like Etty, Zahra, and Banu. I was happy Momman didn't have to worry about Motty as much this time, as I knew it would be terribly exhausting to carry her up the long trail.

By noon, we had started distributing the soup, and only after every visitor had been fed were we allowed to eat, similar to what happened the previous year. In accordance with the routine, after our meal was finished, all the women cleaned up and gathered their things to leave for home. And, as always, just before heading back down the hill, Belquees Khanoom approached the shrine keeper and thanked him: "Yusef Agha, forgive me for troubling you for seven years. We won't be coming back next year. My promise to God is complete. Banu turns seven today."

He smiled at Banu. "May Allah bless you and keep you for hundred years." He then reached in his pants pocket and pulled out a string of beautiful turquoise prayer beads, with small yellow flowers painted on each one. He handed it to Banu as a keepsake. She wore it as a necklace.

"Look, Momman. Isn't it pretty?" She pulled her long, shiny black hair back over her shoulder so her mother could see it. Its color perfectly matched her shirt.

Belquees Khanoom nodded and said, "*Azizam* (my dear), this is for you to use when praying to God. It's not a piece of jewelry. I'll show you how to use it later today after our evening namaz."

Banu shrugged, not quite comprehending the seriousness in her mother's voice. Then she turned to me with a smile so genuine and sweet it took all my attention away from her vibrant new necklace. I smiled back, looking into her bright eyes, and as if by instinct, prayed a quick thank you to God for blessing me with such a lovely friend. Being around Banu gave me a feeling of satisfaction and comfort.

"Mohsen, let's go!" She patted me on the shoulder, then turned and began running down the hill, giggling loudly all the way, as I ran closely behind her. The thought of the first day of school was in the far corner of my mind as I sprinted down the lush green hill. Her laughter only became louder as I jokingly made guttural animal noises and stretched my hands toward the glistening ripples of her hair. I let her think she was outrunning me, while I ran in exaggerated zig-zag motions, purposefully missing each time I pounced at her.

The next day, the day before the first day of school, Momman laid out my uniform—a white shirt and the gray suit Aghajoon had bought for me from the bazaar. My stomach sank whenever the thought of school popped into my head. I wondered how Banu felt. That night, before I slept, I put a pencil, eraser, notebook, and pencil sharpener into a brown bag Momman had sewed for me from blue, green, and yellow fabric remnants she had saved. I left the bag next to the shiny black shoes Aghajoon had made especially for this occasion. The new clothing made me feel like it was New Year's, except I had a queasy stomach instead of being lighthearted and cheerful.

I had a tough time sleeping that night, haunted by nightmares of evil teachers hitting me for unknown reasons. In one, I got lost on my way to school and completely missed my first day.

I awoke the next day so nervous I couldn't eat anything for breakfast. Momman forced me to take a couple sips of the sweet tea and eat a little fresh naan with feta cheese; she knew I would be hungry later if I didn't have something in my belly, even if it was a small portion. My queasiness made it hard to swallow, but I finally got through breakfast and rushed to put on my school uniform. Once I was all dressed, I took a deep breath and headed slowly toward the door.

Etty stood in the way and stopped me for just a moment. "You don't look like yourself with your uniform on," she said, holding her cloth doll.

We didn't have a mirror, so I couldn't see what Etty meant. I looked over and saw Momman staring at me, smiling but not saying a word. I mustered up a nervous smile in return and headed into the yard to call Banu.

"Banu, Banu! Let's go!" I hollered.

I heard the faint clicking sound of her quick little footsteps as she came down from her room to meet me in the front yard—wearing her black uniform and white long stockings. She had a white collar over her uniform collar, and I noticed that her black shoes were shiny like mine. She was carrying a red handbag, and on top of her long black hair, she had pinned a white ribbon bow, a mandatory requirement for all elementary school girls. The bow colors were different for each grade: white for first, yellow for second, and pink for third. Banu looked so grown up. I wondered if that's what Etty meant when she said I didn't look like myself.

Our walk to school that first day was quiet, and our behavior not as playful as usual. This is when I knew for sure that Banu was just as nervous as I was. Otherwise, she would have been talking up a storm or teasing me about already knowing how to read. As we got closer to Sareh Elementary School, we noticed girls walking hand in hand, laughing and talking.

Suddenly, Banu started crying. "I'm scared of going to first grade," she sobbed. "What if they give us a lot of homework and we can't play anymore? What if my teacher is mean and hits me if I do something wrong?"

It astonished me to hear that Banu had the exact same worries I had. I was just as scared as Banu, but I didn't want to let her see my fear, because I knew that would only frighten her more. I knew I needed to be strong and confident for her, so I tried to comfort her. "I'm sure our teachers are meaner to us since we're boys. My father always spanks me, but he never hits my two sisters. Plus, you've been to kindergarten, and that will make things easier for you."

She wiped her tears. "Well, maybe in the afternoon we can do our homework together and then play." She mustered up a smile.

The thought of being able to play with Banu after the first day of school made me instantly lighter. I smiled and took a long, deep breath, and suddenly my playful spirit came back. "Race you to school!" I shouted.

As I ran, I could hear Banu's footsteps far behind me. She screamed, "Not fair! Wait for me!"

I didn't listen to her pleas and ran as fast as I could. It felt good to let out my nervous energy. Occasionally, I glanced over my shoulder, with a smile, to make sure she was still following me. Panting as I reached her school, I could see groups of girls entering through the rusty yellow door. Some of the younger ones, the first graders, were holding their mother's hands.

Banu arrived shortly after I did. She rolled her eyes and stuck her tongue out at me before going in.

"Bye, Banu, see you at home after school!" I yelled. I could tell she was genuinely mad at me for not waiting for her, but I knew we would talk again as soon as we started working on our homework together later that day.

I walked another two blocks to Daryush Elementary School. I knew Banu would want me to describe my school to her, so I walked around to check it out. It was an old building in a residential area, with broken windows and chipped yellow paint on the front of the building. The two wooden doors at the front were wide open to the playground, where boys of all ages were standing around talking and laughing, while a handful stood alone crying. I assumed that was because, like me, they were afraid, and this was their first time away from home. At one end of the school were five swings connected to a pole, most of them by rusty chains. A couple of older kids were rocking back and forth slowly, while chatting with friends. Next to the swings was a blue slide, or what once was a blue slide. Now it was old and covered with rusty brown stains.

A middle-aged man and a small boy in uniform came out of a tiny dark room, located close to the swings and the slide. *The older man must be the* baba-eh madreseh (*keeper of the school*), I thought. *They must live in that room.* Later, I found out that they didn't pay any rent, since the father maintained the building. I envied that small boy for having the school playground with its slide and swings in his backyard.

Walking to another end of the yard, I saw rows of bathrooms and water fountains. It smelled foul in this part of the yard, but at least there was plumbing in the school. A variety of trees and shrubs were in the playground, and the colorful leaves that fell from their branches speckled the landscape, like the patches of colorful fabric on my brown school bag.

In the middle was a hooz. I frowned as I stared at it. The ugly, rusted metal fence around it didn't make sense to me. What was the point of having a hooz if you couldn't get to it?

A shrill bell rang and took away my attention from my surroundings. The kids began congregating in the middle of the school, waiting to be told what to do. I ran back to join them. An angry-looking man wearing a black suit and a blue shirt was standing at the top of the stairs that led to the classrooms. He was carrying a wooden stick in one hand and a big megaphone in the other. He paced back and forth as he watched us, with his brow furrowed and a scowl on his face. Shortly after the bell rang, he screamed into the megaphone, overpowering the squeaky sounds of all the kids' chatter: "Shut up!"

Suddenly everything was quiet. Even the birds stopped chirping. He paused for a moment, then said, "I'm Mr. Aalamii, your assistant principal." He looked at us sternly and continued: "Form six lines. First graders here, second graders there, third graders on this side, and ..." He gestured to different sections of the playground with his stick. "There are two first grade classes. The first group goes to classroom one, and the second group to number two. Each class has a representative who will take you to your class."

He called out our names and gestured with his wooden stick where we should each stand. I prayed that I would have a nice teacher.

"Mohsen Fazel Fashandi." He pointed to the first-grade line, and I walked over quickly, with my head bent toward the ground, desperately hoping he would not say another word to me. He was even more intimidating than my own father.

After all the lines were formed, the assistant principal motioned for each line to move upstairs, following the representative for that class. Ours was a tall, chubby fifth grader with beady eyes.

We climbed the stairs and entered a narrow, dark hallway. Our representative stopped abruptly at a room next to the principal's office. I stepped out of line just enough to peek inside. A group of women, both young and old, were sitting on old wooden chairs, each with a cup of tea in her hand chatting and laughing. They seemed happy to be back to school. I wondered which of them was my teacher.

Before I had much time to ponder that, we were led into a dimly lit, musty room with two rows of large wooden benches. We were instructed to sit, four kids per bench. I took a seat in the second row, close to the door in case I needed to make a quick run for it. As soon as we all sat down, a young, kind-looking woman entered the classroom.

"Stand up!" our chubby representative commanded.

The teacher approached the wooden desk in the corner of the room and put her belongings down. She turned around and smiled at us. I already knew I was going to like her. She resembled my mother—short, with long light brown hair, a fair complexion, and light brown eyes.

"You may sit down," she said softly, while gesturing to our seats. "My name is Mrs. Naserii," she said and wrote her name on the blackboard.

When she called the roster, I found out that the boys sitting next to me were Ali, Masood, and Mehdi. I made a mental note of their names so I could tell Banu about them. They seemed to be good kids from poor families, like mine; I came to this assumption based on their hands—they were just as dirty and cracked as mine were.

While she was calling out our names, the baba-eh madreseh brought a medium-sized box and put it on Mrs. Naserii's desk. "The books, Khanoom," he stated firmly.

After taking attendance, Mrs. Naserii chose a front-row student to help her hand out the books. When I received mine, I cracked it open right away. The aroma was amazing—a chemical, glue, and ink smell, mixed with wood, plastic, and cardboard, emanated from the cover. The stiff spine and clean, glossy pages promised new adventures and learning experiences. It was so exciting. I couldn't wait to be able to read and write. I wanted to show off to Banu.

The teacher wrote ten alphabet letters on the board. She took out a long wooden ruler and asked us to repeat after her. "Aleph, beh," she said pointing at each letter. After going over them five times, Mrs. Naserii pointed at a letter randomly and asked, "What's this?"

"Beh," we screamed happily.

"Good!" She smiled. "And this?" She pointed at another.

"Peh."

"Bravo!" She beamed at us with pride for catching on so quickly. By the time the bell rang for recess, we all knew the first ten letters by heart. After recess, we stayed in the classroom until noon, writing and reading the letters repeatedly. I was exhausted and starving by the time the final bell rang.

"Today's homework is to write these letters ten times. Write neatly," Mrs. Naserii said.

I collected my book, notebook, and other school supplies; shoved them into my bag; and ran through the narrow hallway. I hopped swiftly down the stairs, hoping to catch Banu on the way home.

When I reached her school, the rusty yellow double doors were locked. A couple of girls were walking hand in hand down the alley. *She must have gone home already*, I thought. I was disappointed but still ran the rest of the way home, excited to tell Banu about my school and my teacher, Mrs. Naserii, and how much I liked her, and about my new book, my homework, and the boys who sat next to me in the classroom. I was sure she would want to tell me about her day as well, and I would be happy to listen.

By the time I reached the entrance to our yard, I was out of breath, but I could sense something was not right. None of the shop owners were in their stores, and I heard noises coming from the yard. *Were people crying?*

I saw Ramazoon wiping Mamad Agha's outside windows. He didn't even turn around to acknowledge me, but I knew he had seen my reflection in the glass. My heart was racing. I took a deep breath and reluctantly pushed open the gate to the yard. It was crowded with all our neighbors: the shop owners, the butcher, the fresh produce vendor, the kababii. Every single person was crying, some harder than others.

Momman was sobbing uncontrollably, with her face in her hands. Aghajoon tried to comfort Banu's father, Ost Gholam Reza, who had dropped to his knees on the ground. He was shaking as he shouted questions I could barely understand through the unnerving sound of a grown man's sobs. Next to him was Belquees Khanoom. I had to force my eyes to look toward her, knowing I didn't want to see what she was doing. Her eyes were red and swollen, her mouth hanging open and lips quivering. I could see a glisten from the stream of tears flowing down her cheeks and dripping off her chin like raindrops.

Belquees Khanoom was holding Banu's wet body in her arms, rocking back and forth, sobbing.

My heart dropped inside my chest. I couldn't understand what was wrong, but I knew from Banu's unmoving form that something terrible must have happened. Her lips were blue, and her long black hair hung off her limp neck in thick, wet strands.

I stood there motionless, with my jaw dropped, able to breathe only in short, jagged breaths.

Momman must have sensed my presence. She picked her head up from her hands and turned to me. She gently pulled me aside and solemnly explained to me, while trying her best to hold back tears. "Mohsen Jon, Banu fell into the hooz in our backyard while she was washing her hands. Her mother looked for her everywhere, but by the time she found her, it was too late. Banu had drowned." She patted my head. "Your sisters and Banu's sister are with a neighbor. Do you want to join them? You must be hungry too; she'll give you lunch as well."

"No!" I pulled away from her, feeling sad and confused, my eyes filling with tears. For the first time in my life, I refused food. My hunger had vanished.

My brain knew what had happened, but my heart didn't want to accept it. I kept rubbing my eyes, thinking I was imagining things. Banu appeared so beautiful and calm in her mother's arms. I thought any minute she would stand up to surprise us. But she didn't.

How had everything changed so quickly? Just this morning, Banu was walking with me to our first day of school, and now she was gone. She had died just like that.

I sat down quietly next to Belquees Khanoom. She was caressing Banu's long wet hair, murmuring, "My Banu, my Banu, why did you leave me?"

Belquees Khanoom turned and saw me, "Mohsen Jon, Mohsen Jon. Do you see what happened to your friend? Banu was so excited to tell you about school. Oh God, why did You take her away from me?" She tilted her head toward the sky. "What have I done to deserve this?" she shouted, in between sobs and kissing Banu's forehead.

I stood up and walked mindlessly around the yard, as if I could get away from this scene and then come back to find none of it had happened, and our beautiful Banu was laughing that contagious laugh of hers and asking me to play.

As I walked toward the stairs of our building, lost in my grief, something caught my eye. The cloth doll I had made for Banu was sitting neatly at the edge of the bottom step. Banu must have placed it there before she decided to wash her hands. I picked it up and sat down, stroking its face with my thumbs, as tears silently slid down my cheeks. I would never get to hear her sweet, innocent laughter again; feel my heart jump when she smiled at me; or watch as her tiny, chubby fingers followed the words of a book when she was reading to me. I'd never again see the way she rolled her big brown eyes at me when she got mad at my constant teasing.

The sound of Belquees Khanoom's sobbing and moaning brought me back to reality: "God, why did you take away my angel? What about all those nazri soups I arranged for her over the past seven years? I kept my promise, why didn't you keep yours!?" Belquees Khanoom shouted.

I shook my head. She was right. *Why didn't God keep His promise?* Suddenly my sadness turned to anger. I couldn't understand why he had taken my dear friend. *How selfish of Him,* I thought.

The next morning, I didn't immediately remember yesterday's tragedy. I felt like I was waking up from a bad dream I couldn't recall. As soon as I heard Belquees Khanoom sobbing, however, I knew I had lost Banu and she was gone forever. I felt sick to my stomach again. My eyes quickly filled with tears, and my heart filled with sadness once more.

I didn't eat much of my breakfast. Food wasn't appealing; I just wanted Banu back. *How can I go to school without her today?* I thought.

"Momman, I want to stay home today," I pleaded.

"No," she said firmly.

She wanted me to get back to a normal life, and she thought school would distract me from the sadness.

Disappointed, I put on my uniform, picked up my school bag, and reluctantly walked to school. I tried taking a different route so it wouldn't remind me so much of Banu, but that didn't help at all. Her angelic voice was in my head all the way,

During the week, I sat by the hooz, remembering Banu and how she comforted me all the time. When I was cold, she would have me go to their room upstairs until Momman's students left, and when I was hungry, she would share her snacks with me. I sat there with my thoughts as I stared deeply into the water and my tears created tiny ripples in the murky pond. I heard footsteps coming up behind me but stayed focused on the pond.

Belquees Khanoom sat down next to me, in her long black dress and black scarf. I turned to see her pale skin, teary red eyes, and solemn face. She managed a smile for my benefit and wiped her tears away. She didn't say anything, but her eyes spoke to me. I knew her sorrow was much deeper than mine. I had lost my friend, but she had lost her sweet daughter. I wished I could do something to make her feel better.

Some of the women in the neighborhood blamed Belquees Khanoom for making her nazri to God for only seven years. They said, "As soon as Banu turned seven, God took her. Do you think this is a coincidence?"

I wondered, *If Belquees Khanoom had promised to make the soup at the shrine every year instead of just seven, would Banu still be alive today?*

To help Belquees Khanoom with her grief, one afternoon Momman invited her for tea. Madarjoon, my grandmother, joined us since she lived close by. I sat in the corner, with my textbook in front of me, eavesdropping on their conversation and occasionally peeking at them.

"You know, Belquees Khanoom, God knows what is best, and you should trust Him. Have faith in Him. He took Banu only because there was a reason behind it. We, the servants of God, can't comprehend His knowledge." Madarjoon's voice was soft and kind, but Belquees Khanoom continued to cry. I wondered how many tears one could shed. Undoubtedly, more than I ever realized before.

Finally, Belquees Khanoom wiped her eyes with the corner of her black scarf.

Madarjoon moved her concerned, wrinkled face closer to Belquees Khanoom's and whispered, "Banu is watching you from heaven. She is now an angel. If you keep crying like this, you will break her heart." Then she poured some tea in a cup and put it on a saucer with two sugar cubes. She put it in front of Belquees Khanoom. "As hard as it might be, you need to pick yourself back up. You still have your other daughter, Zahra, to care for."

Belquees Khanoom held Madarjoon's petite hands. "I know, I know. My emotions are so strong that my body can't manage them anymore, so I weep. It isn't like Banu was sick and died. She was healthy and happy." She wiped her eyes. "I had her for only seven short years. How should I deal with that? God, forgive me for saying this, but what You did to me was so unfair, taking my child exactly after seven years when I was done with my nazri. What did You want to prove to me? That You have all the power, and I don't?" she shouted.

Madarjoon shook her head and said, "Don't say such evil things. God knows best."

My grandmother's advice comforted me more than it did Belquees Khanoom. Knowing that Banu was still here in some way, watching us from above, elevated my mood. I smiled, thinking she might be looking down at me, sitting there with my new schoolbook. I flipped through the pages, hoping she could see the contents of my first-grade textbook. Sometimes I read the words aloud for Banu to hear.

Banu was with me, hopefully proud of me for being able to read.

Belquees Khanoom became very depressed after Banu's death. She often sat in the corner of the backyard, mumbling under her breath. Eventually, her family sold their house and moved to the village where their relatives lived. Years later, we heard that Belquees Khanoom gave birth to a baby boy. We didn't see her again, but I am sure the new baby replaced her sorrow with joy.

To Lose a Brother and Gain Another

Age Nine

Do I believe in destiny or fate? I still don't know, but what happened in 1956 in our household makes me wonder if fate or destiny is just another term for God's will.

It all started when Momman's stomach began growing big. Every time she stood up, she would place her hands on her back for support. She continued to give sewing lessons daily but spent a larger portion of her day lying down and often wore a look of queasiness on her face. Something strange was happening to her, something I couldn't quite understand.

Etty, Motty, and I wondered what had caused Momman to change. But everyone else, especially Aghajoon, seemed to be elated when they were around her.

One day, Madarjoon caught me looking at Momman with a worried look. She patted my head and said in her usual kind, comforting tone, "Mohsen Jon, don't be concerned. Your mom will be fine. She is just pregnant, dear."

I stared at her with a puzzled look on my face. I wasn't sure at nine years old what this strange word pregnant meant.

As if knowing my thoughts, she smiled and explained: "You are going to have a baby sister or a baby brother soon."

Is this supposed to clarify something for me? I wondered. I still didn't understand what the connection was between Momman's big stomach and having a new sibling. Though I knew better than to question her.

A few days after my grandmother's strange explanation, I heard my mother moans in the corner of our room as I was busy doing my homework. I looked up quickly to see her rubbing her big belly, her eyebrows furrowed, and tears rolling down. She seemed to be in great pain.

"Mohsen Jon, get Madarjoon quickly." She sounded nervous.

I put on my shoes with haste and ran out of our room as quickly as I could to my maternal uncle's house, where my grandmother lived.

Momman hadn't told me why she needed her mother, but I sensed it had something to do with her big stomach. I quickened my pace and ran for about ten minutes until I reached the narrow alley that led to my uncle's house. When I arrived at their worn-down, small wooden door, I knocked frantically. My cousin Asghar opened it.

"Salam, is Madarjoon home? My mom wants her to come to our house," I said, panting.

Madarjoon was in the yard sitting by the hooz, washing dishes. She stopped when she saw me. "Nana, Mohsen Jon, what is it?" She wiped her hands with the chador she had wrapped around her waist, a look of concern on her face.

"Salam, Momman keeps rubbing her belly and wants you to come to our house."

Madarjoon nervously untied her chador from around her waist and put it over her head to cover herself from head to toe. "Okay. Okay. I'll go to your place. I want you to go to Nobar Khanoom's house and bring her with you." Madarjoon was already rushing out the door as she told me what to do.

Nobar Khanoom was the midwife who had delivered me and my sisters. Every time she saw us, she would pinch our cheeks and say, "*Bah, bah, mashallah* (good, good, God willed it), what beautiful children I brought into this world. Each one is cuter than the other."

I stood in the doorway watching my grandmother move faster than I had ever seen her before. I was quite amused at the sight. When she reached the end of the alley, she turned around and yelled at me, "Mohsen, what are you waiting for? *Move!*"

I had briefly forgotten the urgency of the matter and wanted to stay and play with my cousin. I waved goodbye to him and ran toward Nobar

Khanoom's house, about fifteen minutes away. I banged on the door. Her daughter opened it.

"Salam, my mom keeps rubbing her stomach and wants Nobar Khanoom to see her," I said, out of breath. The constant running had winded me.

"She isn't here. When she comes back, I'll send her over," she replied, adjusting her chador.

I rushed back home. Madarjoon and Sima Khanoom were with Momman—I knew Madarjoon must have asked Sima Khanoom to come downstairs to help. We had moved to a room in a new house, and Sima Khanoom and her husband were our landlords now. Momman was crying and twitching in pain. Sima Khanoom was rubbing Momman's feet to calm her. It was hard to watch whatever was happening to her.

"Nobar Khanoom wasn't there, but her daughter assured me she would send her as soon as she comes back." I took off my shoes and nervously entered the room as Madarjoon beckoned me forward.

"Nana, Mohsen Jon, take your sisters and go outside to play. Nobody can come in until I tell you." Madarjoon closed the door behind us as soon as we left.

In the yard, we sat on one of the steps, listening to Momman's cries and moans. We looked at each other, teary eyed and concerned. We all knew we were helpless. As the eldest, I took it upon myself to distract my sisters from the moans by suggesting we play hide-and-seek, although I could tell nobody's heart was in it. As we played, my thoughts were with our mother.

An entire hour passed before Madarjoon stuck her head out of the door and hollered my name, "Nana, Mohsen, go back to Nobar Khanoom's house and find out why it's taking her so long."

I ran the whole way; grateful I could help somehow. I arrived in less than ten minutes. I knocked on the door, and almost immediately Nobar Khanoom opened it. She reminded me of my grandmother; she was petite and had truly kind eyes, a wrinkly face, and grayish short hair.

She looked as if she were ready to go. "Let's go. Let's go," she said, grabbing her black chador. She walked so fast that I had to run to catch up with her. She seemed to be in more of a hurry than I was to get back to the strange event that was taking place at my home.

Once we reached our place, she went straight to the room and closed the door behind her. Momman's crying and groaning had gotten much louder since I left. I went to the yard, looking for my sisters, but they weren't there. They must have gone upstairs to play with the landlord's other tenant's daughters, Saba and Sara.

Alone, I paced up and down the backyard, worried about Momman. Every time the door to our room opened, I heard her loud and painful cries and my grandmother's recitation of the Qur'an. I assumed she recited it to ease her daughter's pain with her prayer. I hoped it was helping.

I thought that maybe if my father were present, he would be able to help our mother with the pain. I couldn't understand why nobody had bothered to ask me to get him. I contemplated going to his shop myself but decided against it. I didn't want to get into trouble . . . I always got into trouble if I did something without asking first.

I reasoned with myself: *Okay, the next time Madarjoon pokes her head out, I will ask her opinion.* I waited and waited, but she never came outside to check on me or allow me to voice my question. It was late in the afternoon when I heard the cries of a baby.

Finally, the door opened and Madarjoon walked out smiling, with a bucket in her hand. She put it down by the little garden in the yard and started digging a hole in the ground. I peeked into the container. It was filled with blood and a strange swollen purple sac with a long cord attached to it.

I had never seen anything so foreign and weird looking. I got very scared. *What could that strange thing be? Where did it come from? Was that what made Momman cry? Was this thing inside her stomach, causing her discomfort?*

My grandmother dumped the contents of the bucket into the hole and covered it with dirt. I asked with a sense of urgency, "Madarjoon, can I go inside now?"

She kissed me on the cheeks and said, "Nana, Mohsen Jon, you have a chubby baby brother now. I'll tell you when you can come in."

Sima Khanoom, Nobar Khanoom, and Madarjoon continued to go in and out of the room, carrying buckets of water from the hooz. I wondered when I'd get to see my new brother and Momman. It seemed everyone else was going in, why couldn't I?

At last, Madarjoon poked her head out of the room and instructed me to do the very thing I had been so anxiously waiting to do the whole time: "Nana, Mohsen, go get your father."

At the shop, Aghajoon was busy polishing shoes. He looked up. "Why are you here?" he asked in an irritated voice.

I knew immediately it must have been a dreadful day for him. We all understood that if our father didn't make much money during a workday, he would be in a grumpy mood. On those days, I tried to stay out of his way, otherwise he would slap me or spank my butt so hard it would hurt for days. It wasn't an event I favored. "Madarjoon is at our house," I said. "I have a new baby brother. She wants you to go home."

Aghajoon got up, jumped over the counter of his shop, and left in a hurry. He called to me, "Watch the shop until I come back and don't let anyone come in." He seemed more excited than I had ever seen him.

I watched as he crossed the street and headed toward our place. I sat outside by the front door of Aghajoon's store and waited for Ramazoon to come out so I could tell him about the new addition to my family, but he never did. I sat there for what seemed like an eternity. To keep my mind entertained, I decided to imagine what my new brother looked like. *Will he look like me and Etty, with olive skin, dark eyes, and dark hair? Or will he look more like Motty, with her lighter complexion, eyes, and hair?*

Finally, Aghajoon returned. He had a big smile on his face. Before he sat behind the counter, he gestured to me that I could go home.

At home, I stood by the door, not knowing if I could go inside. I was still worried about getting into some sort of trouble. I had to knock two times before anyone seemed to hear it—the place was filled with women's voices and the new baby's cries. Everyone was more concerned with admiring the newest addition than letting me into the room. Sima Khanoom finally came to my rescue and opened the door, motioning for me to enter.

Momman looked pale and tired but happy. She was beaming with pride as she lay on the floor in the corner of the room. When she saw me, she smiled and pointed to my crying new baby brother. Nobar Khanoom had him in her arms and was reciting something in Arabic. I assumed they were verses from the Holy Book. She said it first into his right ear and then his left, keeping her eyes fixed on his. This ritual was a tradition to which we were all accustomed. It was a special chant to help ward off the evil eye and prevent children from being harmed by jealous or unkind people. In Islam, we believe that God is the only one who can protect people from the evil eye. That's the reason Muslims always say, "Mashallah, what God has willed," whenever they admire someone or something. It lets the other person know their compliments don't come from a place of jealousy.

I suspect my brother just got tired of screaming and finally calmed down, or maybe the verses from the Qur'an quieted him down. I waited till Nobar Khanoom had completed the recitation to ask if I could see my new baby brother.

He was fair and pink. His small red lips and cute button nose made him beautiful and gave him an angelic look. I suddenly understood what all the fuss was about. This tiny little baby had completely captured all our hearts.

Madarjoon took the sleepy infant from Nobar Khanoom and calmly put him down next to Momman, who had begun to doze off. All the hours of labor had finally caught up with her.

Etty and Motty came in full of excitement. As we all sat next to our mother, she smiled faintly and said through weary lips, "Did you see your little brother? You know, you were once as tiny as he is."

I looked down at my hands and legs. It was hard to believe I used to be as little as my new brother. Had I also been inside my mother's tummy, as my brother had been?

"Momman, why does he keep sticking his tongue out?" Etty asked.

"I think he's hungry," Momman replied. She sat up and placed a small blanket over his head in a way that covered her upper body as well. I could tell she was moving the baby closer to her chest. After some time,

Momman fell asleep with the baby in her arms. Motty, Etty, and I sat next to her with sad looks on our faces, waiting for her to wake up.

Madarjoon noticed us and said sweetly, "Don't worry! After eating this *kachi*, she will regain her energy and be fine in a couple of days." She showed us something that looked like pudding, made with sugar and cooked flour, covered with grease. She put the kachi down next to Momman and patted our heads, "What's this frown on your faces? For God's sake, you should be happy and jumping up and down to have a new sibling. Go outside and play. I'll stay with your mom in the meantime."

It was a relief to hear that Momman would be okay. We knew our grandmother would make everything better. She always did. We loved her very much, and she was so wonderful. Every morning, she asked one of us what we wanted her to make for lunch. It was always our favorite: lentil rice with sugar one day, cutlets another day, fried potato patties the day after that. She took out the money from her inside jacket pocket and gave it to me to buy the ingredients for the meal every day.

Everything she made was delicious. I could tell that her presence put Momman at ease as well. When the baby cried, Madarjoon calmed him down by pacing around the room with him in her arms, softly stroking his back and mumbling something in his ears. I watched her with such fascination that, at the time, I believed she must be an angel. There simply couldn't be any other explanation. No one else could calm an entire home with their presence the way she did.

Our room looked brighter when Madarjoon was in it, and the atmosphere felt more relaxed. Our dear, kindhearted grandmother had a distinct way of taking the worry and stress from the room. She could transform the saddest feeling into pure optimism and lightheartedness. I was happiest in her presence. We all were.

Once when we were getting ready to sleep, we fought over who would sleep next to her. I suggested, "Why don't you sleep in the middle? Etty can sleep on your left, I'll sleep on your right, and Motty on top of you. That way, we'll all have you."

The adults started to laugh, but I didn't think it was funny. It made perfect sense to me and my sisters.

A couple of days passed, and Momman was up more often; her cheeks went back to their usual pretty rosy color. Her radiant smile returned too. She had a contagious smile that warmed your entire soul and seeped into your heart.

When our baby brother turned a week old, my parents invited some of our neighbors and relatives for lunch to show him off and announce the name they had chosen for him.

Early one Friday morning, we had the gathering at our place. Momman's sister, Khaleh Afsar, came there with a large copper pot and brought Akbar, my six-year-old cousin, with her. He wanted to spend time with me and my sisters before the rest of his family joined us later in the day. We didn't have a kitchen, so we cooked outside for our guests. Aghajoon, Akbar, and I put two rows of bricks, three stacks high, in the yard. I added dried wood between the bricks to start a fire, and before long, the scent of burnt wood filled our backyard. I loved the aroma. It indicated that a delicious meal would soon be prepared.

After setting the fire, Aghajoon went off to work. Although Fridays were a day off in Iran, all the shop owners in our neighborhood kept their businesses open till noon or sometimes all day. Akbar, Etty, and I became Khaleh and Madarjoon's helpers. Motty was too young to help, so she stayed with Momman and the baby inside the room, while the three of us chopped and peeled the pile of potatoes and eggplants Madarjoon had placed before us. We rushed to finish our chores so we could play, but as soon as we were done, Madarjoon brought out a round metal tray.

"Bah, bah, mashallah, mashallah, what good kids. This is the last thing for you to do," she said as she poured many cups of rice onto the metal tray.

I divided the rice into three piles: one for Akbar, one for Etty, and one for myself. All the while, Akbar and Etty shifted their eyes back and forth, comparing the piles to make sure we all had an equal amount. It took us one hour to clean the rice, removing all the little pebbles and black grains. By then, the fragrance of fried eggplant and potatoes filled the air, making our stomachs rumble with hunger.

I was looking forward to having *gheymeh bademjan* (beef stew with eggplant) with fried potatoes and rice for lunch. It was a delicious dish, one of my many favorites.

By noon, all the guests had arrived: my maternal aunts and uncles with their families; Nobar Khanoom, the midwife; and Sima Khanoom, her husband, along with their other tenants and their daughters, Saba and Sara. Our tiny room was crowded with at least twenty people, but everyone was happy and wanted to see the baby, who was sound asleep in Momman's arms. He looked so peaceful and content.

Madarjoon asked me to spread the sofreh on the floor and put plates and tablespoons down for everyone.

After Aghajoon came home, everyone helped with taking out the food and putting it on the sofreh. "Please. Please. Let's begin," he said.

Everyone sat down. The elders sat away from the door and at the head of the sofreh. We were seated so close to one another that our shoulders were constantly rubbing up against each other. Once we started eating, we had to be careful not to elbow the person next to us in the face as we brought the food up to our mouths!

Aghajoon stepped onto the sofreh in his bare feet, as he usually did when we had guests, and began serving everyone. He poured rice onto each person's plate and gave them a soft, steaming piece of bread, then picked up the stew bowl and poured some for everyone; usually, the most meat went to the adult guests. The more meat we served to the guests, the more respect we offered them. Although secretly I wished I could have more meat on my plate, I never voiced this.

Momman sat next to Aghajoon, trying to eat while holding the sleepy baby. She seemed quite happy and fully back to her old self.

After our meal, I looked around the sofreh. All the bowls and platters of food were empty; there wasn't a single grain of rice left.

Then Aghajoon and Madarjoon slipped away to bring in the tea. On a silver tray, they had placed many small tea glasses filled with tea and a bowl filled with sugar cubes. I got up, grabbed a platter of cookies, and followed closely behind them, offering the dessert to the guests.

Everyone was still drinking tea and talking when the baby finally woke up. Momman smiled and gave him a gentle kiss on his cheek. "Agha and I decided to call him Morteza. According to Madarjoon, it means 'the chosen,'" she explained, as she handed him to her brother.

Etty and I exchanged a look and smiled. I was happy our brother finally had a name, and we didn't have to call him Brother anymore. Now we referred to him as Morteza—a fine name if ever I'd heard one.

My uncle, Daii, took out some money and slipped it into the waist of Morteza's tiny pants. He kissed him on the forehead and handed him over to another guest, who followed suit. Little Morteza was passed to every adult in the room. Each kissed him gently and stuffed his pants with money. By the time the baby was returned to Momman, he resembled a tiny little scarecrow made of toman bills instead of straw. I couldn't help but smile at my little brother as he passed by me.

After most of the guests left, Nobar Khanoom approached Momman, who was holding the baby. "May God give you a long and happy life," she said, kissing Morteza's forehead. She thanked Momman and opened the door to leave, "Come and get me when you are having another baby and refer me to other pregnant women," she said as she bent down to put her shoes on.

"More babies?" Momman replied incredulously. "I have two girls and two boys. That's enough for us. But don't worry, I'll spread the word about you and how skillful you are, Nobar Khanoom." Momman smiled.

Nobar Khanoom slipped her shoes on and stood up to face Momman, a curious twinkle in her eye. "Something tells me you will have more children."

Momman's smile disappeared. "Bite your tongue, Nobar Khanoom."

Nobar Khanoom apologized for her troublesome prophecy and headed out the door, but with that same look in her eyes and a confident smile on her face. Part of me wondered why my mother had resisted the thought of another child. This one had certainly brought much joy to our home.

After Nobar Khanoom left, Etty and I began to clean up our tiny room. We overheard Madarjoon telling Momman that she was planning to leave later that day. Etty and I looked at each other with sad faces. We begged and pleaded with her not to leave, but Madarjoon was insistent.

"Etty, let's hide her shoes. How can she go home without them?" I whispered in her ear. She smiled in agreement. So, I took our grandmother's shoes and put them on the top of the stairs in the hallway of our building, where she couldn't see them. I was confident this would keep her here, as we wished.

A few hours later, after the conversation began to die down, Madarjoon headed to the door. She opened it, looked down, and paused, before turning around to face Etty and me with a playfully angry look on her face.

Etty and I couldn't stop giggling.

"Nana, Mohsen Jon, I promise I will come back soon. Now give me my shoes."

I shrugged and told her I didn't know where they were.

"Madar, what's the rush? Stay here. The kids love you, and Agha told me to keep you here," Momman chimed in.

Etty and I were praying that Madarjoon would agree, but Saba ruined our plans. She came walking down the stairs, holding grandmother's shoes. "Do these belong to you?"

I angrily snatched them from her and once again begged Madarjoon not to leave.

She shook her head and said matter-of-factly, "Nana, Mohsen Jon, I've been away for a week and have thousands of things to do." With that, she kissed Etty, Motty, and me on the cheeks, then kissed Morteza's forehead. "Azam jan, send Mohsen if you need me," Madarjoon said sweetly, as she turned around to hug and kiss her daughter.

As soon as Madarjoon left, so did the sense of happiness in our room. Her presence made such a big difference through her affection, cheerfulness, and kind eyes. I think that's why the joy in our home left when our grandmother did.

Days later, Nobar Khanoom came back to read more Qur'an verses in Morteza's ears. Momman put one sugar cone and fifteen tomans on a square-shaped cotton cloth and brought the four corners together to tie them in the middle. She then handed it to Nobar Khanoom for her services.

A couple of months passed, and I kept getting flashbacks of the day Morteza was born and what Madarjoon buried in our yard. I had to ask Momman about it. I needed to know what it was. One day, when she was knitting a pair of yellow socks for my baby brother, I quietly sat next to her.

She looked up and smiled.

"Momman?"

"Yes?"

"How are babies born?"

She looked at me, puzzled. I could tell she was shocked to hear my question.

"How?" I asked again.

She continued knitting, her fingers missing a step or two in the process. "Umm, you see, God puts a baby inside a woman's tummy after she's married," she explained. "And then the baby grows inside her until it's time for it to be born."

"So how does the baby come out?" I asked, still curious.

"Well." She cleared her throat. "Someone like Nobar Khanoom comes to cut the woman's stomach open and take the baby out. That's how."

I now understood the reason for the blood in the bucket, but I was still uncertain about the purple thing with the cord. I didn't want to tell her I had seen what Madarjoon buried. I didn't think she would like that. The conversation ended when Morteza started crying and Momman set down her knitting needles on the floor, before getting up to tend to him. I left the room, still not completely satisfied with the answer she gave me. I knew there was more to it. There had to be.

Over time, Morteza grew and began to know us more. He smiled every time I came back home from school, and he held out his arms for me to pick him up. On one warm summer day, I took Morteza to Aghajoon's shop to show him to Ramazoon. He wanted to see him.

"What's his name?" Ramazoon pinched my brother's cheeks softly with his dirty hands.

"It's Morteza," I said, wiping the dirt off my baby brother's face.

"He is so beautiful. He looks like a foreigner, so white, and his eyes are light brown. He doesn't even have black hair. He has blond fuzz." He touched Morteza's head. Ramazoon took a small rock from the sidewalk and threw it into the joob. The plop sound as the rock hit the water caught Morteza's attention.

"You know what would taste good right now?" my friend asked with a mischievous grin.

"I don't know. Ice water?" I said with a chuckle, wiping the beads of sweat from my forehead.

"No, my father's cold doogh. You should try it. It's so refreshing, and it cools every part of your body as it goes down."

Morteza started fussing, so I got up to head home, without responding.

As I was crossing the street, Ramazoon shouted, "One day, I'll take you to our house to try the doogh."

I looked back to face Ramazoon, smiled, and nodded in agreement.

Morteza was getting bigger, chubbier, and so playful. His beautiful face was getting rounder and cuter. He was beginning to look more like Momman—fair and rosy. As tough as things were back then, we enjoyed ourselves and life was good—until Morteza turned about four months old. That is when things started to change again. I noticed Momman's strange sickness had come back. She was throwing up and looked tired again, except this time neither my father nor my mother looked happy.

When Madarjoon came to visit, I eavesdropped on their conversation, hoping to find out what was going on.

"Azam Jon, why did you let this happen? Two babies so close to each other?" Madarjoon complained as she shook her head.

"They told me that as long as I am breastfeeding, I am safe," Momman replied with an angry voice.

I didn't understand what they were saying. *Was she going to have another baby?* That was how it started last time, with Momman throwing up every morning. Unlike the adults in the family, I really liked the idea of another baby sibling. Morteza was so much fun. My sisters and I played with him every chance we had.

A few months passed, and Momman's belly grew. This I was happy about. But Morteza's changing behavior upset me. He was six months old and appeared to be getting weak and pale. He had lost his chubby cheeks and looked very frail. Momman began to get frustrated with him because he would no longer take her breast, and it was hard on her body to be pregnant and produce sufficient milk to feed an infant at the same time. Plus, she didn't eat much. We couldn't afford that much food. I was certain Momman wasn't getting enough to eat since she was basically eating for three.

Momman pumped her breasts, but there wasn't enough milk to fill up Morteza, so sometimes she mixed some sugar and water and poured it into the bottle to temporarily satisfy his hunger until she could figure out how to make more milk. I'm sure it was difficult for Momman to deal with her pregnancy and her fussy baby. Weeks went on, and Morteza's condition got worse. He was no longer interested in anything and didn't like to be touched or held. Increasingly, he would clump up into a ball in the corner and cry himself to sleep. Everyone felt sorry for him and tried to come up with some remedy to cure him.

Khaleh Afsar's advice made the most sense to me. "*Khahar* (sister), why don't you take him to the doctor?"

"We took him to Lulagar Hospital, but they didn't have a children's section, so they refused to see him," Momman explained.

My aunt looked at her curiously, "There are other hospitals here in Tehran, you know. Lulagar isn't the only one."

Momman didn't respond to that.

A doctor's visit cost a lot of money. None of us had ever gone to one, even when we were seriously ill, like when all the children in the neighborhood developed diarrhea from contaminated drinking water. Momman simply boiled some *gol gav zaban* (a purplish herb) and gave the concoction to us to drink—one small teacup per child. It tasted and smelled horrible. I had to put a lot of sugar cubes in my mouth and hold my nose before I swallowed the bitter, medicinal dark tea. Surprisingly, it cured us in a day.

Momman brought some tea and rice cookies and put them in front of Khaleh Afsar, who softened a rice cookie, rolled it into a little ball, and put it in Morteza's mouth. He scrunched his nose and pulled his head away defiantly, before making a squealing sound that soon turned into a full-blown tantrum. Khaleh Afsar was able to get some of the food in, but

Morteza ended up spitting most of it out. He didn't want to eat. He had become dependent upon the sugary beverage my mother fixed for him.

Momman glanced at her struggling sister and said harshly, "Leave him alone. He won't eat anything, only sugar water."

That's all he wanted. Etty and I took turns filling his bottle and were thrilled when he drank most of it. Every time Momman changed his cloth diaper, she'd say, "I don't know why I even bother with this. You don't eat enough to have a dirty diaper." Then she wrapped him back up and resecured the diaper with two large safety pins.

I'm sure it must have been exceedingly difficult for my twenty-three-year-old mother to take care of the household, raise four children, teach sewing classes in the mornings, and continue to stitch clothes for her customers at night, while working under the oil lamp. Still, she did it somehow. But despite her strength, she grew tired and irritable. Momman's frustration got to a point that she would listen to anyone's ideas about how to treat Morteza—no matter how ridiculous the idea was.

One customer of Momman's, an elderly woman, came over with some fabric so Momman could sew a dress for her. She noticed the sickly looking Morteza in the corner of the room staring at her. "What's going on with this boy? He should be climbing up the walls. How old is he?" She clicked her tongue, scoffing.

My sisters and I were quietly doing our homework in the corner of the room when we heard the question. We stopped, trying desperately to hear Momman's reply. She told her that since she had become pregnant with another child, her son wouldn't take her breast anymore and didn't have the energy to do anything but to sit quietly.

"*Saghfesh oftadeh*" (the roof of his mouth has fallen), the woman replied.

Etty and I exchanged confused looks. We had no idea what she meant by that. Who is she? A doctor? What kind of disease is this? We had never heard of anything like this and wondered if Momman had.

"I can fix it," she claimed. She asked Momman for some butter. We didn't have any in our room, so my mother sent me upstairs to get some from Sima Khanoom. The old woman put some butter on her thumb and forced her finger into Morteza's mouth, pressing hard.

My poor fragile brother's face turned red, and he screamed at the top of his lungs. It must have hurt him horribly. I wanted to kick that woman out of our room for causing pain to Morteza. But I was only a kid and couldn't do things like that, though I wished someone would have. Momman should have made her stop, but surprisingly she didn't.

To make matters worse, this sadistic ritual became the old woman's routine. Every time she came over to try on her outfit, she took some butter and pressed hard on the roof of Morteza's mouth. He hated it. Eventually, whenever Morteza saw her come into the room, he would pull himself into a little ball as if he wanted to disappear. My heart ached for my little brother. I wanted to help him. Why Momman trusted this stupid woman and allowed her to torture my poor brother was beyond me. The only thing I could think of was that she must have been so desperate for something or someone to cure her son that she allowed this to continue out of pure desperation.

The day the old woman paid for her dress and left, Etty and I were happy. Morteza would no longer have to tolerate her archaic treatment, which had done nothing to improve his condition. His torture was over, though his situation worsened when our mother gave birth to our new baby brother, Majeed. Nobar Khanoom delivered him just as she had Morteza.

When I ran once again to Nobar Khanoom's house to get her, she smiled and said matter-of-factly, "I told your mother she would have more children. This won't be the last either."

The new baby looked like my sister Etty. He had olive skin, deep brown eyes, and lots of dark hair. In the middle of his hair, he had an interesting curl that twirled around from one side to the other—a cowlick. No matter how many times we dampened it or combed it, the curl would perk back up. It was a cute signature look that set him apart from other babies.

With the arrival of Majeed, everyone gave up on Morteza. We fed him only what he didn't struggle to eat, usually sugary water since that was the easiest and cheapest means available to us. Every morning when I woke up, the first thing I did was check on him to find out if he was still breathing. Momman used to point at him and say, "*In ke mordaniieh*" (this one will die soon). That scared me. I loved my little brother and didn't want him to die.

It was amazing how this little, fragile, thirteen-month-old boy hung onto life. His tummy grew big, as if he had hidden a small ball under his shirt, and his legs were small and wobbly. He had to rest his hands against the wall and pull himself up to stand. He gradually started walking but still didn't like anyone touching him. I wondered if that hurt him.

Now, instead of Morteza, I took Majeed outside to show him off. Everyone would pinch his fat cheeks in admiration of his beauty. The old-fashioned and ornery elderly women would kiss his forehead and claim that babies with this kind of curl running through their hair were "children of God" and would be returned to Him in a short time. At comments like these, I scowled, squeezed my baby brother closer to my chest, and walked away with haste. I didn't understand why anyone would say things like that about an infant. Didn't they know he was my brother, and it upset me to hear those kinds of remarks?

Majeed grew bigger and cuter by the day. He was a very interactive baby and very astute for his age. He blinked hard with both of his eyes and didn't stop until he made us laugh. Then he laughed right along with us, with his mouth all the way open, showing his toothless gums. I taught him different games. I held him, stomach facing the floor, and said, "Majeed, Majeed, *mahii*" (fish).

When he heard *mahii,* he giggled and brought his arms to his sides and secured them there very tightly.

"Mahii, mahii!" I repeated as I wiggled him around and moved him up and down like a fish. While the whole family was having fun with Majeed, in the corner of our room, Morteza was sitting, with his big belly, watching us enviously. Those sad eyes followed us everywhere, but I couldn't understand what they were saying. *Does he wish he were the one going up and down, receiving all the attention? If so, then why does he shudder and shy away from us whenever we try to touch him?*

Majeed, on the other hand, loved to be around people. Whenever I had time, I took him to Aghajoon's shop to be with Ramazoon to play with him during his break.

Majeed was growing rapidly. At nine months, he began to crawl quickly. We had to watch him constantly because he was so fast. In the blink of an eye, he could go from one side of the room to another. Whenever he reached Morteza, he teased him by pulling at his legs or hands. Poor Morteza didn't even have the energy to scream. He just let him yank his limbs around. At this point, Morteza was about fourteen months older than Majeed, but Majeed looked much stronger, with his chubby arms and legs. I didn't know what to do to help Morteza. It appeared he was giving up, that he had lost the will to live.

Meanwhile, Momman kept waiting for Morteza's teeth to come in so she could give him solid food. None of us understood how his body continued to function on sugary water.

Summer was upon us again, and Ramazoon kept reminding me about his invitation to take me to his place so I could try his father's refreshing doogh. I really wanted to go, but between chores at Aghajoon's shop and taking care of Majeed, I had no time. I didn't want to take Majeed with me, because Momman was still breastfeeding him and Majeed seemed to be hungry all the time.

It was a sweltering summer day and Majeed was uncharacteristically fussy. Momman asked if I could carry him around the block so he would fall asleep. I held his heavy, chubby body in my arms and walked around the neighborhood. He pointed at everything he saw, and I told him what they were—*olagh* (donkey), joob, and *motoor seeklet* (motorcycle).

I saw Ramazoon across the street outside Mamad Agha's shop. He must have been on one of his breaks. I headed to Aghajoon's shop to greet him. Majeed put his head on my shoulder and began cooing and babbling quietly.

Aghajoon saw me approaching with my baby brother, and his usual gruffness transformed into an unusual softness. He gestured for me to bring Majeed near him. It was apparent that Majeed was our father's favorite child. He became a completely different person whenever Majeed was around. Aghajoon smiled at Majeed sweetly and kissed him softly on the forehead, before continuing his work of polishing a customer's shoe.

I walked over to Ramazoon.

"Do you want to come over to our place to have some doogh? I have some free time," he said excitedly.

"I don't know if I can. My mom asked me to entertain Majeed until he falls asleep."

"His eyes are closed. I think he's napping." Ramazoon looked over my shoulder.

It was a balmy day, and I really did want to try some doogh, so I said, "All right, let me put him down at home. You wait here for me."

I placed Majeed on a blanket on the floor next to Morteza, who was asleep as well. I walked quietly to Momman, who was by the hooz, washing the cloth diapers, and got her permission to go to Ramazoon's place to try some of his father's doogh. My parents knew his family well. Aghajoon used to go there to buy ice blocks when the heat became unbearable.

Momman gave me a little money to pay for my beverage. As I was about to leave, she hollered at me to brew some tea so she could have it later.

I placed the teapot on top of the samovar to brew, put my shoes back on, and ran outside, hollering as I went, "Momman, I did it. I'm going to Ramazoon's. When I come back, I'll take Majeed out. He is sleeping next to Morteza now."

She looked up, gave me a contented smile, and nodded.

Ramazoon and I headed for his house. We passed by a woman in her chador, tapping on watermelons at the fresh produce shop to select a sweet one. Then we passed the bakery, its counters stacked high with fresh steaming bread. The workers were on a break, smoking cigarettes and drinking tea while lounging outside. These were the usual activities one might see on our streets.

We noticed a mulberry branch hanging into the street from one of the residents' houses as we continued toward Ramazoon's home. We took off our old torn-up shoes and threw them at the branches. A handful of mulberries fell onto the ground. We scooped them up for a sweet snack.

We continued to walk for another five minutes or so, happily eating our berries, until we reached his house, a small clay structure his father had built on barren land. We took off our shoes before entering the dark room Ramazoon called home.

It took my eyes a few minutes to adjust to the lack of light before I could observe the unpaved floor, covered with torn, thin blankets. In one corner, their bedding, blankets, and pillows were piled high; in another, a few pots and pans were scattered about. There were no windows and absolutely no ventilation. I felt I could suffocate. It was no wonder Ramazoon smelled sour during the sizzling summer days. *How could they stand to live here?*

The outdoor bathroom was poorly constructed as well. The hinges on the metal door were rusty and didn't completely shut. I didn't understand how anyone could go to the bathroom with no privacy. I don't think I could have proudly shown this place to my friends, as Ramazoon did, if I lived there. I would have been too embarrassed, but Ramazoon showed no shame. I realized how lucky I was to live where we did. Compared to this filthy, dark, and stuffy place, our room seemed spacious, clean, and bright. Across from their living area was a stall his father had built from shabby wood.

Ramazoon told me they stored ice blocks there and conducted their business—selling doogh and ice blocks. "My family has to work fast when we get ice delivered in the early mornings. We chop them into smaller blocks and then put them into sacks before transferring them here in the shade. They don't melt or stick together." He pointed to the inside of the shack, as we approached it.

Both his parents were working inside the stall, wearing clothes that were just as dirty and shabby as Ramazoon's. We greeted them, and they smiled back sweetly and looked genuinely happy to see me.

"Are you the son of the kafash whose shop is next to Mamad Agha's?" his mother asked.

"Yes!" I beamed with pride.

"Ramazoon really likes you and tells me you always help him."

I wondered if she was referring to the time we had made a little money from the joob and I gave Ramazoon half of it. I didn't say anything. I stood there and continued to smile.

Ramazoon's father wasn't paying any attention to our conversation and was attending to his customers, putting ice into aluminum tumblers and pouring the yogurt drink into them.

"Mohsen would like some doogh," Ramazoon told his father.

I handed two rials to his dad, and he gave me an icy doogh.

"How about you, Ramazoon? Do you want to share?" I asked.

His father gave him one too. I couldn't see how much doogh Ramazoon got, but I knew he didn't get as much as I did since he didn't pay for his. It felt good to hold the cold container. I gulped all of it down in seconds. Ramazoon was right: it cooled me down immediately. If I had more money, I would have bought more. I am sure I could have asked for another one without paying, but I didn't want to take advantage of my friendship with Ramazoon. His family was poor and needed to sell as many of those drinks as they could to make a living.

Ramazoon had to go back to Mamad Agha's shop, so we said goodbye to his parents and left. We had just arrived at my father's shop when I saw Etty running frantically toward us. As she got closer, I could see tears streaming down her face. She ran right past Ramazoon and me, into Aghajoon's shop.

"Aghajoon, Aghajoon, Momman wants you home! Majeed is burnt badly! He dumped the tea pot on himself," she yelled through her sniffles.

Etty's words made no sense to me. *How could he have been hurt?* I was holding his sleepy body in my arms not long ago. I watched Aghajoon shoot up and jump over his counter, crossing the street to go to our place. Without realizing what I was doing, I followed Aghajoon, but he looked back at me and told me to stay put until he returned.

I sat on the front steps of Aghajoon's shop and began to cry. I didn't care who saw me. I didn't want to act tough; I wanted to cry. I needed to cry. For my brother and for myself. Ramazoon wanted to sit and comfort me, but Mamad Agha told him to come back to his shop.

What a cruel man, I thought. *Did he not care that my brother was hurt, and I needed some support?*

Only a few minutes had passed when I saw my parents rushing toward Lulagar Hospital. I heard Majeed's wailing and noticed his tiny body hung over Momman's shoulders.

Etty came to Aghajoon's shop and sat next to me. We were both silent for some time. I was haunted by the echo of my brother's wails, while Etty stared, teary eyed, into the distance at the shrinking silhouettes of our parents.

"Mohsen, I was busy playing upstairs with Motty, Saba, and Sara when we heard a scream. I couldn't tell if it was Majeed or Morteza." She wiped her tears with the back of her hands as she continued to explain, "I ran down and, in our room, I saw Majeed. The empty teapot was next to him. His face and head were red. The skin had peeled off his hands and part of his neck." Etty breathed in deeply and choked on her sobs. She continued, her voice becoming more frantic. "I didn't know what to do. I was afraid touching him would make it worse. He was in a lot of pain and screaming so hard."

I said nothing but put my arm around her to comfort her. It wasn't her fault. As soon as Mamad Agha left his shop, Ramazoon came out to check on us. "Is it bad?" he asked in a sad voice.

I shrugged and quietly said, "I hope he'll be okay."

The three of us sat in silence, each in our own thoughts. Hours later, we saw my parents get off the bus, without Majeed. Aghajoon helped Momman go back to our place and then crossed the street to come back to his shop, walking faster and harder than normal. When he reached us, he looked directly at me and pointed his finger at me. He was shaking. His eyes were cold, angry, and dark. "Mohsen, it's *your* fault!" he screamed. "If you had kept an eye on him, this wouldn't have happened!"

I stared up at him, terrified, tears silently streaming down my cheeks. Didn't he realize I was only a child and needed to be comforted rather than reprimanded? Couldn't he see my red and swollen eyes? Didn't that tell him all he needed to know?

"Go home and see if Momman needs your help," he said coldly. Somehow, he saw me as the one who had hurt his favorite child. Somehow, he felt I was to blame.

At home, everyone was crying—even Morteza looked sad sitting in the corner of the room. He felt that something wasn't right.

Momman told us with teary eyes that they had taken Majeed to Lulagar Hospital. They wouldn't admit him there, because they did not have a pediatric department—the same thing they told my parents when they took Morteza there. This time they suggested Neekokar Hospital, a children's hospital, where he would surely be treated. My parents had taken a taxi there. I couldn't imagine how much they had to pay for the fifteen-minute ride or how they were able to pay at all. Momman said we would have to wait to find out how Majeed did. "I pray he'll be okay," she said, looking up into the sky.

Two times every day, Momman took a bus to the hospital to nurse Majeed. When she came back, my sisters and I gathered around her to hear about Majeed's progress. Even Morteza was listening to what she was saying. I don't think he comprehended the conversation; he just wanted to be part of everyone gathering together. We all sat there hoping Momman's news would be good.

"The nurses are very nice, and they are treating him kindly. He is drinking my milk, and they have a tube with some kind of liquid inserted in his arm, making sure he has enough water in his body," Momman said, smiling.

About a month passed. Then, one day, Momman came home with a huge smile on her face. She looked as if she would burst if she didn't get this news off her chest. "Majeed is doing really well considering how badly he burned himself. There is only one small scar, the size of a pea, under his right eye." She pinched the tips of her fingers together to show us the size of the mark. "His front teeth are coming out too; the little rascal bit my breast today."

We thought that was the funniest thing we had ever heard and laughed hard.

The next day, Momman came home with even better news. "Majeed is coming home soon," she said joyfully.

Overwhelmed with relief and excitement, I thought about the first thing I would do when Majeed arrived home. *What games should we play first? Should I put him on my shoulders and walk him around our neighborhood or should I play mahii with him? Maybe I should take him to see Ramazoon.* Majeed liked him a lot. Ramazoon entertained him by making funny faces or tickling him. I was so happy Majeed was well again. I wouldn't have been able to forgive myself if we had lost him. I constantly blamed myself for what happened to him and prayed to God for his recovery.

Momman sewed a blue shirt and a pair of pants especially for Majeed, smiling the whole time while making it.

The day of Majeed's return home finally arrived. It had felt so empty without hearing the precious baby's giggles; without seeing Momman cradling him in her arms, a tranquil smile on her face; and without the calming effect Majeed had on all of us, especially Aghajoon. Momman took the little blue outfit with her when she left for the hospital.

We waited patiently and excitedly for Majeed's arrival and started cleaning the room. We took turns to go outside to look for Momman and Majeed. It was taking longer for her to get home than usual.

"Mohsen, what's taking her so long? Can you walk over to Aghajoon's shop and ask him to go to the hospital?" Etty pleaded worriedly.

I was getting worried myself, so I agreed. As I crossed the street toward Aghajoon's shop, I saw Momman getting off the bus. Something was not right. There were two women on either side of her, helping her down the bus steps. I could see Momman muttering something, repeatedly wiping her face with the back of her hands. Then I noticed Majeed wasn't with her.

I ran to her. "Where is Majeed?" I asked frantically.

"Mohsen Jon, Mohsen Jon," she put her shaking hand on my shoulder. "Your brother died last night." She was sobbing and breathing with difficulty

"Died!?" My jaw dropped. *How could that be? After a month of waiting, he was finally going to come home.*

Momman couldn't talk anymore. The pain of my brother's death was too much for her to bear. With the news of his death, the guilt and the sadness came rushing back to me. Our little game of mahii would only be a memory now. I felt numb and hopeless. I mustered up the courage to ask the two women next to her if they would leave her with me.

They nodded.

I took her hand to lead her home. Her eyes were red and teary, her hands weak and trembling, her back hunched over. The five-minute walk home from the bus stop was long. I tried my best not to look across the street at Aghajoon's shop.

As soon as Etty and Motty saw Momman, they knew something was wrong. I think even little Morteza could sense it. He pulled himself up to get closer to his mother to comfort her as well.

Quietly, I told Etty what had happened.

She simply stared at the floor and walked outside to cry alone.

"What's wrong?" Motty held the corner of Momman's skirt.

"Nothing, nothing. Go upstairs and play with your friends Saba and Sara," Momman said quietly, as she patted Motty's head.

Our father came home earlier than normal. One of the shop owners had seen us and told him about his wife's condition.

"Khanoom, what happened? Where is Majeed?" Aghajoon looked panicked.

Momman had a tough time speaking but managed to tell Aghajoon that Majeed had developed diarrhea and began vomiting the night before. The doctors couldn't do anything for him, and by midnight he passed away. "We lost Majeed." She burst into tears as she shared the grim news with my father.

Never in my life had I seen such a look on my father's face. His eyes filled with tears, his lips started to quiver, and his eyebrows furrowed. He immediately left the room, without saying anything; he wanted to mourn alone.

Majeed was in our lives for only nine months, yet we had so many fond memories of him. He was a sweet boy who loved making everyone laugh. Anyone who saw him couldn't help but pinch his cheeks or play with the unusual curl in his hair. I thought of those elderly women who said that he was a special boy, and children with a cowlick like his would be returned to God soon. This had made me so angry. I couldn't understand why God would bother to give Majeed to us if He was planning on taking him back in such a short time. Did God like to see us suffer?

Our grandmother had always told us, "Human beings can't understand God's logic, but there is always a reason for everything. We should accept what He gives us."

I imagined God as an old, fat man with a long white beard, sitting on fluffy, white clouds, holding Banu in one arm and Majeed in the other. I imagined God laughing at me as if He enjoyed punishing me for something I had not done. God had taken away two of the people who were dearest to me in the world. He was cruel and heartless. How could God do this to us?

The next day, our room was filled with my maternal family, uncle, aunts, Madarjoon, and Sima Khanoom. Aghajoon and Momman's brother went to the hospital to bring Majeed home. It was a custom then to bring the deceased home before burial so their spirit could say goodbye to their home and family.

Aghajoon carried Majeed home wrapped in a white cotton cloth. The bag was tied, and no part of his body was showing. They placed him in the corner of the room, away from everyone. An uncomfortable chill itched its way through my body, starting from my upper back—the boy who had brought so much joy and laughter into our lives in such a short amount of time was tucked inside a piece of cloth, lifeless. I lost control of myself; tears streamed heavily down my cheeks and dripped from my chin.

Aghajoon and Momman's brother took the body to the Darasht Cemetery—a cemetery for poor families, where none of the plots had any gravestones. To date, we don't know where Majeed's grave is. We had no place to visit and remember him, other than the remnants of a happy memory deep within the corners of our minds.

"Where are you taking my son?" my mother cried frantically as they took his body away. "He's too small, and he's afraid of the dark. God, why did You do this to me? What did I do to deserve this!?" Momman screamed as she ran after my father and uncle, who were carrying Majeed in the white cloth.

Madarjoon whispered something in my mother's ear. Momman immediately nodded and calmed down. I suspected Momman could now empathize with Belquees Khanoom and everything she went through when she unexpectedly lost Banu. I looked around the room: everyone was crying. Some of the elderly folks were reciting verses from the Qur'an. My aunt Khaleh Afsar was offering *halva* (a dark brown sweet dish made with flour, oil, rose water, and sugar) with tea. Someone tapped on my shoulder, and as I glanced back, I saw Ramazoon. He smiled and sat next to me on the floor.

My father kept reminding me that if I hadn't taken Majeed home to nap, he would have been alive. He didn't understand that I already felt guilty about that. All I really wanted in that moment was for my father to comfort me, instead of adding more guilt to my shoulders.

With Majeed's death, Momman started paying attention to Morteza again. I don't think she could have withstood losing two of her children.

Thankfully, a new pediatrician, Dr. Eshraghii, had recently opened an office in our area; he was a Godsend. Khaleh Afsar insisted we take Morteza to him to be examined.

Momman agreed and asked me to accompany them.

A fifteen-minute walk brought us to his office building. The office was ridiculously small for a medical establishment, but it was well organized, with three chairs and a small table arranged in the corner of the front room. There was nothing fancy in there or on the walls, except a black-and-white poster of a nurse in a white uniform. She had her forefinger on her mouth, a sign to be silent. Momman, Morteza, and I sat in the creaky wooden chairs. Morteza had his face down and looked scared of the place but didn't cry.

After several minutes, a short and portly old man with a gray mustache walked into the waiting room. He reminded me of my maternal uncle. The stethoscope around his neck and his white coat told me he was the doctor. I looked at his name tag, Dr. Eshraghii.

He looked at the three of us and guided us to his exam room.

Dr. Eshraghii barely had to check Morteza before he knew exactly what treatment was needed. His big belly and thin arms and legs were enough evidence. He shook his head and asked Momman why it had taken her so long to bring her son to see a doctor. Momman just started crying and didn't say anything. He figured out on his own that we were too poor to afford it. All he had to do was look down at my torn shoes.

He gave Momman two cans of dry formula, Keegose. "Dilute three scoops in this much water." He pointed to the second mark on the baby bottle. "Give it to your son three or four times a day. Follow my instructions *exactly* as I told you. Don't give him less powder because you want to save money. I will know if you do that," he said in a serious tone.

He then looked inside Morteza's mouth. "Where are your teeth, boy?" He sighed and told us, "I want to see him here every week. If you don't show up, I'll come to your door. I know where you live."

"What's wrong with him, doctor?" Momman asked, afraid it might be more serious than she had previously thought.

"Too much sugar and no protein in his diet. You are lucky he's alive."

I decided to take charge of making Morteza's formula because I knew Momman might be tempted to give him less powder to save money, even though the doctor asked her not to.

We had to visit Dr. Eshraghii a couple more times after that initial visit so he could check on Morteza's progress. He was happy with the results. Momman complained about the cost of the powder and asked the doctor if we could substitute something else for it.

Dr. Eshraghii shook his head in disagreement, but he was kind to us. He charged us only five tomans per visit, half of his regular rate, and even gave Momman one free can of formula every time we went to his office.

Before too long, Morteza had pink cheeks again, and the shine had returned to his eyes. My happy brother had finally reappeared. He was laughing and running around now. The size of his belly shrank, while his limbs became chubbier and stronger. He turned into a joyful two-year-old boy whom we could barely get to stop talking and playing around.

Some days when I went to see Ramazoon, I took Morteza with me. One afternoon, as Ramazoon and I were talking, Morteza grabbed a stick and stabbed it into the water in the joob. He liked to see the water splash and loved showing off his accomplishments to us.

"*See?*! Ama-une, Ama-une." Morteza looked at Ramazoon.

"It's Ramazoon, not Ama-une." Ramazoon walked over to give Morteza's chubby cheeks a kiss, then he turned to me. "You know, I always thought he would be the one dying. I never imagined it would be Majeed," he said, swinging Morteza back and forth.

"I know what you mean, Ramazoon. There were days when Majeed and I would be playing and Morteza would look at us jealously from the corner of the room. I felt sorry for him, but he didn't want to be touched, so we left him alone." I shook my head. "Sometimes I wonder if he prayed that he could be the one having fun with us, and then God granted it."

Ramazoon shrugged and said, "That's strange for God to take one and let the other stay. Why couldn't you have both brothers?"

"I don't know. I'm glad Morteza is back, but I miss Majeed terribly." My voice trembled, and tears filled my eyes. I turned away from Ramazoon to hide my face. I didn't want him to see me cry.

Luckily, Motty and Morteza didn't quite understand the meaning of death. Occasionally, Motty asked where Majeed was. We told her that he was with us, but we couldn't see him. She was happy with that answer.

Around the time Morteza was beginning to get better, some of the more superstitious neighbors told Momman that the reason he became sick was because of jinns, supernatural beings God supposedly created from fire, who stole the healthy boy and replaced him with the ill one. "You need to change his name to something else for him to be fully healthy again," they ordered.

My parents weren't very superstitious, but they figured it wouldn't hurt to follow their recommendation. I think they couldn't bear losing another child, and truthfully, I don't know if I could have handled the loss of another brother either. The loss of Majeed was exceedingly difficult for all of us.

My parents started looking for a good name for Morteza. One night, when everyone was asleep, I heard them discussing their choices. "Khanoom, how about Masood?" Aghajoon asked.

"Masood? I like it, but my cousin named her son that. We can't have two babies in the family with the same name. It's a bad omen, and one of them will die," Momman whispered. I didn't remember Momman being so superstitious before.

"How about Saeed? That's a nice name."

"Saeed . . . Saeed. It means, happy," Momman said.

I smiled and repeated the name in my head. It felt appropriate, since we were all so happy God gave us our baby boy back. As much as I wanted to stay mad at God, I couldn't. I needed Him and I still prayed to Him whenever I wanted something very badly.

The next day during lunch, my parents announced in front of all the children as well as Madarjoon that we were changing Morteza's name to Saeed. Madarjoon clapped her hands in delight.

The following Friday, my grandma, my cousin Akbar, and my aunt Khaleh Afsar came by to make *ash-e reshteh*, the same soup Banu's mother made for seven years as an offering to God for giving her a daughter. When somebody's name was changed, it was customary to offer food to neighbors and family members. I helped Aghajoon prepare the fire for cooking the ash under two rows of bricks in our yard. I liked the smell of the wood getting red and burnt. The whole family pitched in to clean the ingredients, which included all kinds of greens, lentils, and beans.

By noon, the pleasant scent of smoked wood was replaced by the even better aroma of sautéed onions and garlic. It reminded me of when we were at the shrine, making soup for Banu. I thought back to when I jokingly stole the sparkly headband she had received as a birthday gift, and how she chased me down the hill to grab it. I remembered her teasingly telling me she was so mad at me that she wouldn't speak to me until judgment day. The idea of judgment day didn't seem as scary as it once did. I would be able to see Banu and Majeed again.

The sound of Madarjoon's voice brought me back. "Nana, Mohsen Jon, get Etty and Akbar to take the ash to people." She ladled the thick soup into bowls. My cheeks were damp. I hadn't even realized I was crying. Akbar, Etty, and I distributed the soup among our neighbors as well as to the shops near Aghajoon's place. "We changed Morteza's name to Saeed," we said each time we handed a bowl to a person.

"*Mubarak basheh*" (congratulations), they all replied.

And with that, Morteza's name had officially been changed to Saeed.

Dr. Eshraghii's office was our final stop. I brought Saeed with me for this trip, and surprisingly his office was open on a Friday. Dr. Eshraghii greeted us warmly and looked at my brother with joy. I gave the bowl of soup to the doctor and looked down to Saeed. "We changed his name to Saeed."

"Welcome back, Saeed Agha." He pinched my brother's chubby cheeks as he took the bowl of soup from me.

New House

Age Nine

We have a saying in Farsi: "The bird of Amen was on the way when you made your wish."

It means that if, as one makes a wish, an invisible bird from heaven hears it and responds with "Amen," then God grants that person's wish at that very moment. That must have been what happened to our mother when she made her wish to buy a house, because I cannot understand how else it would have come true.

The new room in Sima Khanoom's two-story house was bigger than our last one and had two large windows that overlooked the front yard. It was quite a change from the small room we previously rented from Ost Gholam Reza, with its one tiny window we covered with a raggedy old cloth.

In the new room, the windows were so big we could see the sky through them. Some nights, while lying in our roll-up bed on the floor, we looked out at the beautiful night sky and all the glittering stars.

One night, Etty pointed to the three brightest stars and said, "Mohsen, do you see those three big stars next to each other? The middle one is yours, the one on the right is mine, and the left one is Motty's."

I smiled because she had placed our stars in the same order that we slept. "So, what about our baby brother, Saeed? Where is his star?"

She pointed to a little star that was in the same area of our three and whispered, "That twinkling one. Do you see it? The left one?"

There were so many little stars on the pitch-black sky that night, and I didn't know which one she was referring to. But just to make her happy, I said, "Yes, I see it."

I wondered if Momman ever heard our conversations while she was sewing late into the night under the light of the kerosene heater. Something told me that she did, because later that night, I woke up to find Momman standing by the same window looking up at the night sky. This happened more than once, and sometimes I heard her sigh in a longing, exaggerated fashion. Other times, I heard her sniff as if she were crying. I wondered if she were trying to find her own star or if she were making her own wish. If it was the latter, I knew her wish must have been to have a house of her own.

For as long as I could remember, buying a house was one of Momman's top priorities in life. She knew that if she left it up to Aghajoon, with the little money he made, it would never happen. She saved every toman she earned from sewing garments for women in the area or teaching them how to sew. She wanted to buy a house to raise her growing family in, and she was determined to make her dream come true. There were six of us by now, four kids—Etty, Motty, Saeed, and I—plus our parents all living in one room.

In that room, in addition to eating, cooking, and sewing, my sister and I now had to do our homework. We spread our books on the floor, lying close together, side by side, as we read, wrote, or memorized our lessons for school. Saeed's crying underscored the messy and cramped circumstances. To make things even more tiresome, various guests—such as Momman's sisters, brother, or mother—often stopped by with their families to visit. Momman kept working through the constant noise and distraction, with the hope that someday she would be able to buy a beautiful house with its own yard and multiple rooms.

Living downstairs from Sima Khanoom was nice for me because she always gave me little snacks—such as nuts, sweet bread, or candy—when I looked after her infant boy while she cooked or cleaned. She would finish her work, walk over to her pantry, and ask me what I wanted to eat. Obviously, I always chose the biggest treat I could find: the sweet round bread her parents made in their village. I took it downstairs and divided it into four portions and gave each of my sisters and my brother a piece. Etty and I shared the chores in our household and helped Momman whenever she needed anything, so I always gave her a slightly bigger portion than the rest.

One day, Momman asked me to bring Sima Khanoom down to our room to try on her dress before she did the final stitching.

I skipped upstairs to find Sima Khanoom sweeping the balcony that overlooked the backyard as well as some of the neighboring yards. "Salam, my mom wants you to go downstairs to wear your outfit one last time before she does the final stitching."

Sima Khanoom looked up from her work. "Mohsen Jon, ask your mother to come up to me; it's better that way. I'm making lunch, and I don't want to burn it."

"Momman, you have to come upstairs, Sima Khanoom can't!" I hollered from the hallway of the second floor.

"If I wanted to scream, I could have done it myself," Sima Khanoom said, smiling.

After a minute or two, Momman came upstairs, carrying Sima Khanoom's flowery dress, still speckled with safety pins. It was the first time Momman had come up to the second floor.

After Momman and Sima Khanoom greeted one another, Momman handed the dress to her. As Sima Khanoom disappeared into the other room to try it on, I started playing with Sima Khanoom's two-month-old son, who had just woken up, while Momman became transfixed by something she saw from the balcony. "Wow, what a beautiful house, Mohsen. Do you see the lantana, the red roses, and the jasmine plants? That mulberry tree is so beautiful too. I wish we had a house like that. Soon, *inshallah* (God willing)." Her gaze was pointed at the yard of the two-story house across from Sima Khanoom's balcony. Her eyes were teary.

I had seen that house many times before from Sima Khanoom's balcony and didn't think much of it, but the combination of white jasmine flowers; red roses; and clusters of small yellow, orange, and pink flowers on the lantana plant made the yard look exceptionally beautiful. It made my heart ache to see Momman so pitiable, to see her wanting something so badly that she could not have. To comfort her, I immediately said, "Our yard is just as beautiful as this one." My voice was not convincing even to me, let alone Momman. Plus, I knew this was not our yard—it was the yard of our landlords, Sima Khanoom and her husband.

My parents continued working hard and saving money—never stopping to relax. Years later, Momman told me that she and Aghajoon had to save their money for twelve years so they could eventually buy a house.

Sometime early in the fall of that year, I overheard Aghajoon telling Momman that one of his customers won the lottery. The money Aghajoon's customer had won was enough for him to relocate to a better area than our neighborhood, so he decided to sell his house. The price was 17,000 tomans.

In those days, in addition to the price of the house, the buyer had to pay the closing cost, the cost of a notary, and all the seller's other expenses. With all these costs, my parents had to come up with about 17,500 tomans. The seller didn't have to spend any money in the process.

"This is such a low price. Agha, find out what we need to do to purchase it!" Momman said excitedly. She didn't even ask where the house was located. She just wanted to buy it since the price was right and she could finally have her own home.

When Aghajoon approached his customer about the house, he told Aghajoon that he wouldn't change the price even by one rial, since he was already selling it so cheap.

A few days later, Momman and Aghajoon went to see the house. When they returned, I turned my head toward the door so I could gauge their reaction.

Momman walked inside, head held high, with a smile from ear to ear. She walked proudly to our window and stared in the direction of the house with the beautiful yard. As it turned out, the house Aghajoon's customer was selling was the house she had seen from Sima Khanoom's balcony. When she looked at that house, wishing for one like it, the bird of Amen must have been passing through.

The realtor was also one of Aghajoon's customers, so he graciously gave Aghajoon ten days to come up with the money to buy the house.

After that, he would let his other customers know about it. According to Momman, that house would sell in one day since its price was so low. Momman and Aghajoon needed every one of those ten days to come up with the 17,500 tomans.

My parents had saved 6,000 tomans over the years. We were short 11,500 tomans, but they weren't about to give up. Aghajoon sold the five rial silver coins he had collected over the past ten years for five hundred tomans total. Some were one-of-a-kind, and he might have made a significantly larger profit if he had waited a decade longer.

Then Mamad Agha, the butcher, bought our handmade carpet for a thousand tomans. Madarjoon had given it to us as a gift not long before. I think she had gotten tired of sitting on the bumpy floor in our room. I felt so bad the day I rolled up the carpet for Mamad Agha. It was the only fancy thing we owned.

From that day onward, my parents sat together every night under the kerosene heater to figure out how much more they needed to buy the house and how they were going to get it. With their savings of 6,000 tomans and all the other things they sold, they had about 7,500 tomans. They still needed a lot more to make it to 17,500 tomans.

Momman regrettably handed over some of her wedding jewelry to Aghajoon to sell to a jeweler nearby. It was as if she were parting from one of her children when she gave him that bag containing three gold bangles, four gold necklaces, and two solid gold rings.

After selling all Momman's jewelry and a few other prized items, my parents had barely 9,000 tomans. We still needed another 8,500 tomans to buy the house. Luckily, one of Aghajoon's customers worked in the Saderat Bank and was able to tweak the paperwork so my parents could borrow 7,000 tomans. Unfortunately, the loan came with a high interest rate, making our monthly payments 140 tomans. Even at my immature age, I knew my parents would have a challenging time paying this amount every month.

We needed another 1,500 tomans to make our total of 17,500 tomans, and we had only one more day to make up that difference. We didn't know anyone in the family who could lend us any money—their financial situations were the same, if not worse, than ours. As a last resort,

Aghajoon told the realtor he really wanted to buy the house but was a bit short of the total amount. The realtor found a man by the name of Mr. Ghozii, meaning Mr. Hunchback, who did in fact have a hunchback. He lent us the remainder of the money, with a significant interest rate, which meant we had to pay him about 270 tomans per month. Momman wanted a house more than anything and knew this would be their only big opportunity to own one. Miraculously, we managed to produce the total amount, cutting it extremely close to the end of our grace period. We moved into the two-story house immediately.

The first things Momman wanted us to take there were the Qur'an and a bowl of clean water to bring "good omens and happiness" to the house and our family.

It only took Aghajoon and me five or six trips of less than a block each to bring over the rest of our things: a kerosene heater, a samovar to brew tea, some pots and pans, some copper plates, our clothing, our bedding, the dry food, a tin oil can, and some nonworking appliances Aghajoon wanted to repair and use some day.

Once everything had been moved and we finally had a chance to take a break, we roamed around the house excitedly. To us, our new place looked more like a mansion than a house. It had three upstairs rooms and three downstairs rooms. The narrow hallway on the first level led to our new backyard, with the beautiful roses, the lantana, and the jasmine plants. It felt a bit surreal to step outside into a yard that not so long ago had been only a dream.

The first thing Momman did was to go into the backyard, and we came out to enjoy it with her. She inhaled the scent of the roses and the jasmine, and her eyes tracked the colorful butterflies as they flew off the clusters of lantanas. I could tell she was mumbling something under her breath, and I wondered if she was thanking God for granting her wish.

In the middle of the backyard—as was the case for other similar houses—was a hooz with a faucet hanging over it. In the corner of the backyard was a bathroom. By then, the city had begun to bring plumbing and electricity to parts of our neighborhood; we couldn't wait to finally enjoy clean water, and looked forward to a day, hopefully soon, when we no longer had to work under the light of the kerosene heater.

Upstairs, Etty, Motty, and I kept going from one room to another, calling each other's names. We loved to hear our voices echo in the rooms. The upstairs had a wide-open space that led to three rooms, one of which had two windows overlooking an alley and the neighbors' front yards.

Eventually, I got to know all the kids in the neighborhood, including a girl named Maheen, who was crippled and walked with crutches. I found out later that she had caught polio at the age of six. Polio might have taken her ability to move her legs, but nothing could take away Maheen's spirit. She was a cheerful, energetic girl who participated in all our games and moved just as smoothly and swiftly as all the other kids in that alley. Her voice sounded so beautiful that by the time she was fourteen, she could sing the songs of Hayedeh, a famous Iranian singer. Every time Maheen came to our house, Etty asked her to sing. Closing our eyes, we could imagine Hayedeh had come for a private concert without her musicians.

The other two upstairs rooms overlooked our backyard. From there, we could see Sima Khanoom's house and our previous room in her house on the first floor. I wondered if she would continue giving me treats when I visited her. I soon found out, however, that wasn't the case, as she rudely asked me not to come to her house anymore. I really thought she loved me like her own child, but I was wrong. She wanted me only when my parents paid her rent. I wondered, *Is Sima Khanoom jealous that we moved into our own house? How can a person change so drastically from one day to the next?*

From the upstairs windows of our new home, we could see two of our neighbors' houses. The one to the right belonged to a family whose father was a teacher, but we later found out he belonged to the Sāzemān-e Ettelā'āt va Amniyat-e Keshvar (SAVAK; National Intelligence and Security Organization), also known as the secret police.

Mohammad Reza Shah established SAVAK with the help of the United States Central Intelligence Agency. SAVAK operated from 1957 to 1979, ending when the Pahlavi dynasty was overthrown. While it was still in operation, this organization was described as Iran's "most hated and feared institution," because of its practice of torturing and executing opponents of the Pahlavi regime. Ironically, I thought of this man as being naive and simple-minded. He never caused any problems in the neighborhood and always minded his own business. My family was shocked to find out he was part of SAVAK. I never thought of our neighborhood, as poor as it was, as having any people from SAVAK. Its members must have gone through extensive training to be able to gain people's trust. It certainly worked on us.

The house to the left of ours belonged to a family with six beautiful girls. The oldest daughter, Iran, was eight—a year younger than me.

On the second floor of our home, there was a stairway leading to a door that opened to the rooftop. During the hot summer days, my sisters and I used to sleep there, gazing up at the black sky. Surprisingly, Etty remembered exactly where the cluster of three stars that represented us were and pointed them out to us.

Per Momman's instruction, we placed the pots and pans, the kerosene heater, the plates, the samovar, the tin oil can, and the little amount of dry food we had in a room we called "the small room." We cooked and ate in the small room, using the kerosene heater; we chopped and cleaned the vegetables in the corner of the room on the floor. During summertime, we took the kerosene heater into the backyard and cooked there, but still ate our meals in the small room.

The two rooms on the first floor became our sleeping area. For the first time, Momman and Aghajoon slept separately from their children. Etty, Motty, and I slept in one room, continuing to share the bed rolls on the floor, while Momman and Aghajoon slept in the front room, located next to the entrance, with Saeed, who was still a toddler.

My parents had mixed feelings about our living situation. On one hand, they were delighted that they had finally bought a house, but on the other hand, they were always worried about how they would make the next month's payments to the bank and to Mr. Ghozii.

Aghajoon came home so late from his shop and left so early in the mornings that sometimes we didn't see him for days, especially when school was in session.

We didn't eat many meals throughout the day. Momman was working so hard teaching and sewing that she often forgot to feed us. Other times, we just didn't have anything in the house to eat, not even a piece of bread. Every bit of money had to go toward the house payment. In fact, most nights, we went to sleep hungrier than when we lived in a rented room.

It got so bad that Etty used to cry herself to sleep. All she could do to protest her hunger was cry. I held her tight at night and tried to comfort her, but tears continued streaming down her face. Every morning, she woke up with crusty eyes. Sometimes she couldn't even open them. Momman used to wash them with lukewarm tea and a cotton ball.

Poor Momman had her moments too. Many times, I saw tears rolling down her cheeks while she was sewing. Most of the time, she didn't know I was watching her. And if she did happen to notice, she pretended they weren't tears. "There is a lot of dust in here and it irritates my eyes," she said as she wiped her face with her sleeves. She didn't want to worry me, but I knew about their immense financial burden. My parents both had circles under their eyes and were growing thinner.

I used to go to Aghajoon's shop and express my concern. "Aghajoon, Momman is crying."

"It will get better; it will get better," he said, although not with the most reassuring look.

During those rough days, I tried extra hard to look for ways to make additional money to help with the expenses, but school was open, and I had too much homework and not enough free time.

One day, when I was standing in line at the nanvaii waiting to buy bread, I noticed a few people go into a dark store across from the nanvaii, with metal appliances: plates; round, rusty trays; metal pipes, etc. They would come out empty-handed. I wondered what they did with the things they carried into the shop. After paying for the bread, I walked over to the seedy looking shop and opened the door; a dingy, foul smell emanated from inside.

A deep, gruff voice rudely grabbed my attention before I got the chance to walk in. A tall man barked at me: "What do you want? We don't buy naan here." He pointed to the bread in my hand. "Where is the metal you want to sell?" he asked harshly.

"Nothing. I'll come back later," I said, nervous and a little scared.

I knew exactly what I wanted to do once I reached home. I picked up the metal appliances Aghajoon wanted to repair someday—an iron, a little primrose, and other metals. I had no idea how much I could get for them, but I was hopeful, so I put them into a sack. I felt very sad thinking about our situation and how we were better off before we bought the house. Now we couldn't afford even to make abgoosht, we consistently skipped meals, and the few dinners and lunches we scraped together consisted mostly of bread and homemade jam Madarjoon had brought for us.

On the way to the scrap metal shop, I stopped by Aghajoon's to tell him what my plan was. Surprisingly, he agreed and told me to bring the money back to him. At the gloomy, rancid-smelling scrap metal shop, I stood in the line behind three men, waiting for my turn. I glanced around the small shop and saw piles of junk metal that appeared to be separated by material—copper, aluminum, and iron. One pile had mostly pots, pans, and trays. Another pile consisted of pipes of all sizes, and a third pile had heavy items, such as banged up heaters, irons, and sewing machines.

My turn finally came, and I did exactly what the other people in front of me did. I opened the sack and dumped the metal contents onto a large, dirty scale in the corner of the shop. The hands of the scale pointed to a number that was much less than I thought it would be. The cranky owner checked the contents on the scale to make sure that everything was metal and I hadn't cheated him by mixing non-metal items, such as rocks and stones. He sorted them by hand and threw each into its appropriate pile, making loud noises. The things he could not use, he threw into a large metal trash can.

He handed me seven tomans—not a large amount of money but just enough to put some food on the sofreh. I took the bills happily and walked back to Aghajoon's place.

From then on, that became my job—my part in helping to provide for our family. I constantly kept my eyes open for scrap metal on the corners of streets or other places where people dumped their nonworking household appliances. The more metal I sold, the more I began to figure out the shop owner's "system." I realized that copper and brass were the most expensive items; then aluminum; and last, iron. I did my best to collect as much copper and brass as I could. To make it more entertaining, every time I picked up a metal object, I tried to figure out how much I would earn. At the scrap metal shop, some people bargained with the owner to get more money for their metal pieces, but the owner was a stingy, selfish man who wouldn't budge.

"It is what it is. If you don't like the price I offer you, take it elsewhere," he said with a frown. He knew all too well that there were no other shops nearby and most people, like me, really needed the additional money. Every time I handed the money to Aghajoon, I told him that if he went to the metal shop, he would get more money than I did. I knew the shop owner would cheat a kid but not an adult. Aghajoon simply waved me away as if it were a horrible idea—maybe he was too embarrassed to go there.

The memories I cherish from that house, some happy and some sad, will stay with me forever.

Going to the Movies

Age Ten

The power of imagination is free, entertaining, and costs nothing.

It was the middle of July. Etty and I were coming home from the produce store, each carrying a basket filled with all kinds of greens. I could smell the fresh cilantro, parsley, green onions, and small red radishes, all wrapped in newspaper. My basket held heavier stuff—for example, potatoes, yellow zucchinis, and eggplants. Although we both had thin clothes on and were walking in the shade, our bodies were drenched with sweat, and we were red in the face. Tehran turned ridiculously hot and humid that time of the year. People who had money escaped to the northern parts of Iran to be closer to the Caspian Sea.

At home, we spread the newspaper on the ground under the mulberry tree, where there was shade, and started cleaning the vegetables. That day, the produce shop happened to put the vegetables in the movie section of the paper. I glanced at it to find out if any action movies were showing in the theaters nearby. "John Wayne and the Indians," I said, excited. "They are showing John Wayne, Etty." Like most boys, I enjoyed watching action movies with guns and shooting.

Etty looked at the newspaper. "Are you going to see it?"

"I don't know, maybe." I shrugged

"Can I go with you? I have some money to buy candies or lavashak."

I couldn't say no to my sister when she was offering to buy me snacks!

My two sisters often followed me around, like ducklings following their mom. Most of the time when I wanted to leave the house, I took off my shoes and placed them under my arm before going outside, just to avoid making any noise and having my sisters tag along. Sometimes when I knew my cousins were coming to pick me up, I instructed them to meet me at the end of our alley. That trick didn't last long, because Etty and Motty figured it out; they would go early and be there waiting for me. My cousins were as shocked as I was to see them there before me.

Etty and I finished our work and left the house. We headed to Meehan Theater, about half an hour away on foot. On the way, I asked her, "Did you bring your money?"

Etty opened her small hand for me to see the shiny coin.

I smiled, happy we were going to get to eat either candies, or lavashak. There were too many choices and extraordinarily little money. Usually I walked to the theater, but it was getting too close to the show time, so I told Etty we should catch a bus instead. We reached the station and waited in line behind a young couple until the bus arrived. I whispered to Etty, "Stay close to this couple and pretend we are their children. This way, we don't have to pay the bus fare."

Akbar and I had found this out by accident one day when we entered the bus at the same time as a woman who was carrying her infant, and the bus driver let us on without asking for a ticket. We looked at each other, surprised we didn't have to pay. It saved us one rial, which was a significant amount of money for me; I could buy a lot of candies with it.

Every chance Akbar and I had, we used the same trick—accompanying older people to make it look like we were their children. Sometimes we talked to the older person as we entered the bus, pretending they were our parent. Some of these people knew what we were doing and played along, but others frowned, pointed at us, and said to the bus driver, "They aren't with us and have to pay their share of the fare."

I still wonder why some people double-crossed us like that. The bus fare didn't go to them. Didn't they see our shabby clothes and skinny faces? Couldn't they tell we were poor? It wasn't about being honest or dishonest; we just wanted to use that money to feed ourselves. I liked that Etty was a team player. She figured that the worst thing that could happen was that the driver would not let us in or would just make us give him the fare. Most of the time, I carried one or two bus tickets in my pocket.

Sometimes, if I didn't have any, I bought them from other passengers; most people carried extra ones.

I held Etty's hand as we climbed up the steps right behind the husband and wife and successfully got in. The driver saw us but thought we were with them. Etty and I smiled together at our victory. We sat down, and I noticed that she kept opening her hand to make sure her money was still there. I could tell she was happy to be with her big brother. When we reached our destination, I stood up and said, "We are here. Let's go."

I knew we couldn't afford movie tickets, but I wanted to take my sister for a special outing. In the theater lobby, smiling young boys holding their dad's hands waited patiently in line to enter. I envied them. The only contact Aghajoon ever made with me was to slap my face—sometimes so hard that traces of his fingers remained on my face for days.

Etty's voice brought me back. "Hey, Mohsen, look at these." She was pointing at the pictures of scenes of the movie displayed behind the two glass cabinets outside the theater. One was on the right and the other on the left side of the entrance door. One showed John Wayne in his cowboy hat sitting around a firepit with some bare-chested Indians in feathered hats. They were drinking something from a cup. In the corner, two white guys whose hands were tied with ropes sat kneeling. It looked like they were negotiating to release their two captives. The other picture showed John Wayne on his brown horse, galloping after some bad guys; he had a gun in one hand and the reins in another.

I looked at every corner of those images to try to imagine the story. In my mind, it felt like I was watching the movie. Etty looked at all the pictures too, but I could tell she was not as enthusiastic as I was. She preferred cartoon characters like Betty Boop.

After spending fifteen minutes outside, we went inside, where we would have to buy tickets before being allowed to enter the theater. Etty followed me, and we looked at the pictures of future showings. We both said loudly, "Tarzan!" Two large banners on two opposite walls showed a nearly naked Tarzan in skimpy shorts, swinging from the branch of a tree like a monkey. In the background, there were elephants, lions, and some other jungle animals. The title was written in big letters in Farsi: *Tarzan, marde e maymoonii farar meekonad* (Tarzan the Ape-Man Escapes).

After some time, I figured out that the movie must have started, because the woman selling tickets in the glass booth had closed the window and left. Only boys like me, who were poor and couldn't afford to buy tickets, remained in the lobby to continue looking at all the fascinating posters.

During summer, there was no air conditioning, and a few theaters showed movies on the roof; it looked the same as an indoor theater, with rows of chairs and a large white screen, except there was no ceiling. After looking at those posters, Etty and I stepped outside, and I climbed an electrical pole—just like a monkey—to watch the movie. I tried to pull myself as high as I could, but even so, the most I could see was John Wayne's hat, his two eyes, and part of his nose. His eyes were looking down, so I assumed he was talking to someone. From up there, I could not hear any sound either. This was a normal thing for poor young boys to do. We were content to be up on the pole, in our own world. On unlucky days, a policeman showed up with his baton, and we all came down and ran before he smacked us.

After some time, my arms and legs got tired. I jumped down to take a break and asked Etty if she wanted to get on my shoulder to see the movie a little better, but she refused. Maybe if it were a cartoon, she would have agreed. Then I climbed back up to see more action. From the top of the pole, I occasionally looked down and felt bad for Etty, who was patiently waiting on the sidewalk, pacing up and down.

Before the movie ended, I jumped down, took Etty's hand and asked her what she would like to eat.

There were many stores around us—bakeries with displays of chocolate and vanilla pastries; an ice cream parlor that carried chocolate ice cream bars and bastanii Akbar Mashtii; all kinds of candy stores with bags of colorful hard and soft candies; and nut stores with sacks of cashews, pistachios, and hazelnuts. We both knew ten shahi wasn't going to buy us much.

As we got closer to our neighborhood, the streets became more crowded with people, and the fancy shops turned into carts or metal trays with a variety of snacks on them. None looked as good as the ones we saw in the shops we had passed earlier. Everyone was shouting what they were selling. Etty and I walked by each vendor to figure out what we wanted. Some were selling *shancii* (a soft, circular, caramelized candy). Some vendors had *goosh e-phil* (a soft square candy with sugar coating).

We walked up to a man with a thick mustache, bald head, dirty fingernails, and a cigarette in the corner of his mouth who sold shancii.

"One shancii," said Etty.

He handed it to her, and she unwrapped it and bit it in the middle. She kept one half for herself and gave me the other. The rest of the way, we savored the candy and did not talk much about anything.

I really wanted to share my imagined John Wayne movie story that I had just watched from the pole with someone. The next day when I saw Ramazoon, I told him that I had seen a movie. His eyes widened as I asked, "Do you want me to tell you what happened? John Wayne was in it."

He smiled and said, "Yes."

I made up the story based mostly on the poster pictures I had seen at the door. "You know, Ramazoon, John Wayne was shooting at the Indians, and he killed most of them all by himself. He jumped from one hill to another while riding on his beautiful brown horse." I lay on the ground, pretending to shoot people with my finger gun. I surprised myself at how interesting my made-up story was and started believing I had seen that movie.

Ramazoon stood there, wide-eyed, chiming in now and again with "Woah! What happened next?"

We were both satisfied with the outcome of the movie.

"Mohsen, can I go with you next time?"

I paused for a moment, then nodded. "Yeah, next time," I said, knowing there would never be a next time.

Things Happen for a Reason

Age Eleven

Madarjoon always told us, "Things happen for a reason, and God has good plans for us."

One summer, one of Aghajoon's customers—a tall muscular man with kind green eyes and a thick mustache, whose name I later found out to be Mr. Shirveah—stopped by where I was selling candies. That year, I had decided to sell sweets, gum, and other junk food that people would buy on the go for their small children. He bought a piece of gum from me.

As I handed it to him, he asked with a big frown if I were his son. He pointed at Aghajoon.

I looked at him quizzically and said, "Yes, Agha."

He shook his head disapprovingly and entered Aghajoon's shop. Knowing he was going to talk about me, I moved closer to the shop to eavesdrop.

"*Agha kafash* (Mr. Cobbler), it's a pity your son is selling candy on the street. Why don't you let him learn something useful? I could take him to Pahlavii Hospital and teach him how to do electrical wiring or fix hospital equipment and appliances."

Aghajoon laughed and said, "Mohsen already knows how to do wiring. He did the wiring for our house, and it works perfectly."

I smiled, remembering how I had watched an electrician to learn the ins and outs of wiring and electrical work. When we first moved into our house, we had no electricity. We used oil-operated lamps to bring in light at night. After owning our house for a while, we noticed many workers installing tall wooden poles in our neighborhood. We had heard electricity was coming to our area but didn't know exactly when.

Since Momman sewed into the late hours of the night, she asked Aghajoon to figure out how we could bring electricity into our house. A couple of days later, I heard Aghajoon tell Momman that we would have to pay 250 tomans to Forozan Electrical Company for them to bring in wires and install a meter for us. But that wasn't the only expense: we also had to hire an electrician to do the rest of the work—adding switches, light bulbs, and outlets to the main wire for us to be able to use the city electricity.

One of Aghajoon's customers, Mr. Kangevarii, worked as an electrician in a company and moonlighted in the evenings. Aghajoon spoke to him, and he agreed to work at our house after his regular job was done. He gave Aghajoon a significant discount, one thousand tomans for the entire house, which was a good deal.

Mr. Kangevarii gave Aghajoon a list of items to buy—switches, outlets, ten-meter pipes, long wires, light bulbs, and some other items he needed to complete his work. On that day, I rushed home from school so I could observe Mr. Kangevarii. He arrived shortly after I did and immediately got to work. I stood in a corner and watched him very carefully as he pulled wires here and there and connected them to different outlets and switches. He took one step; I did the same. I followed every move he made; I didn't take my eyes off him. I even resisted the urge to go to the bathroom to pee because I didn't want to miss anything he did. He brought light to the first floor of the house in a short time. Before he began the second floor, he asked Aghajoon for half of his payment.

Later that day, Aghajoon told Momman he had an argument with Mr. Kangevarii. "He wanted more than we agreed on, and I fired him. What a rip-off! He thinks I'm sitting on a treasure. He wanted me to pay for the supplies too. I said, 'You have to deduct that from your wages.'"

Momman asked Aghajoon, "Who is going to finish the job now? We can't have only half the house with electricity."

"I can do it. It's simple," I said with confidence.

Aghajoon laughed at my suggestion and said, "No, this isn't a joke. You'll be playing with 220V. You will either electrocute yourself or set the house on fire."

Since Momman hung out at the lower level of our house, and Aghajoon was at his shop most of the time, I thought I would surprise everyone by bringing electricity to the second floor. After finishing my work, which only took two days, and checking that all the lights came on without breaking the fuse, I called Momman and asked her to come up to the second floor.

She refused because she had things to take care of, but I assured her it wouldn't take long. When I heard her footsteps climbing the stairs, I turned the lights on and waited to see her reaction. "Eh, Mohsen Jon, you did it!" she said, satisfied, moving from one room to another.

I relived this memory while Aghajoon and Mr. Shirveah discussed the idea of his taking me as an apprentice.

"Why not?" my father said. "It will be good for Mohsen to learn new things, including how to fix hospital equipment."

And so, with that decision, I stopped selling candies on the streets to make money. Around six o'clock on a Saturday morning, the first working day of the week for Iranians, Mr. Shirveah picked me up on his bicycle. The first time, I was a bit nervous. I didn't know him well, and I also didn't know what was expected of me. I hopped onto the back of his bicycle and hung my arms around his waist to hold on. He quietly pedaled for about an hour to get to the hospital. We passed many shops in our neighborhood, all bustling to open for the day. The streets weren't very crowded yet; there were just a few early risers headed to the nanvaii. The produce vendors were pulling their carts filled with peaches and nectarines onto the street. The *ghahveh khaneh* (coffee house) owners were sweeping the area in front of their shops and putting cushions on the benches and chairs outside—getting ready for their morning customers.

All the places we passed looked the same as my own neighborhood, with small shops and lots of dirty, unpaved roads. I periodically closed my eyes to enjoy the soft breeze, which felt good on my face and neck. Poor Mr. Shirveah started to sweat, and I noticed his back and underarms were wet with perspiration. Another hot and muggy day was on the way.

I could tell we were getting closer to the hospital as there were no more shops to be seen. Instead of dirt streets, there were clean and nicely paved roads and trees everywhere. I didn't see a single donkey or horse, as I was used to seeing in my neighborhood. In fact, one time as I was conducting my candy business on Khosh Street, a donkey pooped right in front of my display. I immediately removed it with a piece of cardboard. We may have been poor, but that was unacceptable.

I was astonished at the size of the hospital, a large, two-story building with beautiful, lush green surroundings and sparkling fountains in the front. The sound of water dripping was soothing. The temperature even seemed much cooler in this area, by about ten degrees.

This serene and beautiful scene brought me back to a time when my cousins and I went to where the "rich people lived." It was a Friday in 1958, and I had just turned ten. My cousins Asghar and Akbar came by our house to pass the time. Asghar was the son of my maternal uncle and was a year older than me, and Akbar, the son of my maternal aunt, was a year younger than me.

Akbar always relied on me to pay for his expenses—for example, bus fares, snacks, and anything else we did together that required spending money. I didn't mind it at all since I liked him better than I liked Asghar. Akbar was an easygoing kind of guy, and after he turned eleven, he spent most of his summer days with me just hanging out and helping me with projects I happened to be working on at the time—such as developing pictures or making a gun or anything else. Asghar, on the other hand, was a bit of a snob and only hung out with us if his other friends did not have time to spend with him. His father spoiled him by paying him an allowance—something that was foreign to Akbar and me.

On that Friday, Asghar suggested we go to Takhteh Jamsheed Street to see how the rich people lived. Excited, we left the house, all three of us in shabby and torn clothes—Akbar's being the worst looking, with visible holes. Mine had holes but were patched up, and Asghar's looked the best, still old but without any holes or patches.

We took two buses to get there. The first bus station was in our neighborhood, and the bus was old and rusty. The seats had holes, and the passengers looked like us—not exceptionally clean—and the air was filled with an unpleasant body odor.

The three of us sat next to each other and looked out the window. We passed our neighborhood's unpaved, dirty streets, with very few trees; the small old shops; the bakery; the pharmacy; the pedestrians; some women in chadors holding their children's hands; bicyclists peddling hard and fast to get to wherever they were trying to go; donkeys and horses pulling carts carrying various items: fruits, furniture, and dried bread. It was a lively neighborhood; I thought it had personality.

We finally reached our destination and walked to the second bus station. On the way, we passed Tehran University. I gazed through the tall metal gates that had been left open and saw groups of young male and female students holding their textbooks, talking, and laughing. Some were walking hand in hand in the garden-like campus. They looked so carefree. Being only ten, I had a long way before I could attend college, but if this was what it was like, I couldn't wait.

At the second bus station, things looked a lot different. The bus we got on was beautifully painted, and the driver was nicely dressed, with a yellow tie. The seats looked new and shiny, and the fragrance of cologne filled the air. The men wore crisp, ironed suits, while the women shone in colorful one-piece dresses or miniskirts; none covered themselves with a chador. As we stepped onto the bus, some of the passengers stared at us, pulling themselves out of our way, as if we carried contagious diseases. I don't know if my cousins noticed their looks and decided, like me, not to mention anything. We sat at the back of the bus, next to a window, and as we passed interesting things, we pointed them out to each other.

"Look at those tall electrical poles." I said.

Akbar and Asghar got closer, their heads near my face to see what I was referring to.

"I wonder how they change the bulbs and what kind of equipment they use," I said. I wished I could live there to see how they replaced those bulbs. I was certain it would be an exciting job.

The streets were paved, clean, and beautiful, with trees and flowers everywhere. Instead of donkeys and horses pulling carts, I saw shiny cars traveling here and there. I didn't see any old and dilapidated shops, only large supermarkets with shopping carts lined up outside, cafés, and nice restaurants. None looked like the kababii next to Aghajoon's shop; the nanvaii where I stood in the line every morning to buy fresh bread; or Mamad Agha's butcher shop, where one or two sheep carcasses hung at room temperature, ready to be cut for the customers.

The bus stopped and we decided to get off. There were so many interesting things to see. As soon as I stepped outside, I felt as if we had arrived in another country. I couldn't understand how one hour of driving could make such a difference. The air didn't smell foul and dirty. Everything looked clean, even the people. I knew I was in Tehran because people spoke the same language as I did and all the signs for streets, restaurants, and supermarkets were in Farsi. People tried not to get close to us, as the people in the second bus had done. I felt very strange in this part of the city, as if I didn't belong there. But my curiosity made me continue. I wanted to see what else was there.

We strolled from one side of the street to another, trying to soak in every sight, smell, and touch we could. We didn't have the money to appease our sense of taste, but we could still admire the food on display and take in the smells. We saw an interesting restaurant and watched the man behind the counter cut meat from a rotating cylinder and place it on a piece of bread topped with tomatoes and a white sauce. We'd never seen meat cooking around a cylinder, only skewers when grilling kababs. My stomach growled just looking at his customers' expressions as they bit into their sandwiches.

Akbar looked at me. "Do you wish you could eat one of these sandwiches right now?"

"No. It looks like it's made of dog meat, and who wants to eat that?" I replied sharply. Of course, I wanted to taste the meat, the sauce, the tomatoes, and the steaming fresh bread. In my heart, I envied these people who had money to buy the kind of food I could only dream about. I tried to imagine what it would taste like.

Akbar pointed to a deli with round tables and wooden chairs inside. The sign above the counter had the names of foods we weren't familiar with: hot dogs, sausages, and bologna. The different shapes of meat—

some round, some cylindrical—were nicely arranged in the refrigerated deli cases, but we still couldn't tell what anything was.

After we had effectively confused ourselves speculating about what these meat products were made of, we noticed a crowd of people leaving a supermarket close by. A bag boy wearing a white uniform pushed the customers' shopping carts filled with grocery bags, while other boys helped them carry their bags to their cars. I was amazed at the amount of food these people had in their carts. I wondered how they could afford so much food or how many days it would last them. I tried to imagine where my family could store this much food, without throwing most of it away since we had no means of keeping it cold. We had no refrigerator yet, but if we did, this much food would have fed all of us for at least a month.

Even though we probably looked like beggars, we managed to enter the supermarket. We were constantly worried they might kick us out. We touched the canned food and vegetables as if they had come from another planet. There were so many shampoos, soaps, and detergents. The seemingly endless number of brands confused me. I wondered how people knew which one to get. "No wonder this store is so big—how else are they going to fit these many brand names?" I chuckled.

We began pointing at various objects, making comments about their ridiculous advertisements and laughing. I noticed out of the corner of my eye, however, that one of the customers was speaking to a store manager. Shortly after, he approached us.

"What do you boys want?" His voice sounded angry.

"We want something," I said nervously.

"Maybe I can help you if you tell me what you are looking for."

"We don't know what we want, but we're looking for something." I exchanged looks with Akbar and Asghar, hoping they would help me.

"Get out of here and don't come back. Do you hear me?! Don't come back!" He raised his hand.

We ran out, thinking the manager planned to hit us. Outside the store, we laughed it off, but I felt truly humiliated; my pride was crushed. If we had been wearing designer clothes with lots of cologne and pockets bulging with money, he would have treated us differently. He would have bowed to us and constantly replied with, "Yes, sir. Yes, sir. Would you like this, sir?" as he did with the other customers. That day, I learned that how you appear on the outside determines how people treat you.

At Pahlavi Hospital with Mr. Shirveah, I felt the same way—out of place and maybe even ashamed of how I looked compared with everyone else. The only difference at the hospital was that nobody looked at me as if I had committed a crime, as the people on Takhteh Jamsheed Street did.

As Mr. Shirveah and I continued our walk toward the entrance, again my attention was caught by the visually stunning ambulances parked near a huge roll-up door with a big red emergency sign on it. The area was crowded with all kinds of people—old, young, healthy, sick, pregnant women—either going to or leaving from the hospital. Later, I found out that there were one thousand beds in this hospital and most of the patients came from poor families and were treated for free.

We entered the building, and I once again gawked at my surroundings. Doctors in white lab coats, with stethoscopes wrapped around their necks, whizzed past me, with their nurses following closely behind them. Almost immediately, I was hit with the sharp, stinging scent of isopropyl alcohol.

We took the elevator to the second floor, where Mr. Shirveah's shop was. I had never ridden in an elevator before; it felt like an adventure. I looked very carefully at how Mr. Shirveah operated the elevator so I could come and go by myself if necessary. He pushed the No. 2 button when the door closed. The elevator made a hissing noise, gave a kick, and pushed us up. I was amazed at the things available in the hospital, while my own neighborhood had only just obtained electricity and running water.

Mr. Shirveah's store was large enough to fit ten compact cars. He had arranged six white benches parallel to each other around the room, each with a rolling chair in front of it. All kinds of electrical tools were hung on the walls; wrenches, screwdrivers, drills, and electrical wires decorated the room like paintings. Each bench had its own cabinet filled with all kinds of other electrical gadgets, switches, lights, screws, plugs, and anything we needed to fix the hospital equipment.

Over the next few weeks, I learned how to fix the hospital instruments, the sterilizer bath, centrifuges, incubators, office equipment, telephones, fans, and anything else that had to do with electricity. After a while, I learned how to repair things all by myself. Mr. Shirveah and his coworkers were impressed with how quickly I picked up the techniques and skills. I smiled as they complimented me. I appreciated some of the attention, but mainly I just liked my new job and set of new skills.

Soon all the nurses, some of the doctors, the floor staff, and the kitchen staff knew me by name. They constantly asked me to go to various locations of the hospital to do this or that. All this attention and praise from the hospital crew gave me a sense of self-confidence. Nobody seemed to care that I wore old clothes; had dirty, cracked hands; or even sometimes smelled. It felt good when they patted my shoulder and asked, "Mohsen, how old are you?"

"Eleven!" I would proudly reply.

"How do you know all this? You must be a very smart boy."

I would just smile and walk to my next assignment, carrying all my tools in my small hands.

Gradually, I learned the culture of the hospital. The department heads had roomy air-conditioned offices complete with beautiful chairs and an expensive-looking desk. I rarely saw these doctors; the only time I went to their offices was when something needed repair. Except for one or two, they were arrogant people, never responding when Mr. Shirveah or I greeted or smiled at them. It didn't matter to me. I continued to be polite and said "salam" every time I saw them.

Besides the new skills I was learning, the best part of my new job was the food. The nurses fed us whenever we fixed something for them, and the kitchen staff fed us when one of their appliances was broken and needed to be repaired. Everyone was kind to us because they depended on us to repair their equipment.

Although Mr. Shirveah never paid me, he let me take wires, microphones, switches, or any other electrical gadgets the hospital could spare. Later, I found out that the hospital paid Mr. Shirveah and his coworkers extraordinarily little money. I saw them taking a lot more supplies than what he gave me. They wrapped the wires around and around their torsos, underneath their shirts, before leaving the hospital. I was perpetually amazed that nobody noticed these slim men coming into the hospital, leaving at least five kilos heavier, and then coming back the following morning, having lost it all from the previous night.

By the end of that summer, I knew how to fix just about anything, but getting the wires, lights, switches, microphones, and miscellaneous electrical items was the real reward for me. With these supplies, I could fix the neighbors' appliances or do wiring in their homes. Working at the Pahlavi Hospital in the summer of 1959 opened doors in my life's journey and altered my destiny. It got me interested in the field of electronics, and it helped me with other creative projects for years to come. It also helped me earn a little extra money later on so I could ease the burden on Aghajoon and Momman.

GREEN IS GO, RED IS STOP

AGE TWELVE

Necessity is the mother of invention.

It was exceedingly difficult for my parents to come up with the payments they owed the bank and Mr. Ghozii after we moved into our new house. They both worked extremely hard to make ends meet— Momman sewing and teaching, and Aghajoon repairing and polishing shoes.

One day, Momman suggested to Aghajoon that we should rent the upstairs rooms. My parents found three tenants for the rooms. Most of the rent we received from them went to paying off the loans and paying for the training classes Momman had registered for. She wanted to open a sewing institute to teach professionally and issue sewing certificates to her students. This way she could make more money. Shortly after we rented the upstairs rooms, my parents decided to rent the two rooms downstairs to make extra money. Aghajoon knew two couples who wanted to move in.

One couple had just gotten married and wanted to save money to buy their own house someday. The other couple had moved to Tehran to be closer to his wife's relatives. Both couples promised to move out within a year because Momman wanted to convert the downstairs into her sewing institute.

My sisters and I moved all the bedding items, bedrolls, blankets, and pillows to the small room, so we once again lived in one room cramped together, but this time it was our choice. That year, fourteen people lived in the house. There were seven tenants: three single men upstairs (one pharmacy student, one dentist, and one engineer) and two couples downstairs. In addition, there were seven of us: five children and our parents.

Momman became very protective of my younger sisters, keeping them away from the men. She always told them not to hang out in the backyard too much. They had to have an adult look after them while they were washing their hands or using the bathroom. I don't know why Momman was so concerned about my sisters going outside; most of our tenants were very shy men and avoided eye contact with us, especially with my sisters and mother. Every time the pharmacy student saw my little sisters in the hallway, he turned red.

The most difficult part of having all these people in the house was the bathroom—especially during evenings before everyone went to sleep and first thing in the morning. Like many houses in our neighborhood, the bathroom was located outside, in the corner of the backyard. Ours was built so we couldn't see if its door was open or closed unless we were few steps away. Whenever my sisters and Momman came out of the bathroom, to minimize their contact with the male tenants, they ran hurriedly to the small room that was nearby. Frequently they fell and scraped their knees or elbows.

In Iran, to clean ourselves after using the bathroom, we had to fill the aftabeh. We poured the water with one hand and washed ourselves with the other. We had no bathroom tissues to dry ourselves, so we had to pull up our underwear while our bottoms were still wet. During the cold winter months, the water in the aftabeh was freezing. When it hit our bottoms, it woke us up like a shot of adrenaline directly into our blood.

I hated it when I heard a knock on the door as I was using the bathroom. Even though the door was locked, I had to say something like "Ah-hmm, ah-hmm" or cough to indicate I was in there. It made me nervous knowing someone was waiting for me to come out, and it took me longer than it should have to finish my business. Sometimes I came out earlier than I wanted, with the intention of going back when the bathroom was available.

On warm days, the person who knocked stayed in the backyard until the individual in the bathroom came out. In cold and snowy weather, they went back to their room and came out later, with the hope of getting in then. At some point, I got tired of all the knocking on the bathroom door and all the embarrassing moments. I had to come up with a solution to make it easier for all of us. I didn't know what that solution would be, but I kept my mind open for ideas.

A couple of months passed, and I continued to think about how to resolve the bathroom challenges. One day, while sitting outside Aghajoon's shop with Ramazoon, I was talking about school and how every year classes were getting harder, when Aghajoon told me to deliver one of his customer's shoes to his house, which was many blocks away. I decided to catch a bus instead of walking so I could come back soon and spend more time with Ramazoon.

The bus was very crowded, and I was squished between many people. I stood in the aisle, holding onto the metal pole for balance with one hand and onto the customer's black leather shoes with the other. I looked out the window to distract myself from the inside of the bus and the aroma of sweat around me. I saw women at the fruit stand picking apples, and at another corner, two men talking while smoking cigarettes.

Suddenly, the bus screeched to a halt, and the people around me were pushed together in the aisle. As I was trying to keep my balance, I noticed the traffic light on a pole outside. It had turned red for stop, but none of the drivers was paying any attention to it. In Iran, the traffic was always ridiculous, and drivers made up their own traffic rules as they drove. They didn't pay attention to traffic lights, they only stopped when they were about to hit something or somebody. In this case, a woman with her child had appeared in front of the bus, causing it to stop with a jolt to avoid hitting them.

As bad as the traffic looked, I was glad that it had given me a new idea for our bathroom: green for available and red for occupied. That idea made me so excited that I got off the bus two blocks before my destination. As I walked the rest of the way, I repeated, "Green for empty and red for busy." I forgot about Ramazoon and returning to Aghajoon's shop. On the way home, I was focused entirely on my new project and what I needed to install the lights.

The next day, under the mulberry tree, I started working. I made a square box large enough to screw the two light bulbs on it—red at the top and green at the bottom, exactly like the traffic light I'd seen the previous day. Occasionally, Etty and Motty would kneel next to me, wondering what I was doing.

"This will make all our lives so much easier. You'll see, no more scabs for you," I promised.

Using a ladder, I was able to reach the highest wall outside the bathroom door and install the box with the lights. The box was visible from all the rooms in our house. I attached the electrical wire so that when the latch on the sliding bolt was moved to lock, the red light turned on to indicate the bathroom was occupied. The green light came on when the latch was released to open the door, meaning the bathroom was vacant. This little device made everyone's life so much easier. We all used the bathroom more comfortably, and nobody rushed anyone by knocking at the bathroom door anymore.

Pretty soon everyone in the neighborhood—my aunts, uncles, and even some of Aghajoon's customers—found out about our bathroom light and asked me to install one for their house. Some suggested they would pay me for the materials, but the installation would be free.

"Free, no," I said, shaking my head. "Maybe I can give you a discount, but I won't do it for free."

Momman had taught me to never provide my services to anyone free of charge.

Confronting Masoom

Age Twelve

Knowing the facts of life can save your life.

One day, when I was about twelve years old, I was talking about diverse topics with my cousin, Asghar, when the subject of sex and how babies are made came up.

"Do you know what sex is?" Asghar asked wryly.

"Yeah, I do. Why?" I said, fully knowing that I had no idea about any of that stuff.

Asghar whispered in my ear, "After the wedding ceremony, the bride and groom have sex."

I had heard the word sex before but wasn't curious about it. I wasn't much into girls yet.

Asghar continued: "When the bride and groom are alone in the room, they get naked, kiss each other on the lips, and touch each other's private parts." He looked around to make sure there were no adults coming our way and continued, "Then they sleep on the same bed, holding each other's private parts."

I looked at Asghar. He had a big smile on his face, probably imagining himself next to a girl on a bed, holding her private part. I, on the other hand, just wanted to leave and play, but Asghar continued. "How about babies? Do you know how babies are made? I want to ask my mom, but she would beat me up instead of answering my question."

"Having sex leads to having babies," I said with a sarcastic tone.

"But why does it take so long for a baby to be born?" he asked.

I hurriedly explained so we could stop talking about the subject. "Well, every time the couple has sex, part of the baby's body is made. The more often they have sex, the faster the baby is developed and born."

Asghar nodded, and my explanation made sense to him. Although I didn't have any facts for what I said, I believed my own reasoning.

Shortly after that conversation, my aunt, Akbar's mother, came to our house to give us news about her oldest daughter, Masoom, short for Masoomeh.

"Khahar," she said to my mother, "Masoom gave birth to a baby boy yesterday."

Masoom had been married for a year to a man who was in the military. I knew that her husband had left home a few weeks after their marriage to go to another city. There had been an uprising by the tribes in Shiraz, one of the main cities in Iran. They wanted to be an independent country, so the government had sent military groups there to keep things under control. He was stationed there for about half a year.

Momman was delighted to hear the news and told her sister that she would visit Masoom and her new son very soon. My aunt didn't stay long, because she had to go to her brother's house, Asghar's parents' family, to give them the same news.

My aunt's voice kept echoing in my head. "Masoom had her baby yesterday." I was so confused and shocked that I decided to speak to Asghar about it. I walked to his house, which was a couple of blocks from ours. On the way there, I kept thinking, *How did the baby develop without her husband around? Whom did she have sex with? It must have been another man or different men every night.*

In the distance, I saw Asghar walking toward our house. He also wanted to talk to me about Masoom and her newborn baby.

"Salam, Asghar, how are you?" I said.

"Did you hear about Masoom?" Asghar whispered

"Yeah, I did."

"What should we do now?"

"We have to confront her, so she knows we aren't stupid kids. You know Asghar, she can lie to other people but not us. We must stand for our family's dignity. She can't embarrass us and ruin our family's reputation. This is ridiculous," I said as I kicked a small rock on the ground.

At that moment, I thought I was a detective and my cousin, Masoom, had committed a huge crime. Asghar and I walked to my house. We tried to figure out when we should go to her house, so she would not have any other visitors. We did not want to embarrass her in front of other people and wanted to keep what she had done a private matter among us.

Masoom was only two years older than I was. She looked very tomboyish, with big bones, and was a head taller than me. She was a very carefree girl, with long brown hair, which she never combed or moved away from her face. She always joked with us. Whenever she saw me or any other boys in the family, she wanted to race with us. "Let's see who gets to the house first," she would say as she zoomed passed us. Sometimes she wrestled with us, and most of the time, she knocked us down shortly after we tangled. She could kick a soccer ball so far that it made the boys envy her strength. Unfortunately, after she married Mr. Mohammadi, we hardly saw her. She busied herself with chores around the house.

Asghar and I wanted to pay a visit before anyone else did. In our culture, people visited the new mother a week after the birth. "Asghar," I said, "we should go there in two days. I come to your house to walk there together." We discussed how to break the news to her. I volunteered to tell her that we knew she had sex with other men while her husband was away.

Two days later, I went to Asghar's house. On the way to Masoom's, I practiced what I was going to say. I began to get nervous; it was going to be hard, but I had to do it.

When we reached her house, I paused. Asghar gave me a nod to indicate he was ready, so I knocked at the door like a policeman who was about to arrest a criminal.

It took her some time to open the door. Maybe she was putting the baby down or maybe she was not expecting any visitors yet and was hesitant. She looked surprised but gave us a big smile when she saw her two cousins at the door. "Mohsen, Asghar, salam, come in, come in," she said as she stepped aside and opened the door wider for us to enter.

Asghar and I both looked at each other, speechless. She had grown to be so big, much bigger than before. She had gained at least twenty kilos.

Before going in, I glanced at Asghar with a concerned look. Suddenly we had lost our courage to speak to her about what we had in mind. We looked like two mice in front of an elephant.

We entered, and she closed the door behind us. Asghar and I waited for her to lead us through her yard into a long and dark hallway and then take us from there into one of the downstairs rooms. All this time, not a word came out of my or Asghar's mouth. We were still shocked.

She pointed her son out to us as we entered the room. I looked at the little boy and wanted to compliment his looks, but I couldn't. He resembled a frog more than a human, due to his puffy eyes and swollen red face. I thought the reason the baby was ugly was that it was made of so many different men.

"Sit down. Be comfortable. I will get something for us to eat," Masoom said.

Asghar and I exchanged looks, but we couldn't say anything to each other because Masoom was at the corner of the room pouring tea for us.

"Mohammadi"—she referred to her husband by his last name—"isn't here but, he will be back in a month to see the baby. I miss him a lot," Masoom said as she placed the tea and a plate filled with cookies in front of us on the floor.

I felt she was bribing us with food to keep our mouths shut. Also, how dare she admit her husband wasn't around when she gave birth to her baby? Wasn't she ashamed to admit to herself that she had been with other men?

Asghar and I just smiled. We were both afraid to say anything to this giant woman. We listened to her, smiled, and nodded our heads many times with "Yes, yes."

After eating the cookies and drinking the tea, we said goodbye and left her house.

All the way back, Asghar and I didn't say a single word. We crossed the street, and Asghar continued his walk back to his house and I turned to go to mine. We didn't say goodbye, both embarrassed for being too cowardly to confront Masoom.

Later that night, I was thinking about my theory about pregnancy and babies being developed inside a woman's body. I remembered

Momman's cheerful face when her sister told her about Masoom bringing a baby boy to this world. Why didn't Momman get angry? She also knew that Mohammadi was traveling. In fact, nobody seemed upset by the news. Plus, if she had done anything wrong and slept with other men, this would have been kept a secret, and Masoom's mother wouldn't have gone around telling people about the birth. Mr. Mohammadi would have rushed home to ask for an explanation. At that moment, I realized my theory wasn't accurate. I could not wait to tell Asghar the next day.

Asghar and I laughed when I told him that my thinking was not correct because nobody in the family seemed to be concerned, including Masoom's husband. I whispered to him, "Good thing we didn't say anything to Masoom. Most likely, she would have kicked both of us to death."

"Yeah. Good thing," Asghar said.

I could not wait to find out what sex was and how babies were made.

GOING TO THE BAZAAR

AGE THIRTEEN

A bazaar is the most complex place, filled with all kinds of fragrance, colors, shops, people . . . and more people.

One evening, Aghajoon told me that the next time he went to the bazaar, he would take me so he could show me the tools of his trade, how to properly handle money, and how to get around in the crazy maze of the bazaar.

I had never been there but had heard the bazaar was a huge marketplace divided into several smaller areas separated by the types of goods sold. A maze of alleys and passageways led from one of these smaller areas to another. There were rows and rows of the same kinds of stores within the same section—for example, the copper pots and pans bazaar, the jewelry bazaar, the carpet bazaar, the nuts bazaar, the herb bazaar, and the shoe-supply bazaar.

Aghajoon used to joke with Momman that the bazaar was so crowded that even a dog would not be able to find its owner. As a child, it was frightening to think that if people didn't know their way around, they could come in from one entrance, leave from another and end up on a completely unknown street.

On the day Aghajoon decided to go to the bazaar, he told me to gather two sacks from his shop and meet him at the bus stop.

I gathered up the two large gray sacks Momman had made specifically for Aghajoon to carry the supplies he bought at the bazaar and trudged with them to the bus stop.

As we waited, Aghajoon said, "Mohsen, you must pay attention today and remember every little detail, because next time you will be all by yourself. You understand?"

I nodded, and my already-stiff posture became stiffer as I prepared to take mental note of every place we passed and of everything we were about to do.

After a few minutes, a bus approached. Its door opened. Aghajoon was illiterate and couldn't read the sign at the top of the bus telling passengers where the driver was headed. He asked the driver, "Do you go to Galbandak?"

The bus driver simply motioned for us to enter.

We weaved our way through the mess of people toward the back of the bus. We were now in a crowded mix of all kinds of people, but the majority were men dressed, like Aghajoon, in old shirts and worn-out pants, with tired, sad faces and dry, calloused hands with dirty nails. Like Aghajoon, they held difficult jobs and had to work long hours to provide for their families.

The women, on the other hand, looked less harsh. Some of them were covered with chadors, but the younger ones wore miniskirts, low-cut blouses, and lots of makeup. Before the Islamic Revolution in 1979, women wore whatever they wanted. Some followed the fashions of European countries; some wore chadors; and others, like Momman, wore modest clothing that didn't cover them from head to toe.

Not finding any empty seats on the bus, Aghajoon and I stood next to each other, hanging onto the backs of seats. Once we were settled, I diverted my gaze toward the window to my right and imagined feeling a cool, fresh breeze from outside rather than the stale air that originated from everyone's body heat inside the vehicle.

The streets we passed were just as crowded. People rushed into and out of the various shops. At some point, a row of yarn shops adorned with colorful displays of their wares caught my eye. Then a photo shop with a beautiful display of smiling faces stole my attention. The images were so pristine and engaging. We quickly passed the photo shop, and I noticed a progression of army supply stores with various uniforms, bags, and hats outside on display.

At last, we reached the end of the line and got out. Carrying the two sacks on my shoulders, I followed Aghajoon's heels for about ten minutes. Everywhere we went was crowded with people and shops. As I tried to catch up with Aghajoon, I looked around in amazement. This new and intimidating place looked like a maze, and I had to pay attention to the path we took to get to our destination. People from all levels of society were there: the young, the old, the well-dressed, and the extremely poor. Some people navigated by bicycle, some by motorcycle, and others with their donkeys. I had never seen so many people in one place, not to mention so many expensive and beautiful goods. We passed many fabric shops filled with rows of vibrant green, orange, red, polka dotted, and striped fabrics. I knew Momman would love to come here just to look at the beautiful material arranged nicely on the shelves.

Looking up, I saw the dome-shaped roof made of clay and covered with small openings. The ground got muddy and slippery when it rained or snowed, making it exceedingly difficult to walk around, especially when carrying heavy items. The passages in the bazaar were extremely narrow, especially in relation to the hordes of people who were constantly squeezing through. I had to walk carefully to not get hit by the men pulling wooden wagons filled with heavy loads of leather rolls or by the donkeys carrying large carpets. People constantly warned us, "Watch behind you! Donkey coming! Don't get hit!"

The bazaar began to look like an overwhelming and confusing place. Walking behind Aghajoon, I suddenly remembered I would have to do all this by myself very soon and became extremely nervous. *How am I ever going to do this alone without getting lost?* I tried to make mental notes of places we passed and the landmarks.

At last, we reached the shoe-supply bazaar. I would have known that we arrived even if I had closed my eyes. All I needed to do was take a deep breath and allow the smell of leather mixed with shoe polish fill my nostrils. The merchants in each shop preoccupied themselves with talking and drinking tea, while waiting for their customers to approach them with their purchases—each had a prayer bead hanging from their wrist. Some sat around smoking cigarettes. I recognized the brand they were smoking, Oshnoo, because Madarjoon smoked it once a week and used to give me money to buy her a pack from the street vendors near Aghajoon's store. I used to read the names on all the packages, especially if Ramazoon accompanied me. He liked it when I read aloud the signs that hung in front of each shop or the names on various packages. Since he wasn't allowed to go to school, this was the only way he learned about words and letters.

Approaching one of the shops, Aghajoon greeted a tall, slender, kind-looking man with a short, nicely trimmed beard. "Salam, Haj Agha Mehdi."

"Salam. Agha kafash," the man replied.

Aghajoon shook hands with the shop owner and smiled.

I stood at the entrance of the shop, as Aghajoon stood directly in front of me, blocking me from entering. Only later did I find out that customers could not go inside the shops. It was customary to wait outside while the shop owner and their staff grabbed the items needed.

I peered curiously into the shop and saw two other men. I eventually discovered they were his sons. Haj Agha Mehdi and his sons had organized everything nicely on the wooden shelves that covered the interior of his store: shoe polishes all stacked in one place, shoelaces on one shelf, and shoe insoles on another side. Just from this quick glance, I could tell how efficiently he ran his business. With everything organized so nicely and with every item within easy reach, Haj Agha Mehdi was not going to waste either his or his customer's time looking for supplies.

Aghajoon introduced me as he pulled me to the front. "Haj Agha Mehdi, this is my son, Mohsen. From now on, he will come here to buy my shoe supplies."

I straightened my posture confidently and said, "Salam."

Aghajoon didn't waste any more time and got right down to business, listing from memory the items he needed: "Twenty brown and black shoelaces, three boxes of nails, five rolls of black leather, three insoles, five heels, two brushes, five of each color shoe polish: black, white, and brown."

They gathered all the items quickly and placed everything on the counter for us to inspect. Aghajoon looked over each item carefully to ensure that they had grabbed the correct items and each one was in good condition. Before Haj Agha Mehdi put everything in our bags, he calculated the cost using his abacus; electronic calculators existed at that time but were extremely rare in Iran.

Aghajoon took out the piles of toman bills from his pants pocket and handed Haj Agha Mehdi about one hundred tomans. I had heard him ask Momman for some money before we left for our trip that morning. Her sewing business had picked up recently, and she was now making three times more than Aghajoon per month. The fact that Momman was making more than Aghajoon didn't seem to bother him. Considering all the expenses we had, Aghajoon seemed happy his wife worked, even though it wasn't customary back then. Most women were stay-at-home moms, but Momman was more assertive and goal-oriented than most.

Aghajoon stuffed the rest of his toman bills back into his pants pocket. All merchants only accepted cash in those days. Credit cards were practically nonexistent, and cashing a check was quite difficult. The seller had to go to the same location where his clients banked, because there were no systems to check the amount of money in the buyer's bank account. If the bank returned a check, one could complain to the police to have the check issuer arrested and put in jail. On the downside, it was often the plaintiff who had to pay for the defendant's jail expenses. Therefore, most of the time, the two parties came to an agreement without getting the police involved. It was a potentially messy and convoluted scenario that people tried to avoid at all costs.

After paying, Aghajoon shook hands with Haj Agha Mehdi and said goodbye. I was shocked that Aghajoon hadn't tried to bargain with Haj Agha Mehdi. He paid him exactly what he had asked. That was so unlike Aghajoon and Iranian culture. The art of haggling and bargaining was part of every Iranian's genes.

Bargaining was such an important part of our culture that the merchants and shop owners always asked for a higher price to leave some room for negotiation. It was the closest thing we had to a game that everyone knew how to play in Iran. It didn't matter if you were young, old, poor, or wealthy; everyone learned how to bargain at some point in their lives. It involved skills and know-how, and someone would walk away proud and victorious. When I accompanied Momman to the fabric stores, she sometimes spent half an hour going back and forth with the shop owner to get the best deals.

As we were walking, Aghajoon paced himself so that instead of me jogging vigilantly behind his heels, we walked side by side. I carried one bag, and Aghajoon the other one. I took this opportunity to ask some questions.

"Aghajoon, how come you didn't bargain with Haj Agha Mehdi?"

He smiled, impressed that I had paid attention to the details. "We just don't. Haj Agha Mehdi knows that I am his regular customer and gives me a discount already."

"You mean the prices he offers you might be different for another customer?"

Aghajoon nodded in agreement.

"His shop was so clean and organized too."

Aghajoon raised his eyebrows, probably amazed that I was so observant, "*Bazaariis* (owners of the shops) know our time is precious, so all the shops are orderly. Nobody goes to one if it takes a long time to find things. The shop owners come to buy their supplies and go back to their store as soon as they can. Time is money, Mohsen," Aghajoon said, his voice firm.

I pondered this for a while as we made enough twists and turns to eventually get us out of the maze of the bazaar. On the way to the bus station, we continued talking. He told me that there were many thieves in the bazaar, and I needed to watch my money all the time. "Hold onto your sack tightly. Don't get distracted. Watch your money."

Thinking about Aghajoon's advice made me even more nervous since now I had two things to worry about: getting lost in the bazaar and watching out for the pickpockets.

About a week after my first trip to the bazaar, Ramazoon and I were talking outside Aghajoon's shop when Aghajoon told me I needed to go to the bazaar to get him supplies before he ran out. He gave me a pen and a piece of paper to jot down what he needed: ten black and ten white shoelaces, ten black shoe polishes, a metal shoehorn, a brush, two boxes of nails, three insoles, and several other items. Then he stood up and paused for a minute to figure out how much he needed to give me. He carefully counted each bill.

"Fifty tomans, seventy tomans . . . and this makes one hundred tomans," he said, giving the bills to me one by one.

I put them deep into my pants pocket. As I was heading out of Aghajoon's shop, he called my name, "Mohsen, go to the bazaar, do your shopping, and come back to my shop. Don't go anywhere else, and make sure you always count the change the merchant gives you before you put it in your pocket. And watch your money and the bags!" he shouted as I started walking to the bus station.

I made it to the bazaar without any incidents. I was relieved, but I knew that my job was far from over. Surprisingly, I found my way to Haj Agha Mehdi's shop with ease. All the landmarks in my head helped me. All this time, I kept touching my pocket to make sure the money was still there. I was determined not to disappoint Aghajoon for trusting me.

At the entrance of Haj Agha Mehdi's shop, I waited patiently until he finished a conversation with one of his customers. He acknowledged me with a kind smile. "What supplies does your father need?" I was honestly surprised he remembered me.

"Salam." I took out the list of things I had written down that Aghajoon needed. I read off all the items one by one.

In a matter of minutes, Haj Agha Mehdi had found every item and placed them all down in front of me in a nicely arranged pile. He never asked me to repeat any of the items I read from the list. He calculated how much I owed the same way he did when I was there with Aghajoon.

I carefully took out the money and handed it to him. As per Aghajoon's instructions, I counted the change Haj Agha Mehdi gave me before I put it in my pocket. I picked up the bag and headed back to Aghajoon's shop, while holding on tightly to my pocket and the bag. I managed to navigate my way out of the bazaar the same way I entered, using the same landmark, a kababii restaurant. I didn't have to see it; the fragrance of barbeque meat guided me to the entrance. Sometimes I wished I had money to buy a sandwich to bite on while walking to the shoe-supply store.

Sometimes I had to go to other places because Haj Agha Mehdi didn't have the items on my list, and he gave me directions to other shops in the bazaar. Some of those merchants took advantage of my lack of knowledge and cheated me. They gave me the wrong nails or shoe tabs or substituted shoe polish brands with less expensive ones.

"*Pedar sookhteh* (little rascal), your father was burned! Are you stupid?" Aghajoon would ask, slapping me hard. "They cheated you! Don't you see these are the wrong size shoe tabs?"

How was I supposed to know the difference? I wasn't a cobbler. And if he thought I wasn't smart enough to do the job right, why did he keep sending me to the bazaar to get him supplies?

Over time, my curiosity got the best of me, and I eventually discovered countless ways of entering the bazaar. I even found two large *masjids* (mosques) there: Masjid e Shah and Masjid e Jumeh. Most of the shop owners were true believers of Islam and went there to perform their daily prayers. These bazaariis were more than just efficient workers; they were a vehicle through which business and pleasure alike were pursued in Iran. Their influence expanded beyond such things and reached, rather successfully, into the political arena as well. In fact, bazaariis later became a major force in the Islamic Revolution.

You see, the mood and spirit of the bazaar changed in accordance with the political and economic state of Iran. While I was personally not very political at the time, I often caught wind of some of the heated political debates that resounded through the halls of the bazaar. Sometimes I went to the mosque and just sat there, watching the bazaariis come and go, eavesdropping on their conversations. They talked about politics, the economy, inflation, and what they believed the future of Iran would be. If they weren't discussing these matters, I watched them pray and meditate. Although I didn't grow up in a religious family, the subject of God and the meaning of life always interested me. Plus, it was hard not to enjoy the beautiful sound of the *azan* (Muslim call to prayer) coming from the loudspeakers of the mosque, inviting people to pray and forget about their day-to-day worries. Today, the sound of the azan still soothes me.

Aghajoon sent me to the bazaar every other week, and I began to really enjoy going there, especially now that every time I went, I discovered a new area. Every trip to the bazaar was exciting, but it was time-consuming; it took half a day to go there and come back. I had a hunch that the cobblers around Aghajoon's shop would not mind buying some supplies from him if he sold some of the more popular items.

"Aghajoon, can I buy some extra supplies for you to sell to other cobblers in the area? You will pocket some profits. Who wants to spend half a day going and coming back from the bazaar?"

He raised his brows, his eyes became wider, and his eyeballs moved back and forth. I could tell he was thinking about my proposal, but he didn't say anything about it. Still, the idea stayed with me. I had to give Aghajoon some additional suggestions on how to implement my idea.

One day, when I had returned from the bazaar to Aghajoon's shop, I noticed that he had one empty wall.

"Why don't you install a glass cabinet here to sell shoe supplies to your customers or other cobblers in the area who run out of some supplies?" I pointed at the empty wall. "You could make some extra money." I reminded Aghajoon of my proposal.

Aghajoon said, "I have to talk to Momman about it." He didn't even acknowledge that I had suggested a good idea.

A few weeks later, Aghajoon asked an ironworker who was one of his customers and lived in our area to install a built-in glass cabinet. Aghajoon made it my responsibility to arrange the extra supplies in the newly installed cabinet after every trip to the bazaar. I didn't mind the extra work. I just felt excited and proud that Aghajoon had taken my idea seriously.

Unspoken Secrets

Age Thirteen

My questions about sex and how a baby is born were answered in a magical and educational way.

I first asked the question when my younger brother Saeed was born, but Momman's explanation didn't completely satisfy my curiosity. One day while I was changing the lightbulb for one of the fixtures in the room, I popped the question again, hoping for a more realistic answer: "Momman, how are babies born?"

She looked up from the sewing machine, surprised, and said, "Umm, well, Umm, babies grow in their mom's stomach, and when they mature, the midwife or doctor opens it and takes out the baby. That's how babies are born. Yeah, that's how."

She repeated herself a couple of times, as if she was trying to convince herself of her own answer. She had given me the same answer before, and I was hoping she would change it since I was older and more mature. Besides, what she said did not make any sense: *Where did all the food go if the baby was in the stomach, or did the baby nourish himself from the same food?* I scratched my head and wanted to ask more questions, but she changed the subject: "You'd better finish changing that lightbulb before my customer arrives to pick up her dress."

My curiosity remained but I was not going to lose sleep over it.

A couple of days later, Aghajoon asked me to go to the bazaar to get some supplies for his shop.

I picked up the sack and left after school. I had to walk about ten minutes from the last bus to reach the bazaar. Sometimes if I were not in a hurry, I window-shopped or looked at items the street vendors were selling.

As I was walking, the voice of one of them captured my attention: "Books, five rials."

I liked to buy instructional books to learn how to build or repair things, so I approached his booth. There were many books on the small folding table and stacks of them underneath on the ground. Many people, mostly older, had gathered around; everyone had picked up a book and was thumbing through it.

I started reading the titles of the books; they were books about gardening, carpentry, cooking, and others. None interested me until I came across a brown-covered book with a catchy title: *Unspoken Secrets*.

I picked it up and opened it to figure out why they called it that. The first page had pictures of nude men and women touching each other's private parts. I immediately closed the book and looked around in case anyone had seen me. I felt ashamed and nervous looking at those pictures. That was the first time I had seen female private parts. Momman had always been careful not to change my sister's cloth diapers in front of me.

I held onto the book, hesitant about whether I should buy it. What would the vendor think about me if I got it, or would he even let me purchase it? I decided to buy another book and hide this one underneath it, so he wouldn't notice it. I quickly picked up another book, which happened to be about animals and their habitat. I waited until there was no one around the vendor. "Salam, these two books," I said and gave him the money.

He took the money.

I was relieved that he didn't ask to see which books I had purchased. I don't think he knew the titles of books he was carrying; he probably bought them in bulk and was trying to sell them to make quick money. I threw the books inside my sack and decided to buy the items Aghajoon asked me to get as quickly as possible so I could go home and check out the rest of that book.

Before I went to Aghajoon's shop to drop off his supplies, I went home and hid the book inside my tool sack, where my two younger sisters could not find it. They knew they were not supposed to touch it without my permission. I gave the book about animals to Etty to read.

Later, at home, I went upstairs and took out the *Unspoken Secrets*, along with my history book, in case someone showed up unexpectedly. This way, I could start reading my textbook and pretend I was studying— although I did not think anyone would check up on me. Momman and Aghajoon were always busy with their work, and my sisters were very good students, so they studied a lot. My other siblings were too young to do anything.

Nervously, I opened the book and turned the pages one by one and looked at each picture carefully. There were pictures of nude men and women in different sexual positions. I felt strange looking at those pictures and wondered if my parents did those things to one another. Sometimes, at night, I heard laughing noises coming from where they were sleeping. I thought maybe they were tickling each other.

As I flipped through the pages, there were images of a wiggly tail with a big head called *sperm* and an oval picture named *egg*. They showed how the head enters the egg to fertilize it. The following pages showed stages of a growing fetus inside a sac in a female womb. From this, I figured out that babies don't grow inside the stomach, as Momman had indicated, but in separate place located much lower than the stomach. I wondered if Momman was confused.

This little brown book was more informative than any science book I had read. I was learning new things and kept turning the pages, looking at the pictures and descriptions. I learned that *uterus* is the name of the organ that holds the placenta; it holds the sac that fills with water during pregnancy. The water is called *amniotic fluid*, which both feeds and protects the baby. I realized this was the same purple sac that Madarjoon had buried in the ground when my brother was born. The last few pages showed a woman in labor. Each image showed her private part getting larger, until the baby's head emerged.

Why did Momman say they cut the stomach to bring out the baby? Couldn't she feel the baby coming out of her genitals? The thought that Momman tried not to tell me the truth did not occur to me, so I figured she simply did not know what was happening to her during childbirth.

Then I thought, *Wouldn't she see scars where they cut her open, if that is what she believed happened to her?* Everything was confusing, and I figured that Momman was naïve and needed to know the truth about childbirth. I decided I had to show the pages about how babies are born to Momman to educate her.

A month passed, and I was still reading that book, going back and forth between pages to really understand how babies are made and are born. One day, I decided to take the book to school and show it to one of my good friends, Amir. I wanted him to learn about the facts of life. I hid the book between my other textbooks in my bag. During recess, I took him to the corner of the playground and showed him the book, being careful not to get caught.

His big black eyes got bigger, his round chubby face turned red, and his jaw dropped. "Where did you get this book?"

I told him it was from a vendor close to the bazaar.

He was just as amazed as I was looking at the pictures. A couple of days later, he came back with the same book. I'm not sure if he bought it from the same man I had purchased mine from or maybe paid someone to get it for him. I never asked him. I knew he did not have as much freedom as I did, since he was an only child and his parents were constantly watching him. One time, he told me that as soon as he went home, his mom made him do his homework, which his dad checked after he came home from work. He envied me when I told him my parents didn't have time to do any of that. "They are always busy with their own work," I told him.

For some time, our routine was to go to a corner of the school playground and talk about the things we had seen in the book.

"Mohsen, do you think our parents have done this kind of act?"

"Well, if we are here, they must have."

"Do you think you ever want to do these things to a girl?"

"I guess I have to if I want to have children."

One day, Amir came to school very nervous; he told me his mom had found the *Unspoken Secrets* in his backpack. "Mohsen, I told my mom this is one of our textbooks. She showed the book to my dad, and they are coming to school today to talk about it."

I felt bad for him because I knew he was in trouble.

During class, the teacher asked Amir to go to the principal's office. I got very worried. What if he told them that I also had a copy of the book? Amir was a trustworthy kid, but he might blurt out my name under pressure. I kept waiting for someone to ask for me to go to the office, but nobody did.

I did not see him again that day; he must have left with his parents. I hoped he did not get into trouble with the school or his mom and dad. The next day, he told me he admitted to his parents and the principal that he had bought the book. He promised them he would not lie to them anymore.

I, on the other hand, continued to study the book; I kept learning new things every time I opened it.

One day, when I was helping Momman nail a picture frame on the wall in her classroom, I brought up the subject of the babies again. I wanted to teach my mom about her body. I thought she should know. "Momman, are you usually awake when you give birth to your babies?"

I could tell she was uncomfortable talking about this subject.

"Yeah," she said as she continued guiding the flowery fabric under the sewing machine and turning its handle.

"Are you sure the midwife cuts your stomach, Momman?" I asked her while striking the nail.

"Yes."

Clearly, she didn't know much, and I decided to tell her about it. I stopped my work and climbed down the ladder. I ran upstairs, put the book under my armpit, and came down, skipping a couple of steps to reach her faster. "Momman, that's not how babies are born. Look! This is how," I said, panting. Then I opened the book to the page that showed different stages of pregnancy and labor.

I think Momman was caught by surprise; at first, she didn't know what to say or do. When she came to her senses, she turned red, her eyebrows rose, and her eyeballs were about to pop out. I'll never forget the look on her face when she saw those detailed illustrations of a woman's private parts in front of her. I did not see the pictures as dirty—more as teaching tools. My intention was to educate Momman about her body and how babies develop inside a female. I think she took it the wrong way.

She immediately closed the book and snatched it from me. "Where did you get this?" she asked, while trying to figure out what to do with it. I did not know why she was so angry at me for teaching her new things.

I said, "I bought it from a guy near the bazaar."

"Well, this is not a good book. Go back upstairs. Don't you have homework to do?" she asked nervously.

I was only trying to help her know the facts. I left very disappointed and sad.

I don't know what Momman did with that book; maybe she showed it to Aghajoon, and they tried some of those positions. I did hear laughter coming from their room later that evening.

MOHSEN ON THE RADIO

AGE FOURTEEN

In a win-win situation, you make money while being entertained at the same time. Almost by accident, I found a way to do that.

One day, while I was combing the market for tools and parts, I noticed that a chubby middle-aged man with a thick gray mustache had spread all kinds of second-hand electrical supplies on a black tablecloth. A large corrugated box with random things in it caught my eye. It was filled with wires, fuses, used motors, vacuum tubes, microphones, receivers, some batteries, and electrical tape. I tested each microphone by shaking it; they all worked because they didn't make a rattling noise.

"How much for everything?" I said as calmly as I could, not wanting to let on how badly I wanted this box, for fear that he might raise the price on me.

He stared at me, probably wondering what a young boy would want to do with all those gadgets. "Ten tomans," he said, while puffing on his cigarette.

I took out three tomans from my pocket and said, "Three tomans."

He shook his head in disagreement and said, "Five tomans."

I walked away.

He screamed, "Come back, come back. Four tomans, no more, no less."

I knew that eventually I would use most of the stuff in that box, and four tomans was a decent price. I paid and picked up the box to head home. The box was not heavy, but its size made it little difficult to carry.

Momman looked at me when I arrived home with that big box but didn't say anything. She knew I liked to make things and used my own money to buy the gadgets I needed. I placed the box in the little room in the corner of our backyard to be out of reach of my younger siblings.

A few days later, my cousin Akbar and I were telling each other jokes, and we both were laughing very hard, holding our stomachs.

Aghajoon woke up from his nap. "*Pedar sookhteha*? What are you doing? Get lost before I get up and slap you!"

Akbar and I ran downstairs. Poor Akbar was as scared as I was, even though he knew Aghajoon would not hit him, and only me.

"You know, Akbar, I can make something so we can talk all we want and Aghajoon won't be disturbed by our voices," I told him confidently.

Akbar got excited and asked if he could help. We grabbed the box from its corner and dumped the contents on the ground. Akbar and I started looking for things we needed to make a homemade telephone.

"Akbar, look for a long wire, long enough for you and me to sit at two different corners of this room and be able to talk. Oh, and find me a battery too," I told him as I began hooking two receivers to two microphones and then taping both of those receivers to their own individual wires.

"Here, catch." He threw the battery to me.

I connected it to the wires coming out of the microphone. "Did you find the long wire?"

He handed me a wire. "This is the longest I found."

I attached one end of it to the battery and the other end to the receiver. As I was taping the wire to the receiver, I heard a crackling sound coming from the other receiver.

"Do you hear that? That means this thing is going to work." I pointed to Akbar to pick up one end of the device and sit in a corner of the room to try it. "Hold the receiver to your ear and the microphone to your mouth." I tried to pantomime the instructions as I sat at the other end of the room. "One, two, three," I quietly said in the microphone. "What did I say?"

He repeated, "One, two, three," with a big smile on his face. Then he began whispering into the microphone, as I had just done: "Mohsen, I can hear you in my ears. Mohsen, you made a telephone."

We didn't own a phone at that time, but we had heard about them and vaguely knew how they functioned. Akbar and I moved to various parts of the house and talked using that telephone. Aside from a little giggling, we made practically no noise, which protected us from my father's wrath.

A month passed, and eventually the novelty of that phone faded. If Aghajoon was around, Akbar and I didn't use it; we just went somewhere else to talk.

One Friday, when Akbar was visiting, he noticed the pile of wires, microphones, and receivers in the corner of one room. He asked if I was planning to do anything with them.

"I don't know. Let's disassemble them and put them back in the box," I said.

As we were walking with our pile of electrical gadgets in our hands, the sound of a persistent drip coming out from the leaky tap caught my attention. I saw the wire connected to the water pipe. I had installed it for better reception for our radio. An idea came to me in that moment, and I decided to try it.

In the old days, most households placed a wooden cross on the roof of their houses and connected some wires to it to make an antenna. For better reception on their radios, households like ours wrapped another wire around the antenna and connected it to another metal piece. Ours was a wire coming out of a gap in the window from the room Momman used to sew. This wire was attached to the water pipe.

On that day, I could hear the click-clacking of Momman's sewing machine. She must have been making an outfit for one of her customers, and I knew Etty was most likely beside her, sweeping the floor or doing other chores. She helped Momman a lot. The radio was on, and I faintly heard the beautiful voice of Marzieh, an Iranian folk singer.

"Akbar, I have an idea. Let's see if it works." I took a long wire from the pile and cut out a portion of its insulation to expose the metal piece and then pulled it out. "Please give me the microphone."

I attached one end of the wire to the microphone and walked to the small room to connect the other end to the neutral wire of the outlet there. Akbar cringed when I put my finger in the outlet. "I thought you can't touch any part of the outlet with your bare hands. Isn't it dangerous?"

"I checked it before, using a voltmeter." I pointed at the two different wires. "This wire is neutral, which means it's safe, but this one is dangerous and will kill you if you touch it." Akbar seemed a little frightened. I distinctively heard a nervous gulp from his throat. "Please give me that battery." I connected the piece I had exposed to the negative terminal. "Now hold the microphone, make sure none of the wires come off."

I connected one end of another wire to the microphone and the other end to the positive terminal of the battery.

"Mohsen, I have no idea what you are doing with all these wires going from here to there."

I giggled. "I don't either, but I hope it works." The last thing I did was connect another wire from the negative terminal to the water pipe. "Okay, we're all set." I took the microphone from Akbar and talked into it. "Salam, this is Mohsen. How are you?"

I heard Momman and Etty laugh in the room. Then Akbar snatched the microphone from me and talked into it, "Salam Khaleh, salam Etty. How are you?"

We both waited to see if any other reaction would come from the room where the radio was playing. Our eyes and ears focused on the window of the classroom.

Shortly after, Etty stuck her head out. "How did you do that? We heard your voices on the radio!"

I had no idea why or how my idea worked, but it did, and that made me happy.

Etty came out and said she wanted us to hear it ourselves.

We went to the room where Momman was sewing. As soon as she saw me, she smiled and said, "What have you made this time, Mohsen Jon? Your head is so full of ideas. You will be a big inventor someday."

I chuckled and got close to the window so Etty could see that I was in the room.

"Salam Momman, salam Mohsen, salam Akbar." It was so cool to hear my sister's cute, girlish voice on top of the music that was playing in the background.

From then on, Akbar practically lived at our house so he could sing and hear his voice on the radio. His goal was to be a singer when he grew up. He kept asking if we liked his voice. I nodded and told him he sang well but I knew he needed to take lessons to learn how to manage his range of voice. He ran out of breath easily.

The only drawback about my setup was that the microphone got hot after a minute or two. I had to remove the wire from the outlet to let it cool down and then hook it back up.

Later, I started charging the neighborhood kids one rial to use the device. It entertained me to hear the things they said into that microphone. Some kids told stories, some recited a poem they had written or one from a famous poet. Mostly, they sang their favorite songs, clapping and dancing. It worked out nicely: I made some money while being entertained, and the children felt famous for being on our radio.

Welcome to the World, JooJoo

Age Fourteen

We ended up feeding our chicken, rather than having the chicken become our feed.

Tears pricked my eyes as my siblings and I shoveled dirt to bury JooJoo, our beloved multicolored pet chicken. After everyone left, I sat on the ground next to her grave, which we had decorated with a brick inscribed with her name, with bright red hearts all around it.

While rubbing one of JooJoo's feathers that I had removed from her body before her burial, I thought about how she came to be and the way she had enriched our lives for two wonderful years.

It was an idle summer afternoon in 1962. I was about fourteen years old. On that day, I was walking down Naser Khosrow Street, one of my favorite places in Tehran, weaving in and out of the hustle and bustle of the crowds that often clustered around the vendors on either side of the street. In addition to the vendors, who spread their merchandise on the ground on a piece of cloth, one could also find a variety of shops selling strange-looking herbs, guns, cameras, or books. The bookstores were filled with fancy Western hardcover novels, instruction books, poetry, etc. I couldn't afford anything at these stores, but the books sold by the vendors were extremely cheap and within my economic reach. The instruction manuals were my favorite; they opened all kinds of avenues for my creativity and offered a temporary cure for my restless mind.

As I stood over a vendor, scanning through his books, a guy next to me picked one up, fanned through the pages, and put it back down. The title of that book caught my eye: *How to Artificially Hatch Eggs*. I thought,

Is this a joke? Could chickens be made from eggs without a hen? Amazed and curious, I picked it up to take a closer look. I excitedly flipped through the pages to find more information. I stared at the pictures in awe. The images of colorful chickens with the names of their breeds written underneath them glared back at me.

Food, especially meat, was a scarce commodity in our household, and chickens cost even more than red meat. We ate extremely little red meat and had chicken two or three times a year, only when we had invited relatives to come over for lunch on Fridays, the Iranian weekend. Once, during a luncheon, I noticed how ruthlessly everyone devoured their chicken pieces, chewing even the bones. Another time, my uncle and his son fought over the chicken butt. Aghajoon had to divide it in half to settle the argument between them.

My imagination ran wild with images of our backyard full of chickens and my plate filled with chicken pieces. The harsh voice of the vendor brought me back to Nasser Khosrow Street.

"Hey boy, do you want that book?" He looked at me over the rim of his thick round glasses.

The book wasn't expensive, so I dropped five rial into his palm and placed the book under my arm and happily walked to the bus station. I had a plan.

On the bus ride home, I studied the book. Halfway through, the pages were filled with pictures of large, fancy-looking machines called incubators. They had many knobs, measuring meters, and switches on their front panels. Some had the names of their manufacturers, with prices written underneath. The least expensive cost about two hundred tomans, equal to the price of fifty chickens. *If I had that much money, I might as well buy chickens instead of growing them,* I thought.

One page stood out from the others and intrigued me. There were images of several old Asian men and women, each with five or six eggs stacked tightly inside the sleeves of their garments. Each sleeve had a thick elastic band at the end that, when pulled, closed the opening of the sleeve. It kept the eggs warm and prevented them from falling out. I was surprised to learn that people cultivated chickens in such a primitive manner in Asia. *Does it really work?* I wondered.

I placed the book on my lap and stared out of the bus window, thinking about ways I could raise chickens, as I watched people rush in and out of stores, carrying bags of food. I started making a mental list of the things I would need to construct a makeshift incubator.

As soon as I arrived home, I took the wheelbarrow I had made, which I kept in the corner of our backyard, and pushed it down the street toward a nearby dumpster. I went through piles of junk and picked out as many red bricks as I could find, along with a piece of wooden board, four or five metal barbeque skewers, several hinges, and nails. I placed the materials in my wheelbarrow and headed home to begin working on my invention.

On the way home, people stopped and stared at me as I sweated profusely, pushing the heavy load down the street. They probably felt sorry for me but had no idea that this junk was soon going to bring my family delicacies. As I approached our house, I let out a deep, heavy sigh and set down the wheelbarrow for a moment. With the back of my sleeve, I wiped the sweat that was dripping from my eyebrows into my eyes.

As soon as I opened the door, the voice of Madarjoon brought a smile to my face and washed away my fatigue. I had many questions to ask her about how to raise chickens. I knew she had the answers since she grew up on a farm. I placed the wheelbarrow in the corner of our backyard, cleaned my face and dirty hands, then I ran inside to join Momman and Madarjoon.

"Salam," I said in a booming voice and sat next to Madarjoon on the floor.

She greeted me back and kissed me on both cheeks. "Mohsen Jon, what was that clank-clank noise I heard?"

"I brought some things," I said with a mischievous grin.

"What things?" she asked, knowing I was up to something.

"Some materials to make an incubator," I explained.

"Incubator?" she asked, putting a sugar cube in her mouth to drink her tea.

"Yes, I'm going to grow chickens," I replied with a proud smile.

Momman poured tea in a glass cup with two sugar cubes on the saucer, listening intently. As she placed it in front of me, she exchanged a prolonged look with Madarjoon. Everyone in our family knew about my many projects during the summer. If I saw something interesting that I couldn't afford to buy, I always figured out a way to make it myself. It never surprised anyone when I brought home a variety of gadgets. My parents never complained since I continued to do my daily chores, and if I had to buy any materials for my projects, I always paid with the little money I had saved up.

Madarjoon lifted her teacup to her lips and smiled. "Growing chickens is a lot of fun, especially when you hear the tweet-tweet of the young chicks hatching."

"Is it hard to grow them?" I asked.

"Nothing is hard if you know what you're doing," she replied, her voice firm, and her eyes full of life and intelligence.

"How do I do it?" I asked.

"First, you need eggs that come from a farm where the roosters and hens are"—she paused and looked at Momman, then whispered to me as if she were telling me a secret—"*mixed.*"

I assumed that was her way of telling me the eggs had to be fertilized. I had learned about reproduction from *Unspoken Secrets.*

Madarjoon took another sip of her tea and continued, "You have to keep an egg warm for twenty-one days for it to hatch."

"How do I know it's the right egg?" I pondered aloud.

"You must hold it up to the light, and you'll see thread-like squiggles inside," she explained.

"Thread inside an egg? You mean blood vessels?"

She hesitated. "I don't know what young people call them these days," she said, putting another sugar cube in her mouth while sipping her tea.

"Where do I find eggs with threads?" I asked, chuckling.

"Mohsen Jon, I'll bring you a few tomorrow! They aren't expensive, but you have to give me one of the chicks when they hatch," she said as she smiled and squeezed my cheeks.

In my head, I calculated the timing. Every twenty-one days, three or four chicklets would hatch. By the time they grew and were consumed, we would have another three hatched. With this plan, we would have chicken frequently. My mouth began to water as I imagined eating the delicious chicken stew mixed with potatoes, carrots, and tomatoes over rice.

As soon as Madarjoon left, I started working on the incubator. I wanted it to be ready the next day, when she would bring over the eggs. I tucked the book under my arm and moved the wheelbarrow to the area where I wanted to construct the makeshift incubator. My sisters and brother were playing hopscotch in one corner.

As soon as Etty saw me, she left their game and walked toward me. She was the most curious of all my siblings. "Mohsen, what are you making this time?" she asked, taking the book from under my arm. She sat down and began to turn the pages.

"A box to change an egg into a chicken."

"Like this one?" She pointed to a picture of an incubator.

"Yeah, but not as fancy looking as that."

"Can I help you?" she asked, moving closer to me.

"Pass those bricks to me one by one," I said.

As she handed me the bricks, I stacked them into a thirty-by-thirty cubic centimeter box, then Etty arranged the skewers parallel to each inside the contraption, following my instructions.

"The eggs will go on top of the skewers." I explained.

"How many eggs, Mohsen?" she questioned.

"As many as Madarjoon brings."

"Why does Madarjoon have to bring the eggs?"

Smiling, I told her that we had to use special eggs with thread-like squiggles inside them. I didn't want to say *fertilized* since Etty would have asked me to explain what that meant. She was only eleven and too young to know about the reproductive system and how babies were made. Besides, I would have felt embarrassed discussing the topic with her.

"So, what do we do next, Mohsen?" she asked with an inquisitive tone.

I searched through my tool bag and saw a tiny heating element. I remembered the day I had asked Mr. Shirveah at the Pahlavi Hospital if I could have it. Thanks to his generosity on that day, I now had a device to keep the eggs warm. I nestled the coil carefully inside the brick box, then I connected a series of wires to it. Etty helped me pass each of the wires through the gaps in between the bricks so I could connect them to a plug. I stepped back and stared at my creation. It didn't look anything like the images of fancy incubators in the book, but I had a good feeling it would get the job done.

"Tomorrow we will put the eggs in and turn on the heat to make them warm. Then we will wait for twenty-one days for the eggs to hatch," I said excitedly, patting Etty on her shoulder.

The following day, Madarjoon brought over the eggs in a handkerchief. She found me in the backyard fiddling with the wires. She glanced over at the brick box and shot me a skeptical look. "Mohsen Jon, what's this?"

"Salam Madarjoon. I told you I was going to make an incubator. I'll put the eggs inside it to keep them warm until they hatch." I spoke with a confident voice.

"These days, kids make life so complicated," Madarjoon sighed. "Just put the eggs under a lamp to keep them warm for twenty-one days, and they will hatch."

"If it were that easy, why would any company manufacture such an elaborate machine to hatch eggs?" I said.

After Madarjoon touched the wires and inspected the inside of the incubator, she asked me to explain how it operated.

"Well, I put the eggs on the skewers, then I plug in the heating element to warm up the incubator. After twenty-one days, the eggs should hatch." I clapped my hands with excitement and continued, "Then we'll invite you to have a chicken stew lunch with us."

"Well, what you said makes perfect sense to me, Mohsen Jon." Madarjoon's eyes shone like diamonds, as a toothless smile spread across her face. She unwrapped the handkerchief holding the eggs, and I saw four perfectly white ovals. I wondered what the chicks would look like when they hatched. I held the eggs one by one against the light to see if they were filled with thread-like squiggles, as my grandmother had said. Looking at the eggs in my hand, I felt responsible for the lives of those living chicklets growing inside them. In a way, their destiny and survival depended on whether my makeshift incubator functioned correctly.

"Do you see the threads?" Madarjoon asked, trying to look over my shoulder.

"Yes, I see them," I said excitedly.

When Madarjoon had made sure I was happy with the eggs, she pulled up her chador to her head, wished me good luck, and told me she would come back soon to check on my progress.

Filled with hope and optimism, I carefully arranged the four eggs in between the two metal skewers. I checked and re-checked to make sure the eggs wouldn't fall on the ground before I inserted the plug into the outlet. The orange-red glow radiating from the heating element indicated it was working. Satisfied, I covered the top of the brick box with a piece of wooden board to trap the heat inside. Now I had to sit back and wait for twenty-one days.

The next three days flew by since Aghajoon had an abundance of chores lined up for me at his shoe shop: delivering shoes, hanging shoes on the walls, dusting, and sweeping. On the fourth day, my curiosity got the better of me, and in between doing my chores, I sneaked off to the backyard to check on the incubator. I placed my hand on the top layer of bricks to peer inside but immediately snapped back, inhaling sharply. The bricks felt as if they were on fire.

"*Ouch! Ouch!*" I exclaimed, blowing on my hand, trying to cool down the burning sensation as I ran over to the outlet and unplugged it. I dipped my hand inside the scorching contraption and removed one of the eggs from inside the box. It felt so hot that I had to toss it back and forth between my palms to avoid burning my skin. I sighed in disappointment, knowing very well that the living cells in the eggs were no longer alive.

Once the egg in my hand had cooled down completely, I held it against the light. I knew what I would see but checked anyway. My heart sank as I searched the egg for the thread-like squiggles, but nothing inside was visible. I tapped it against the side of the brick box. It cracked but nothing spilled out. The white and yellow parts had solidified. After all this effort, I had only managed to cook the eggs.

Later that night, we ended up eating the eggs with fresh bread, cucumbers, and tomatoes for dinner. They tasted delicious but not nearly as delicious as chicken stew. Etty tried to tease me about my makeshift incubator: "Mohsen, you didn't have to make such a fancy device to make boiled eggs. We could have put them in hot water. I could have done that easily."

Momman immediately shushed her. "Mohsen will figure out a way to make it work," she assured Etty.

Determined to make my project a success, the next day, I once again flipped through the pages of *How to Artificially Hatch Eggs*. Incidentally, Madarjoon showed up to inquire about my progress. When she saw my long face and gloomy eyes, she knew my project had failed. She sat next to me without saying a word.

I gave her a half-smile and told her the temperature inside the brick box went up so high that by the third day, the eggs were cooked. She gave me a small kiss on my face and said, "You did your best, Mohsen Jon. So what if this one didn't work; make another one. Don't give up." She patted me on the shoulder as she stood up to join Momman in the other room.

Glancing at Madarjoon's back, with the chador wrapped around her waist, I thought she looked like a young girl, twelve years old, petite, and a head shorter than me. However, once she spoke and projected her personality, she looked as tall and strong as a cypress tree. Her words encouraged me to continue with my project and find ways to overcome the obstacles.

Before entering the room where Momman was, Madarjoon turned around and said, "Mohsen Jon, I can bring as many eggs as you want whenever you need them."

I decided to make a new makeshift incubator from scratch—this time a wooden one with a door, a window, and a thermometer, so I could monitor the temperature inside and adjust it accordingly.

Abas Agha, owner of the fresh produce stand, had many empty fruit cartons, so I asked him if I could have one. Aghajoon must have told him why I wanted the box, because the day I picked it up, he jokingly asked me how many chickens he was going to receive in exchange.

Filled with new hope, I took the wheelbarrow and headed to the dumpster again. I picked up a piece of glass, a wooden board, a rusty saw, rusty nails, hinges of all sizes, metal pipes, and screws. As I was arranging the items in my wheelbarrow, I realized this dumpster was like heaven to me. I didn't have much money, but I could always visit here to pick up the junk other people had thrown away and reuse it for my projects. In addition to Naser Khosrow Street, I realized this place had become one of my favorite spots in Tehran.

At home, I cut the board into a smaller piece and connected it to the open end of the fruit box with hinges. That became the door to the box. Then I pounded a nail into the board to hook a small thermometer inside. Next, I cut out a carefully measured square in the middle of one of the side panels. At the sound of Etty's footsteps, I stopped and looked up from taping the glass pane to the box.

"Wow, Mohsen. This one has a door and a window," Etty said, clapping. "Can I help?"

I preferred to work alone, but how could I say no to her pleading eyes? With Etty's help, I made two tiny holes on the two opposite panels of the fruit box and asked her to insert the two metal skewers, leaving the ends protruding outside. I grabbed the ends and turned them to make sure we could easily move the eggs from side to side, allowing their surfaces to warm up evenly. I took a break to wipe the sweat from my forehead with my sleeve and rub my hands together to remove the sawdust from my bruised and achy palms. They throbbed from the cutting, pounding, and sawing, but the excitement I was experiencing drowned out the pain.

"You must be tired," Etty said.

"I'll be okay once we start eating chicken every week," I said, smiling.

"Mohsen, do you think this one will work?" Etty asked in a sweet, innocent voice.

"The little chicklets will definitely hatch. I have thought of everything this time," I said matter-of-factly, certain my invention would succeed this time.

"Are we done?" Etty asked.

"Nope." I took the metal pipe and connected one end of it to the box and the other end to a small kerosene heater. "This will take care of the inside temperature. All I need now. . .."

"Mohsen Jon! What are you doing now?" Madarjoon's voice came from behind me. When she reached me, she examined my hands, turning them back and forth in her own. "Look at your hands, all black and blue and scratches everywhere!" she said, tsking and shaking her head.

After greeting her, I assured her my hands would be fine. Then I asked if she could bring me more eggs the next day. I told her I had enough money saved up to pay for them myself.

Later that night, with Etty's help, I moved the incubator out of the backyard and into the house. We placed it on the last step of the staircase leading to the rooftop and out of everyone's way. This incubator was definitely a big improvement over the brick box; the only challenge I faced with this one was to keep the temperature constant at 37.5°C, on average, for twenty-one straight days.

I could easily monitor the temperature during the day, but at night it was a different story. I asked Etty and Motty to help; they both graciously agreed. We decided I would wake up two times since this was my project, and my sisters would wake only once each night. I made a list of our names and the times of our duty and hung it next to the incubator.

At night, the alarm went off every two hours. Each of us woke up for our assigned shift to check the thermometer and adjust the heater accordingly. Since we all slept in the same room, the sound of the alarm disturbed my entire family. But surprisingly, no one complained about the frequent buzzing noise.

One night, as I lay on the floor half-asleep, anxious for the alarm to go off, my mind drifted back to a time a few months earlier when we had guests over for lunch. We spread the sofreh on the floor and placed the food on top of the sofreh. Momman had prepared a platter of rice and a bowl of chicken stew, along with some greenery—radishes, green onions, mint, and other seasonal herbs. The guests and my family sat around the sofreh, the elders at the head of the cloth and youngsters closer to the door. We all patiently waited for Aghajoon to serve the food.

When we were invited to their homes, none of my uncles gave out food the way Aghajoon did—maybe because he wanted to make sure everyone got something to eat. He stepped onto the sofreh and put a heaping spoonful of rice on everyone's plate. Then he divided the chicken in the stew and gave each person a piece of it; the best parts went to the guests. As he sat down next to Momman to eat, she looked at his plate and gave him a sympathetic smile. Curious, my eyes moved to his plate too, and I noticed he had mostly rice, some vegetables, and only the skin of the chicken. On that day, I felt sorry for my father. The poor man had spent most of his daily wage to buy that chicken, yet his share of it at lunch was only the skin.

The alarm clock jarred me back to the present, but I thought, *Once the eggs hatch and grow into chickens, my father will be able to eat all the chicken his heart desires.*

A week passed, and we all looked exhausted from waking often at night. Still, nobody pestered me over it. Sometimes when the alarm rang, Momman or Aghajoon told us to continue sleeping while they got up to adjust the temperature. This project now belonged to every member of my family. We worked as a team, turning the eggs and adjusting the heat, around the clock.

Twelve days before the eggs would hatch, Etty didn't get up on her turn, and nobody else did either. We were just too tired.

"Mohsen! Mohsen! Wake up," Etty said, shaking me vigorously. "I missed my turn to check on the incubator!" Her voice trembled.

Hurriedly, I ran up the stairs. The first thing I did was look through the window to see the thermometer. The temperature had increased, but it didn't feel as hot as it did inside the brick box, probably because brick absorbs heat better than wood. Nevertheless, I hoped this project wasn't ruined and the eggs hadn't cooked like last time.

Minutes later, my sisters joined me and watched nervously as I lowered my hand into the incubator and took out an egg. I held it to the light. The inside looked cloudy, and I could no longer see any of the thread-like squiggles inside. I shook my head and tapped the egg lightly against the side of the wooden box. A yellow liquid oozed out, followed by the pungent stench of a rotten egg that stung my nostrils.

"What is that smell?" Etty asked, holding her nose.

"I think the eggs got infected."

"Was it my fault?" she asked apprehensively.

"Nah, I think they got infected long ago. It had nothing to do with the temperature rising."

Etty felt relieved that she hadn't messed up the project. "You know what happened, Mohsen. I dreamed I was standing by the incubator, looking through the window. My dream felt so real that I honestly thought I was up and checking the temperature."

We all laughed at her dream. For the first time, I noticed the dark circles around my sisters' eyes. They both looked worn-out. I must have looked the same to them. None of us had gotten a full night's rest in days. It was then that I realized I needed to figure out a less complicated way of monitoring the temperature in the incubator. That night we didn't set the alarm, and it felt good to sleep peacefully with no interruption.

The next day, I picked up *How to Artificially Hatch Eggs* again and flipped through the pages. I stopped to look at the illustrations of people who hatched the eggs inside their sleeves. I felt bad that I was unable to grow them using a more advanced technique, when these people produced them out of their shirt sleeves. Maybe Madarjoon was right, and I had made this project more complicated than I should have.

My goal was no longer just to serve chicken to my family. Now I wanted to overcome the challenge of hatching eggs. Over time, I found out there were other key factors I needed to consider when hatching eggs in an incubator—for example, the humidity and air quality. I filled a tray with water and placed it inside the box to keep the air moist so the growing embryos wouldn't stick to their shells. I also occasionally vented the apparatus by opening its door so the harmful gases produced by metabolic reactions could escape into the outside air.

To avoid the hassle of waking up every so often at night, I bought a used electric temperature-control thermostat from a vendor on Nasser Khosrow Street. Money well spent, I thought. I wished I had used this tool earlier; it would have saved us a lot of agony from waking up every two hours in the middle of the night.

This time I had a good feeling about my project, and everything was going as planned. Periodically, I checked the temperature inside the incubator, opened and closed its door, and made sure I had enough water in the tray. It was getting close to the end of the twenty-one-day incubation period and everyone, including my parents and Madarjoon, was excited and hoped for the eggs to hatch.

One afternoon, Madarjoon and I were having tea together. I was pointing to the pictures of people in Asia in the *How to Hatch Eggs*

Artificially book. "Do you think this can be true Madar—" I asked, then paused, thinking that I heard something. I turned my head to listen carefully. A delightful tweet-tweet emanated from the top of the stairs. I raised my eyebrows and looked at Madarjoon with a big smile. "Did you hear that?"

Her eyes grew wide, and she instantly put down her teacup. I dropped mine onto the floor as I stood up on both feet. My heel bumped the cup, and I heard a splash as I rushed up the stairs, skipping steps on my way. The pounding of my heart and the sound of blood rushing through my body resonated in my eardrums. I took a deep breath and leaned forward, straining my neck toward the top of the stairs, waiting for another tweet-tweet, but heard nothing. I waited a few seconds longer; still nothing. *That couldn't have been my imagination. Could it?* I questioned myself.

Slowly, I walked up one more step and peered through the glass panel. The first thing I saw was the remnants of an egg that had cracked completely open. Next to it was a wobbly, slimy chick struggling to stand on its feet, tweeting quite loudly for its size.

What a pleasant scene! What a beautiful bird! What a lovely sound! My incubator had finally worked, and we had a chicklet. I jumped up and down, screaming, "Madarjoon, come on up. It's here! It's here!"

Madarjoon's slow, gentle footsteps grew louder. She walked up to the incubator. A toothless smile spread across her kind, wrinkled face. "Mohsen Jon, you did it. I told you nothing is hard if you know what you're doing," she said, cupping my chin with one hand and caressing my cheek with the other.

"You were right," I replied, feeling so overwhelmed with joy that I could hardly breathe. I felt so proud for not giving up, especially since I had something tangible to show for my efforts.

Shortly thereafter, Momman and my siblings gathered around to look at the little chick. My sisters looked just as excited as I was. It felt as though we had a new sibling in the family. I couldn't wait to hold the slimy chick in the palm of my hand.

My sisters named the little chick JooJoo. It was a nickname derived from *joojeh,* meaning a little chick. The other two eggs hatched after a few days, but they didn't survive for long.

Under Madarjoon's supervision, we learned how to raise JooJoo. We loved her like a little sister and wanted to be constantly around her, chasing her around the house, holding her, and letting her peck our palms. Momman wasn't too thrilled about the mess and the droppings, but she never complained.

We kept JooJoo indoors, fearing that the stray cats in our neighborhood would eat her alive. Gradually, JooJoo grew up to become a smart and beautiful multicolored hen.

A few times when we were eating our usual dinner of cheese and bread, my parents talked about scarifying JooJoo to have her for lunch. My siblings and I looked at each other, frightened at the prospect of losing JooJoo. Etty and Motty started crying immediately, then Etty wiped her tears, and in JooJoo's defense, stood up, with her hands on her waist, and confidently said, "Momman, we don't mind eating bread for the rest of our lives; please don't cut off JooJoo's head."

To us, JooJoo was a pet, and we considered her part of our family. Sadly, she only lived for two years, catching pneumonia at the end of her happy, spoiled life. My family solemnly buried her under the mulberry tree in our backyard.

While JooJoo was growing up, I realized we wouldn't be able to eat any chickens I hatched in my makeshift incubator. The incubator remained on top of our staircase, collecting dust for two years. Two days after JooJoo passed, I decided to throw it away. I didn't want to add to my sadness every time I passed by it.

I discarded the box in the neighborhood dumpster. As I was crossing the street, I looked back and saw a thin boy about my age, with olive skin, a buzz cut, and torn-up clothes, happily carrying the box I had just discarded. I shook my head, smiled, and wondered what he planned to do with my creation.

The Green-Eyed Girl

Age Fourteen

How could somebody who didn't acknowledge my existence change my life entirely?

That happened to me when I was fourteen years old. There were only about five months remaining till my graduation from elementary school, and I couldn't wait to go to high school. Back then, there was no middle school. I knew most of my friends would attend the same school, but I was also hoping to meet new people.

Classes were in two sessions: one from 8 to 11:30 a.m. and the other one 2 to 4 p.m. In between classes, most of the students, including myself, went home to eat lunch, relaxed a little bit, and then headed back to class. On that day, however, my friends and I decided to get together an hour before our afternoon classes started to play soccer on the street near our school.

After our morning session ended, I sprinted all the way home. Soccer was my favorite game, and I couldn't wait to kick the ball. I scarfed down a meager lunch, grabbed my school supplies, and ran out the door, turning right from our alley on Mones Street and onto Dum Pezeshkii Street. I walked quickly past the Kianii barber shop and brought my hand up to my head. My hair felt thorny. A buzz cut was a requirement for all the boys in our school.

I passed a nearby fresh produce store and noticed a woman in a miniskirt walking out with some greens wrapped in newspaper. *Isn't she cold?* I thought. I was freezing, so I couldn't wrap my mind around the idea that she could be warm with so little clothing on.

I had my books under my arms and pulled my jacket sleeves forward to cover my cracked hands to keep them warm. My toes felt numb and cold. Still speed walking, I crossed Salsabeel Street, weaving between cars and motorcycles. I turned my head down to jump over the joob.

I almost ran into someone and looked up. There she was: a petite, slender girl with rich, brown shoulder-length hair, a fair complexion, and eyes as green as an endless lush field. Her features matched the description of God's angels living in heaven that Madarjoon spoke about in her stories.

Our eyes locked in just a brief moment. What a beautiful face she had —so kind and so lovely. I couldn't get the image of her out of my head. My heart pounded loudly inside my chest. I felt hot—where did the windy and chilly weather go? What was happening to me? I had never experienced this feeling.

I could tell she didn't feel the same reaction. She looked down and began walking on her way, probably forgetting all about me. But I couldn't. I felt that I wanted to be with that girl all the time and nothing else mattered. I wanted to know more about her, starting with which school she attended. She was, no doubt, on her way back to her class too, so I followed her. Her thick, charcoal overcoat and shiny black boots indicated that her family was better off than mine. I knew she would look down on me with my worn-out clothes, old shoes, and dried hands, but it didn't matter. My heart was guiding me, not my brain. I had completely forgotten about meeting my friends to play soccer. It wasn't important to me anymore. This girl had suddenly changed my life.

As I continued following her, all I could imagine as I looked at the long shiny waves of her rich brown hair was her lovely, kind-looking face. I only wished that I could see it again.

She reached the entrance to the alley of her school, still completely unaware anyone was behind her. I stopped and watched her enter the building. I couldn't go any farther for fear the baba-eh madreseh might see me and report me to my own school. My parents would then have been called to school to discuss the matter with the school principal. How would I explain why I was following some girl I didn't even know? What would my parents do if they found out? Aghajoon would definitely slap my face hard, and Momman would give me an endless sermon. "Mohsen, are you stupid? Why are you after a girl? What would people say if they find out about this? Remember, right now all you should be thinking about is your education and getting good grades."

People cared so much about *aberoo* (their family's reputation) and not having any scandal or rumors about them. Moreover, in Iranian culture, having a boyfriend or girlfriend wasn't commonly accepted, especially where we lived. In richer and more modern areas, they may have been more relaxed, but that was a completely different world from the strict and traditional lifestyle my parents adhered to.

I sighed as I watched the last wisp of her hair disappear into the building, then happily ran back to my school so I could discuss everything with my good friend Bahraum before we went into class. He knew much more about love and dealing with girls than anyone else I knew. He lived in those rich areas, had a girlfriend, and was more experienced with these sorts of things.

Bahraum was an only child from a very well-to-do family. His dad was the assistant principal of an all-boys high school, and because of that, all the teachers and the principal of our school knew him well. He dressed well and presented himself with plenty of confidence and charm. It was no surprise to me that he had found a girlfriend. The only reason Bahraum attended the same school as I did was that it was the only elementary school in his area.

"Bahraum, I saw a very pretty girl today, and I'm sure I'm in love with her."

"So, you saw a beautiful girl? And did she see you too?" he asked, interested to hear my story.

"For a moment, but after that, I walked behind her, and I don't think she knew it," I said quietly.

"Walk next to her tomorrow so she sees you."

The next day, as soon as I came home for lunch, I hurried to eat something and rushed out of the house. I was worried I might miss the girl, since I didn't know her schedule. I had completely forgotten about soccer and how much I loved playing it. I made a turn from our alley, walked a block, and crossed the street. I wasn't paying any attention to my surroundings. All I could think about was seeing her beautiful face again and how it would make me feel. I reached the corner where I had seen her the day before, and waited. I knew I hadn't missed her because I arrived an hour before school started!

The cold breeze, like sharp knives, went right through me. My teeth were chattering. I looked down at my pants; the bottoms were torn. The knees were faded and old. I wished my parents had money so I could have better clothing, a nice overcoat, gloves, and a better pair of shoes to keep my feet warm when I walked on icy ground. My hands were cracked and sometimes bled because they were so dry. We couldn't afford moisturizer and only some *donbeh* (fat), which I used to grease my hands before going to the public bath once a month.

I waited patiently, turning my head toward the direction of the street where she had appeared the previous day. I anxiously waited for her face to appear in the crowd of people walking up the street. *Where is she?* I thought, worried, and moving to keep myself warm.

I stood there, looking around, for twenty minutes. My hands, face, and toes had gone completely numb when I finally saw her emerge from the crowd—walking gracefully in her charcoal overcoat and black boots, which she had on the previous day. Her beautiful brown shoulder-length hair was bouncing around. She had some books in one hand, and in the other, she held a yellow briefcase, which contained her school supplies. My heart started pounding, and I could feel my face once again getting hot, as the heat slowly crept up my neck. I waited on the corner until she reached me.

I smiled at her as she passed by.

She glanced at me with indifference and turned right to continue her walk.

I had hoped she would return my smile or greet me somehow; I would have been pleased if she had rolled her eyes at me or even cussed me —anything that required her to acknowledge my existence. I wanted to know how she felt about me, whether good or bad, though I hoped it would be good.

Day by day, this became my routine, waiting at the corner and walking behind her as she walked to school. Sometimes she looked back to check my presence. She seemed to become accustomed to having me around. Whatever the reason, it raised my hopes just the slightest to think that maybe she had grown somewhat attached to me.

Yet every time I encouraged myself to talk to her, I couldn't. I was too ashamed of my appearance. Bahraum became my adviser on this matter and inspired me to speak to the girl. He asked me every day: "Did you talk to her?"

I shook my head or made up an excuse. Until one day, I lied to him. "Yes! I finally talked to her," I said, feeling guilty because I didn't know how to tell Bahraum the reason I couldn't bring myself to speak to that girl. I was too embarrassed. How do you tell your rich best friend that you feel sorry for yourself and are ashamed of the way you look?

Thankfully, Bahraum didn't ask me for any details. He was just delighted about the news. "Mohsen, gradually, she will let you hold her hand in the alley when nobody is looking."

I smiled and nodded. I felt bad for lying to Bahraum, but my pride was important to me, and I didn't want to look like a loser to him.

That girl changed my life. I concentrated all my thoughts on her and forgot about all my other interests. I began to dread Fridays because there was no school and I had to wait till Saturday to see her. Sometimes I wondered if she felt anything at all for me or was even thinking of me. In my heart, I knew she didn't because she wouldn't smile at me when she saw me waiting for her in the corner. *Why would a beautiful girl pay attention to a poor-looking boy?* I wondered.

I wished I had money to buy her a nice little gift, maybe a pair of earrings or a necklace. Then she would be friendlier to me. *Who wouldn't like a gift?* I thought. The little money I made from doing odd jobs wasn't enough for a decent present. As strongly as I felt for this girl, I also knew that spending money I didn't have on a girl I had never spoken to would be a bad idea. *Maybe I should make her something, but how would I do it without anyone suspecting anything?*

One morning, I woke up with the image of the girl's piercing green eyes in my mind before I had even opened mine. I must have been dreaming about her. I decided to finally talk to her. I was determined. I ironed my pants, creating a crease as sharp as a knife, and polished my shoes as well as I could, even though they still looked old and had holes on the bottom, I wanted to look as nice as possible. I practiced my greeting while I was moving the iron up and down my pants legs.

"Salam." I modified my voice to be deep.

"Salam." I used my own voice.

As I gazed down at my perfectly ironed school uniform, my brow furrowed in an overly concerned and worried manner. *God, what if she cusses at me, or worse, what if she won't say anything to me at all? What will I do then?* I decided that I couldn't let any more self-doubt seep in and chose to keep encouraging myself instead. I slipped on my ironed but shabby clothes, hoping they would stay crisp for at least a couple of hours.

After eating a quick lunch at home, I rushed back to my spot at the corner of Salsabeel Street. I stood there patiently, practicing my greeting, trying not to think about the cold. I stared down at my shoes, so thin and worn-out that my toes had gone completely numb. I forced myself to wiggle them to get some blood flowing. When I looked up, I noticed that she had passed me and was walking ahead about twenty meters.

I started a slow jog to catch up with her. When I was within reach, I cleared my throat, took a deep breath, and said, "Salam." I was so relieved and proud of myself for finally speaking to her.

She turned around, her bright green eyes stealing my breath like a hit to the stomach. I felt as if everything had stopped. She gave me an indifferent look and then turned around to continue walking.

Disheartened, I decided not to say anything else and just follow her. When she reached the alley leading to her school, I turned around and headed back to mine.

After our second-class session ended that day, Bahraum and I walked home together. This time he wanted to know the details and began asking questions about the girl. Although my conscience felt heavy, I had no choice but to keep making up stories. I said, "She told me she has two brothers and a sister."

"Ask her how old her sister is. Maybe I can become her friend," he replied, smiling and nudging me on the shoulder.

I laughed, trying to contain my nervousness. Thankfully, my clever brain came up with another lie: "She is married already, Bahraum. You're too late." I laughed and continued, "Why are you looking for another girlfriend? Don't you have one already?"

He didn't say anything, just shrugged.

At home, Momman had noticed that my personality had changed. How could she not? I was ironing my clothes and polishing my shoes every day before going to school. I'd never done that before. Not to mention, she saw me consistently rushing out after every lunch.

One day, she flat out asked me, "Why do you leave so early these days to rush to school?"

There was no way I could tell her I was in love with a girl and followed her to school every day. The lecture and disappointment I would get would not make telling the truth worth it, so I lied. "Oh. Momman, don't worry. I am the representative of my class, so I have to make sure everything is in order before all the students show up," I told her calmly, as I quickly put on my shoes to rush out of the house and avoid any additional questions.

I didn't like making up these stories, but I had no choice. Again, I waited on the corner, shivering, and looking down at my shoes. I was ashamed that I had lied to Momman, but as soon as I saw the girl's face, the guilt of lying to Momman disappeared.

There she was, staring right at me this time and smiling, and what a peaceful and lovely smile it was. Her eyes sparkled even more when she smiled. I wasn't sure if she was smiling at me, so I looked around to make sure.

No one was there. She was smiling at me. Finally, I had caught her attention, and she had responded. However, she didn't say anything and just turned to walk to her school.

I followed her again. My persistence had paid off, and I felt so great. Everything looked different—the snow looked prettier, I didn't feel cold, and the slippery ice didn't bother me. I was sure it was love.

That day, the rest of my classes went by so quickly. My head was in the clouds. I couldn't wait to see her the next day. On the way home, I decided to make her a pair of earrings out of the prayer beads Momman used, the ones I often saw her thumbing one by one, after she was done praying. Madarjoon had recently given her some green beads, which she had gotten at one of the shrines she visited. But I had to wait for the right moment to take it.

The next morning, I woke up, hopeful our relationship was only going to grow from here and that today would be the day when she finally talked to me.

After a hurried lunch, I went about my routine and walked to the corner, waiting for the green-eyed girl. My eyes were on the street ahead as I saw her approaching. My heart started pounding even harder this time. I was so nervous because I was convinced we would have a conversation.

"Salam," I said bashfully and waited for her response.

"Look, I don't know who you are or what you want from me, but if you follow me again, I will tell the baba-eh madreseh," she said loudly and angrily. Her face turned red, and her eyes bulged out.

I couldn't believe my ears. I felt like someone had just dumped a big bucket of freezing water on my head. I felt nauseated, and my legs started shaking. I didn't know what to do or where to go. I was confused. It was a depressing moment for me. I knew I had lost her and would never be able to see her again.

Later that day, on the way home, I told Bahraum what had happened. I could have easily started crying, but I held back, swallowing the hard lump that had formed in my throat all afternoon. I didn't want to show Bahraum I was a weak person.

Bahraum was genuinely concerned about me but didn't say anything. We walked quietly for some time. I constantly had flashbacks of the girl's angry face and was still trying to figure things out in my head.

Bahraum turned to me with a concerned look and asked me what my plans were.

"It is best for me not to follow her anymore. I would get in a lot of trouble if she told the baba-eh madreseh about me. Plus, she doesn't want to see me, and I should respect her wishes," I said with a sad voice.

Later that evening, when I rested my head on the pillow, I told myself that someday I'd forget all about that girl. I wished she had cussed me out or threatened me on the very first day so my feelings wouldn't have grown so much. I thought back to the day she smiled at me, and came to the realization that her smile wasn't genuine. She had smiled either out of ridicule for my appearance or because she thought I was stupid for following her for weeks.

After that, I no longer rushed through lunch, ironed my pants, or waited at the corner. However, I must admit, I did look around and search for her face in the crowd coming up Salsabeel Street on my way to school.

A month later, Bahraum came to my house so we could go to school together. While we were walking and chatting about soccer and how to improve our games, for some reason, I looked over my shoulder. Maybe I felt eyes burrowing into the back of my head, or maybe my habit of looking around for her was still there. Either way, there she was, with all her loveliness, right behind me. I don't think she was as happy to see me as I was to see her. My eyes lit up, and I felt hot in my face. She just gave me an indifferent look.

I whispered to Bahraum, "Don't look now, but that girl is right behind us."

Bahraum dropped one of his books intentionally so he could check her out as he bent to pick it up.

"*Wow!* She is beautiful, Mohsen. I don't blame you for falling in love with her," he said quietly.

I smiled, but my heart felt heavy.

"Say something to her," he said, smiling.

"*No.* She doesn't like me. She asked me not to bother her, remember?" I admitted regretfully. My only hope was that one day, when I turned rich, God would bring her back into my life.

MESSAGE IN A MATCHBOX

AGE FOURTEEN

Had I known I was a messenger of love, I would have taken stronger precautions to protect the lover.

It happened two weeks after Bahraum asked me to fix the wiring in his parents' house. He told me that every time they turned on the lights in the upstairs living room, it triggered the fuse to blow up.

"It could be many things, I will have to see it," I told him.

When we reached the two-story house, he took me upstairs. On the way up, he whispered, "My mom's brother rents the upstairs from us and lives here by himself."

At the top of the stairs, I saw two small bedrooms, a kitchen on the right, a small living room with a TV, and some additional furniture on the left side. The place looked old but clean.

His uncle, who looked to be in his thirties, was a tall, skinny, well-dressed man in a blue suit and yellow tie.

"Salam Daii. This is Mohsen, whom I was telling you about. He is going to fix the electrical problem," Bahraum said as he pointed at me.

I greeted him, and he looked me over from top to bottom, before he said, "You are here to fix the wiring? No, no. It is okay, I will take care of it myself." His half-crooked grin and expression were extremely condescending, as if he felt I was inadequate to do the job. Maybe he thought I was too young to know anything about electricity and was afraid I would electrocute myself or set the house on fire accidentally, or both.

"But Daii, he knows how to fix it. He has done many jobs even more complicated than ours for other people. Haven't you, Mohsen?" Bahraum said as he faced me.

No matter how Bahraum put it, his uncle wasn't going to budge. He didn't even let me look at the problem or touch anything. I left the house, thinking it was his loss and I had plenty of other projects to keep me busy.

Three days later, Bahraum approached me at school. "Can you come to the house to look at the fixture and find out what the problem is?"

"Your uncle said he was going to fix it himself," I said, stuffing my books in my bag.

"Mohsen, he's a dentist. He doesn't know a thing about electricity."

I liked Bahraum, so I agreed. Once again, we walked for thirty minutes to get to his house, and on the way there, he told me that his uncle had brought two electricians to look at the fixture and wiring to give him a price. "One guy said the job was too small for him and was a waste of his time. The other one wanted to charge a ridiculous amount of money."

We went upstairs, where his uncle was reading the Etelaat Newspaper in his small living room.

"Salam." We both greeted him as we entered.

His uncle looked at me, surprised, and said, "You're back?"

"Bahraum asked me to come back to fix the fixture," I informed him. I tried to reason with him for my friend's sake before he could object. I didn't care whether he liked me or not. "Agha, If I can repair it, you can pay me twenty tomans, and if I can't, then it will be free."

He thought about my proposal and decided he had nothing to lose.

Early Friday morning, I stuffed my gray sack with a screwdriver, black tape, hammer, and voltmeter. I picked up a ladder and headed to Bahraum's house.

The shops were getting ready for the day; the fresh produce store worker, Sabzi Fooroosh, was arranging apples, oranges, and tangerines in his carts, while the baker was laying out a variety of cookies and pastries in the window. It all looked so tasty. The aroma of coconut and vanilla was very appetizing.

As I passed the Karoon Movie Theater, I noticed they were showing an Indian movie. Indian movies were shown only in our part of the town. If I wanted to watch American movies, I had to go to the rich areas of Tehran. The marquee said it was a love story starring Raj Kapur and Narges. I personally didn't care for those kinds of movies because they had no action or shooting. To me, it wasn't worth spending any money on them. *Death Wish* was the first movie I bought a ticket to watch in a theater. There was shooting, cars flipping over, and other exciting stuff—what every young boy likes to see. Now, that was a movie I was happy to pay for.

I arrived at Bahraum's house and rang the doorbell. When he opened the door, I noticed immediately how quiet his house was, unlike ours. He was the only child, whereas I had five siblings and a sixth one on the way. The only time our home was quiet was at night when everyone was asleep. Otherwise, it was crowded with children running around screaming or laughing; if it wasn't us, Momman's students or customers were either coming or going.

We walked upstairs together, and I made sure not to bang the ladder into the walls as we ascended to the top floor. After greeting his uncle, Bahraum took me to the room in which I was to work. His uncle briefly explained what the problem was. I could tell from the tone of his voice that he still didn't think I could do the job. I didn't care about his arrogant attitude, though. I was doing this for Bahraum and not him.

I got down to business immediately, since I had to install a fluorescent light at another house later. I removed the fuse for that section of their house so I wouldn't get electrocuted. I knew there was a short circuit somewhere, but I didn't want to go through the trouble of figuring out where, so I decided to change all the wires, starting from the switch and going all the way to the fixture. Most houses had wiring on the outside of the walls, so it was readily accessible.

I worked fast, taking out the old, defective wires and putting in new ones. When I was done, I put the fuse back in, then turned the switch on and off many times. The lights came on without blowing the fuse.

All this time, Bahraum was quietly standing in a corner, observing what I was doing. His uncle occasionally poked his head into the room, following me around with his eyes to check my progress. I could tell he was amazed that a boy my age was pulling wires out and replacing them like a professional electrician, though he never expressed anything.

When I was sure everything was working as it should, I cleaned up the mess, picked up my tools, and gave him a big smile. "Agha, it is fixed. Twenty tomans," I said.

He was in shock as he flipped the switch on and off many times to make sure the fuse didn't blow. He finally said, "I don't have any money today. Come back tomorrow to collect it."

I went to their house three or four times that week, and every time I was told the same thing: "Come back tomorrow."

I was frustrated and didn't know what to do. I told Bahraum about it, and he was so embarrassed by his uncle's behavior that he told his mother about it.

The next day, he told me his mother had agreed to pay the twenty tomans. As we walked toward Bahraum's house to collect my fee, he said, "She thinks her brother didn't pay you because he is renting the upstairs unit from us and thus isn't responsible to pay any repairs."

"So why didn't he chat with her about that and not waste my time by repeatedly telling me to come back the next day to get paid?"

He shrugged. "I don't know. Maybe he didn't know how to tell her. He is a strange man."

I waited at the door while Bahraum went in to tell his mother that I was there to collect my wages. Shortly after, she came out with twenty tomans and a big smile. I'm sure she was happy that she paid so little for something that was done professionally.

On the way home, I stopped by Hussein Agha's grocery store to buy some candy to share with my siblings. His shop was located two doors down from Aghajoon's.

"Salam," I said, as I looked around his store.

In the front were sacks of rice, beans, walnuts, and almonds, as well as green and black raisins. Tin cans of all kinds of cooking oil lined the walls, and behind the large deli display refrigerator, he had many kinds of cheese in open bins with brine. The signs next to each explained the type of cheese: French, Bulgarian, Tabrizii, or Lighvan. All the types looked alike to me, but I'm sure they tasted different. Aghajoon usually bought the Bulgarian. Momman used to say the others tasted salty. I had no idea how she knew that without trying them.

Next to the variety of cheeses, he had arranged brown eggs, butter, and other dairy products. Many shelves behind the cash register were filled with sugar cones, tea leaves, cookies, cigarettes, and various things. In fact, every corner of the place was filled with different items; the only items you couldn't find in this grocery store were fresh produce, bread, and meat.

"Salam, Mohsen. What would you like today?" he asked, as I approached the counter.

"I'd like one rial of these candies," I said, pointing to the colorful jar.

He twirled a piece of newspaper, closed the bottom, and made a cone-shaped bag. Then he weighed the candies on a scale before throwing them into the bag.

I gave him the money and took the candies. I was almost out the door when he called my name. "Mohsen, Mohsen, come back," he said, waving me back inside the store. "Give this to Mali Khanoom," he said, handing me a small matchbox, which he took from his pants pocket.

Mali Khanoom was one of Aghajoon's customers. Every time I saw her, she reminded me of Momman's sister, Khaleh-Hamideh, with her big light brown eyes and hair. Even the way she dressed resembled Khaleh-Hamideh's style—most of the time in miniskirts and low-cut colorful tops. She was a happy and cheerful woman, just like my aunt.

Later, Aghajoon told me she was married to a pharmacist who didn't work in his field. Apparently, he was a hoarder and found all kinds of junk on the streets to sell one day, but never did. He made money by making homemade vodka and selling it for a cheap price directly to the neighborhood men. Hussein Agha was one of his customers; I had seen bottles of vodka in the back of his shop's refrigerator. Most of the shop owners in the area knew Hussein Agha drank on the job. His breath had the smell of vodka. Aghajoon and his brothers always drank it too when they got together, so I was familiar with its aroma.

I held tight to my bag of candies in one hand and took the matchbox with the other. I left his shop, irritated that I had to do one more thing before I could enjoy the candies with my siblings.

As soon as I rang the doorbell, Mali Khanoom opened the door. It seemed as if she was waiting for someone to knock.

"Salam, Hussein Agha asked me to give this to you."

She smiled and took it from me. I noticed that she hurriedly hid it in the palm of her hand.

After that day, I became Hussein Agha's messenger boy—delivering the matchbox to Mali Khanoom or watching his shop when he left for hours.

"Mohsen, Mohsen, come here," he would say as he saw me walk by his store, or sometimes when I was outside Aghajoon's shop, talking to Ramazoon. He gestured for me to come into his shop and would already be out the door before I had time to react, saying, "I'll be right back. Take care of my customers."

I looked around and had mixed feelings about being there alone. I was happy because I could eat whatever I wanted, but at the same time, I was nervous since I didn't know what to do when someone showed up to buy things. I didn't know how to use the scale balance he had in the shop.

Most of the time, people came in with weird requests. For example, "Give me seven rials worth of cheese."

In my head, I tried to calculate what that meant: If one kilo is ten rials, how much is seven rials? I knew it was more than half a kilo, but how much more I wasn't certain. I'm sure if I thought about it long enough, I could have figured it out, but most of the time the customer was in a rush, which made me more nervous. I'd cut a big piece of cheese and put it on top of the paper on the scale and place a weight on the other side. I kept adding cheese until the scale lever came to the middle, which indicated that I had an equivalent amount of cheese as the weight in the other pan. Then I'd wrap the cheese in a page of newspaper and hand it to them in exchange for money. I'm pretty sure I gave them more than they asked for, but at least I didn't rip them off like some of the store owners around Aghajoon's shop did.

The routine with Hussein Agha continued; he either asked me to watch his shop or deliver the matchbox to Mali Khanoom. Sometimes, Mali Khanoom acted a little nervous when I knocked on her door. She came out, looked around, and then quickly grabbed the box, before closing the door on me.

One day, I accidentally forgot to take the matchbox to her and went directly home. I was coming back from wiring somebody's house when Hussein Agha handed me the box to take to her. As soon as I reached home, I remembered the box in my hand. I decided to eat something first since I was hungry and then take it to her, especially since Hussein Agha hadn't shown any urgency about its delivery. I put it next to my tools on the floor.

"What's this?" Momman asked. Her eyes looked worried. "Are you smoking?" She didn't wait for an explanation as she picked it up and opened it. Under a row of matches, she found a note folded many times to fit in the small box.

I was surprised to see it and thought, *Have I been delivering letters to Mali Khanoom all this time?*

Momman unfolded the paper and started reading it quietly. Her eyes were moving rapidly from right to left. I don't know what the letter said, but I could tell it wasn't good news. Momman's face turned red, her eyes grew wide, and she kept clicking her tongue. She tore up the letter and threw it in the garbage. "Mohsen, don't make any deliveries on behalf of Hussein Agha to Mali Khanoom, or to anyone else."

I was still confused, but I didn't ask any questions. Momman was very angry, and I wasn't planning to provoke her.

Later that evening, when Aghajoon came home, Momman whispered to him, "Hussein Agha wrote a love letter to Mali Khanoom, and in that letter, he explained to her what he planned to do to her when he visited her. The letter was inside a matchbox he gave Mohsen to deliver for him."

"Why does he involve our kid in his love affair? I will have a talk with that dirty man. He should be ashamed of himself; he has five grown children and a lovely wife," Aghajoon said.

My parents didn't know I was eavesdropping, otherwise they wouldn't have talked about it. It wasn't an appropriate conversation for a fourteen-year-old boy to hear—a married man writing a racy letter to a married woman.

The next day, Hussein Agha stopped by Aghajoon's shop to have his shoes polished. I was talking to Ramazoon when I noticed Aghajoon speaking to him in a muffled voice. Curious, I sharpened my ears to hear what he was telling him.

"Khanoom found the matchbox you gave to Mohsen to deliver to Mali Khanoom. It's embarrassing for a married man such as you to be with someone else's wife. Do you want to ruin your marriage? What more do you expect from your life? You have five good children and a kind wife!"

When my father finished his speech, Hussein Agha whispered in a pleading voice, "Agha Kafash, ask your wife not to mention any of this to my wife when she sees her. I will be in big trouble if she finds out."

His wife was one of Momman's good customers. My father replied, "If you were a good man, you would have thought about that before you got yourself into this mess."

Some years later, Hussein Agha went bankrupt because he had many affairs with many women in the neighborhood, and eventually people found out. Women in the area sabotaged his store and stopped shopping there; they also forbade their husbands from buying anything from him.

I liked Hussein Agha; he was my advocate. One day when I stopped by his shop, he noticed I was not holding my head up and was desperately trying to cover something up. "Mohsen, what happened? Look up, let me see your face."

When I did, he started clicking his tongue, took my hand, and walked to Aghajoon's shop. "Are you crazy to hit your kid like this. Look at his face! Traces of your fingers are on it!" He screamed at the top of his lungs and continued, "You should be ashamed of yourself. If I see you do this to him, I will smash your face."

Inside, I felt happy that someone defended me. Unfortunately, Aghajoon's behavior didn't change after that encounter. He continued to hit me for numerous stupid reasons.

Eventually, Hussein Agha moved to another location, where nobody knew him, and he asked me to do the wiring of his new store.

On my way out of his store after finishing my work, I turned and said, "Hussein Agha, if you need my help to look after your shop, let me know."

He smiled and nodded.

OUR FIRST REFRIGERATOR

AGE FIFTEEN

When I look back at my childhood, I realize that our relatives were a bunch of crooks.

It was a hot summer day; I was hanging out at Aghajoon's store with Ramazoon when *Amoo* (paternal uncle) Reza walked in.

"How is my nephew doing?" He pinched my cheeks.

When Aghajoon saw his brother walk in, he stood up to greet him. They hugged and kissed each other. My uncle usually showed up when he wanted something that would benefit him. Out of curiosity, I started eavesdropping, while pretending to play with Ramazoon.

"What brings you here?" Aghajoon asked.

"Do you remember Mr. Abasii, Kobra Khanoom's husband? He wants to sell his Zenith refrigerator to buy a bigger one for his house. Are you interested in it?" my uncle said in a whisper, his eyes dashing back and forth as if he were trying to sell something illegal in a back alley.

I didn't think we needed a refrigerator. We never had any food to keep in the house, and whatever meal we made was all gone after we ate.

Aghajoon stayed quiet, as if he were thinking about his brother's proposal. He probably had the same thoughts as I did.

"So, what do you think?" my uncle asked.

"I have to talk to Khanoom about it."

"Okay, but I'm telling you, it's a great refrigerator and you will lose a good offer if you decide not to buy it. He is only asking for nine hundred tomans."

I knew Amoo Reza must be pocketing some money from this deal. Otherwise, he would have bought it himself. His family didn't own one either, so why didn't he buy it himself if it was a good deal?

Later that night, Aghajoon brought up the topic to Momman. I could tell he was a little hesitant to tell her about his brother's visit. He knew Momman didn't care for his side of the family.

Momman said, "Agha, whatever food I make is gone. The vegetables and fruits Mohsen and Etty buy from the market we keep in the corner of our backyard in the shade, and they stay fresh for days. We don't really need one, why waste our money?"

I smiled and thought, *Momman and I think alike.*

Aghajoon didn't insist, because he knew his wife's logic made complete sense. But he looked nervous. I think he did not know how to refuse his older brother's proposal.

Amoo Reza didn't give up; he was at Aghajoon's shop every other day trying to sell the idea of having a refrigerator. "*Duhduhsh*" (brother), just think! You don't have to buy any more ice from the ice merchants. You can have ice all year long. Just throw a few ice cubes in a pitcher of water and next thing you know, you'll have cold water. It's perfect for these hot, muggy summer days. As a matter of fact, I wish I could have a glass of ice-cold water right now." He took out a handkerchief and wiped his bald head. "Have you ever had cold watermelon?" I think he intentionally named Aghajoon's favorite fruit. "They are best coming out of a refrigerator, chilled and sweet."

This routine continued until eventually my father gave in. My parents talked about it a lot among themselves. Momman suggested bargaining to lower the price to 850 tomans.

Interestingly, Amoo Reza immediately raised the price when Aghajoon mentioned he was finally going to purchase the fridge.

Aghajoon got terribly angry when his brother told him that his friend had decided to charge 1100 tomans for it. "Duhduhsh, what are you talking about? I wanted to pay less; you are asking for more. I don't know. I have to talk to Khanoom about it."

Aghajoon told Momman about the increase; it made her furious. She said, "Forget about it. He raised the price because he wanted a better commission. He's trying to take advantage of us."

After going back and forth for a couple more days, they settled on one thousand tomans—one hundred tomans over the original price. I was beginning to agree with Momman that Aghajoon's side of the family always took advantage of us.

Amoo Reza knew my parents struggled financially, which made it difficult to understand his actions. Shortly after the negotiation, one evening, Aghajoon, Amoo, and two other men brought the white Zenith refrigerator to our house, each holding a corner of it. I could tell that it weighed a lot by the way they carried it and their red, sweaty faces.

Momman asked them to put it in the small room, next to an electrical plug. My parents slept in this room, but I think Momman wanted them to put down the refrigerator anywhere so they wouldn't hurt themselves. We didn't have a kitchen; instead, we had a portable kerosene heater we took to any of the rooms to cook.

After the men plugged in the refrigerator, I heard the motor make a sound. It seemed to be in working condition. They all left the house to return to Aghajoon's shop and get paid, as Momman and all the kids gathered around the refrigerator.

Momman said, "Eh! This is so small. We paid one thousand tomans for it, what a rip-off."

It was a rip-off, but I knew we couldn't have afforded a brand-new refrigerator, which would have cost us about twice as much. I opened its door; even though it was a used appliance, I didn't smell anything foul. It had been kept in good condition and looked like brand-new. There were three small shelves, with a side compartment on the door for butter and a built-in egg holder. Above the top shelf was a small door to a compartment large enough to hold two metal ice trays. The ice trays had a latch; when pulled, the ice popped out of the tray.

A metal key hung from a keyholder so one could lock the refrigerator's door. This key created a lot of fights among us children later on.

We didn't have anything to put in the refrigerator, but that didn't stop us from being excited. Etty and I filled a pitcher with water and poured it into the ice trays. We couldn't wait to make our first batch of ice and to enjoy an ice-cold drink on this hot day. We opened the door every five minutes, and all of us put our little fingers in the trays to check for ice. Our constant checking didn't give the freezer compartment enough time to get cold.

After an hour or so, I got very frustrated, so I went to Momman to complain. "This refrigerator is defective. It is still warm; it has not made any ice yet. It's been plugged in for almost an hour. We should return it," I said furiously.

Momman came to the small room to look and said, "I knew I shouldn't have trusted your uncle. That's why he didn't buy it himself."

Later, Aghajoon came home with a big watermelon to put in the refrigerator. As soon as Momman saw him, she started complaining about the appliance. "Mohsen tells me the refrigerator does not cool down and no ice was made yet. Four hours have already passed." Nobody in our neighborhood or family had a refrigerator, so we did not know how a refrigerator worked. We thought that as soon as we put the water in the trays, ice would be made. Momman continued, "Tell that brother of yours we are returning it."

Aghajoon didn't even bother putting the melon in the fridge and served it that night after dinner. We all slept thinking the refrigerator would be gone the next day. It made me sad that this new toy would be returned soon.

The next day, I woke up early in the morning, before anybody else. The first thing I did was check the refrigerator. When I opened the door, a woosh of frigid air hit my face. Excited, I looked inside the ice compartment and saw ice. I screamed, "Ice, ice! We have ice!" I woke everyone up with my loud voice. I made a pitcher of ice water and drank it that morning. It was amazing how refreshing it tasted.

My parents, especially Aghajoon, were happy to hear the refrigerator was functioning. I think Aghajoon didn't want to have to deal with returning it.

As the day went by, I kept checking the refrigerator to make sure it was working. In the middle of the day, I realized the motor in the back felt extremely hot. I told Momman.

She came in and touched it. "Mohsen, it is going to catch fire."

I suggested we unplug it to let it cool down; she agreed. I kept plugging it in when the motor turned off and unplugging it when it came back on. After some time, I brought a fan and put it close to the motor to cool it down.

Momman started complaining about the refrigerator again. "I knew they ripped us off; we can't trust the family. We spent one thousand tomans on a piece of junk."

Later that night, Aghajoon came home with another watermelon, hoping, this time to chill it in the fridge before enjoying it.

Again, he heard Momman nagging about the refrigerator and the fact that the motor got hot. She said, "Please talk to your brother to make arrangements so we can return it and have our money back. Tell him to buy it himself if it's such a wonderful thing to have."

We ate another warm melon that night. I could tell Aghajoon was fretting over asking his brother for a refund.

The next day, I decided to investigate the problem myself. I headed to Naser Khosrow street to find an appliance shop. I found a store filled with all kinds of juicers, televisions, refrigerators, record players, and other appliances. I approached one of the men sitting behind a desk, reading a newspaper. I greeted him, "Salam Agha."

His eyes examined me from top to bottom. No doubt, he was making judgments about my raggedy appearance.

"My dad bought a refrigerator. The motor in the back gets extremely hot. I have to turn it on and off to avoid any explosion."

"You're unplugging and re-plugging it?" he questioned with a frown.

"Yes, because we don't want it to catch fire."

He chuckled. "That's how it works! The refrigerator gets hot so the food inside remains cold! If you turn it on and off repeatedly like that, your electricity bill will be outrageous. Also, it might break your refrigerator eventually."

I thanked the man for his explanation and walked home, relieved the refrigerator was not defective after all. Later that day, I explained to Momman about my conversation with the appliances man.

We were happy to hear that nothing was wrong with our refrigerator and it was okay to keep it. Later in the week, Etty and I decided to put some food in the refrigerator, so I used my money to buy some eggs and butter to put in the appropriate compartments. Those items were meant for decorations only and not to be used or eaten. We went to Hashemii produce market and bought some fruits and vegetables that looked semi-fresh for a price we could afford. On the way, Etty and I talked about where we were going to put them in the refrigerator: cucumbers and tomatoes together on one shelf; apples, peaches, and nectarines together on another. This way, when we opened the refrigerator door, it would look like the refrigerator advertisements we saw in the newspaper.

After we filled the refrigerator, I enjoyed opening the door and looking inside. All the shelves were filled with colorful produce. Occasionally, I saw worms crawling on the walls inside, seeking a warmer place. I picked them off and threw them outside.

One day, Momman's brother and his wife came to check out this new appliance. My uncle did not approve of it and made negative comments about having a refrigerator. "Azam, you wasted your money. The only good thing about having one of these is that you have ice at your home all the time. I heard they put a chemical in these things that is bad for your health." Then, he looked at his wife and said, "We will never buy one of these; we spend our money wisely."

A week later, my uncle bought a brand-new refrigerator that was larger than ours. Momman never asked him why he changed his mind about buying a refrigerator. My uncle and his wife were in some unspoken competition with my parents: whatever we bought, they had to have a bigger and better one.

Occasionally, Momman asked us to collect the ice cubes in bowls and distribute them among the nearby neighbors. Sometimes Aghajoon asked me to take ice water to the merchants near his shop. My parents shared their blessings with other people whenever they could; they did this to please God and express their appreciation to Him.

WORKING AT MIRZA AGHA'S FACTORY

AGE SIXTEEN

You must be a very cruel person to cheat your own nephew.

It was a Friday on a summer day, and we had arranged a family luncheon. In Iran, people took turns inviting their relatives. That day, my aunt and her family, along with my uncle and his family, visited us.

During the meal, Mirza Agha, my aunt's husband, told us that his uniform factory business had picked up and he was hiring a *sar nakhii* (someone who removes the extra threads from the end of the seams of newly made outfits). Mirza Agha bid on making uniforms for government-owned companies—for example, the oil refinery in Abadan and the police department—and sometimes for privately owned companies, such as Saderat Bank. I don't know why, but suddenly he looked at me and asked if I wanted to work for him. "You will make seven tomans per hour."

Everyone looked at him when he said the hourly rate. That was a lot of money for a sixteen-year-old kid. I felt very happy and surprised when he offered the job to me and not to his favorite nephew, Asghar, my uncle's son. I think Asghar was also shocked, because he gave me a jealous look.

Mirza Agha was a cold man and very condescending toward my family. He almost never came to our house, and when he did, he never talked to any of us. I don't think he knew any of my siblings' names. The only reason he knew mine was probably because I hung out at my uncle's house a lot.

Momman looked at me and asked if I wanted to work at the factory.

"Of course," I exclaimed. I would be crazy to turn down such a great offer. I quickly calculated how much I would be earning—at least 2500 tomans, the most I had ever made.

Mirza Agha's voice brought me back to the room: "Come to the factory tomorrow at seven in the morning."

I set the alarm the night before so I wouldn't be late to the factory. When I woke up, the house was eerily quiet. I opened the cloth where Momman usually stored the leftover bread, if there was any. I felt lucky when I saw a small piece. I grabbed the bread and headed for the front door. My siblings' shoes were laid next to mine, all worn out with holes and missing parts. As I slipped my bare feet into my shoes, I had a bit of a change of heart. Instead of spending money on my hobbies, I would surprise my siblings with new shoes and new clothes once I got paid. With that thought, a sudden surge of energy ran through me as I walked out the door, imagining us dressed in crisp new clothes and shiny shoes for school this year.

Every academic year, my parents promised to buy us new clothes and shoes. But every year, due to lack of funds, Momman would patch up our previous year's uniform and sew the holes in our socks, and Aghajoon would repair our torn-up shoes and polish them. Every new school year, I was embarrassed to show up in my old shoes and patched-up uniform, but this year would be different, I thought. This year I was going to look as chic as my classmates.

At the bus station, I hopped on the bus and noticed an abundance of empty seats. I took one at the very back of the bus. The air inside was fresh instead of sour from the smell of body odor. Instead of chaos, there was silence. I leaned my face against the window and gazed outside, watching the streets as Tehran gradually woke up. The fresh produce vendor pulled out his cart filled with nectarines, peaches, and grapes. Women came out of the bakery, holding fresh hot naan by the corners of their chadors, and the local grocers raised their rollup doors, getting ready to do business. As soon as the scenery began to shift from the sparse greenery of my neighborhood to a stagnant sea of dirt, dust, shacks that looked like people's houses, and rows of beggars sleeping outside, I knew we were approaching the factory. We didn't live in the best part of Tehran, but our neighborhood looked a lot more affluent than this area.

When the bus driver called out the street name, I stepped into a cloud of dust and putrid odor, while staring at the ground to make sure I didn't trip over the potholes. The loud wailing of stray dogs made me quicken my pace, and by the time I reached the factory, I was out of breath.

At the entrance, a tall, bearded man holding a cigarette in one hand and a cup of tea in the other greeted me with a condescending smile. Except for his unusually tall posture, everything about him resembled Mirza Agha—his receding hairline, dark beady eyes, thick black-and-white speckled mustache, and bushy eyebrows.

"Salam. Is Mirza Agha here?" I asked, "I'm Mohsen. He hired me to work here for the summer."

"Come on in. I'll take you to his father, Masht Ghara." Masht Ghara was standing behind a counter, talking to a worker. "I brought Mohsen. He says your son has hired him to do work," he said and walked away.

Masht Ghara and I had met at my aunt's house many times. I greeted him and explained about the offer Mirza Agha made at our house.

"Let me show you around before you get started." He put down the garment he had in his hand. I could tell he was happy to have a helper.

I followed Masht Ghara to a room near the entrance. He called it the "factory's cafeteria." The room was tiny and could fit no more than two people at a time. A large counter took up most of the space, but there was nothing on it except a large samovar. The aroma of abgoosht spilled out of the kitchen behind the counter.

Masht Ghara said, "You can buy tea or abgoosht whenever you want. Just ask the cook to add it to your tab. You can pay the cafeteria owner at the end of the week when you get your wages."

I nodded but knew I wouldn't spend any of my salary on food; it would only dip into my clothing fund.

Then he took me inside the factory. It was a huge open room with sleek concrete floors and many windows and ceiling fans. The open ceiling displayed massive steel rafters that made the room look spacious. I noticed that most of the workers had taken off their shirts while they sat behind the industrial-sized sewing machines. The place looked exceptionally clean and orderly, as did the workers. There were at least thirty of them, lined up in precise rows across the room, mirroring the austere structure of the rafters above. The space between each employee was sufficient for one to move about without disturbing the guy next to him.

As we moved through the rows of workers, they all greeted Masht Ghara and seemed to like him. Later, I found out that Masht Ghara was the owner, but because of his age, he had asked his son to take over the business—buying the material and negotiating the contracts with the clients. Through the years, Mirza Agha had learned to wine and dine his potential or existing clients till the early hours of the morning at a variety of nightclubs, to get their uniform orders. Nobody seemed to mind that Mirza Agha showed up at seven o'clock in the morning, although that was late for a shop that started its operations at five. They knew he usually went home to take a nap after entertaining customers the previous night.

According to my parents, Mirza Agha had saved his father's factory from going bankrupt, and it flourished into a multi-million-toman business. No wonder he drove the latest model Mercedes every year and eventually bought a beautiful house in a very prominent neighborhood.

Masht Ghara and I continued to go from one row of workers to another. The loud clack-clack of all the sewing machines whirring together at frantic speeds pierced my ears.

"This is where you and I will be working." Masht Ghara turned his head to yell over his shoulder, before stopping in front of a knee-high pile of uniforms. He bent down, picked one up, and turned it inside out. "It is very important that all of these threads are taken out," he shouted again, as he grabbed an extra piece of thread that hung between the seams and brought it close to my face. "Otherwise, the government inspector will reject the production, and we won't get paid for any of them."

I squinted with concentration as I watched him wrap the thread tightly around his index finger and pull it out in one swift motion. He did a few more garments in front of me, each time showing me the clean, finished product before throwing it onto a separate pile of finished uniforms.

Soon after, a skinny bald man with a thick mustache appeared, picked up the pile of finished uniforms, and walked out. Masht Ghara nodded in the man's direction while telling me, "He irons the uniforms in the back room."

Then, as if we had already fallen behind schedule, Masht Ghara hurriedly handed me a uniform, with his eyebrows raised, and gave me a get-on-with-it nod. And with that, my job officially began.

Soon the excitement I had felt only a few hours earlier began to fade. First came the bleeding. The threads were sharp and rough, cutting my fingers as I pulled them out of the seams. To remedy the pain, I wiped the blood on my pants. A few times I noticed Masht Ghara was watching me, but he quickly looked away when our eyes met.

After a while, the cuts began to sting so badly that I had to continuously switch hands. Next came fatigue. There were no chairs anywhere near my workspace, so I had to stand on my feet while de-threading the garments. After a few hours, my legs began to ache, and I had to switch to standing on one leg at a time, as if I were an indecisive flamingo.

By far the worst part of the day was around noon, when my stomach started growling like a rumbling volcano. The owner of the cafeteria brought out trays of warm, steaming abgoosht and bread. He placed one bowl out for each employee, ignoring me as if I didn't exist. I didn't like abgoosht much, but on that day, the aroma was so appetizing. I watched as everyone grabbed the material they were sewing, turned it inside out, and threw it on the ground to sit on.

I felt like an unwanted outsider, a teenage boy sitting among grown men who were talking and laughing about grown-up stuff I didn't understand. I wished that, at least on that day, I had asked the cafeteria owner to give me lunch and put it on my tab. I was surprised that neither Mirza Agha nor Masht Ghara offered to pay for my lunch, at least on that first day. Somehow, I knew that if Aghajoon had employed his nephew, he would have made sure the kid had something to eat for lunch on his first day at work to feel welcomed.

I stepped outside and sat on the pavement, with my knees to my chest and the sun in my eyes. My fingers stung, my legs ached, and my stomach rumbled. I picked up a piece of rock and threw it into a joob. The splash caused a little bird pecking nearby to take flight. I followed the bird with my eyes, wishing I could fly off and escape this cold, unfriendly place.

After that first day, I woke up every morning with a knot in my stomach, and I dreaded going to work. I missed hanging out with Ramazoon at Aghajoon's shop or working on my projects with Akbar. The only thing that kept me going was the vision of how nice my siblings and I would look in our new outfits on our first day of school.

Near the end of my first week at work, I noticed the man next to me talking under his breath, cussing as he picked up his sewing machine; he rolled it somewhere and came back with another one.

Masht Ghara approached him. "What happened, Hassan Agha?"

"That stupid thing stopped working!"

Repairing sewing machines seemed a simple task to me; I had fixed Momman's many times. Sometimes it was due to a broken motor or worn-out wiring in the foot controller. It could also be a defective plug or outlet. I dropped the uniform I was working on and approached Masht Ghara. "May I take a look? I'm good at repairing electrical appliances and have fixed my mom's sewing machines many times."

I could tell Masht Ghara didn't believe me, but he didn't have anything to lose.

"It is in the storage room," Hassan Agha said and pointed.

Smiling, I stood up taller and raised my head as I walked confidently over to that room. Mash Ghara followed me. I plugged in the sewing machine and noticed that the lightbulb turned on, so the plug and the outlet weren't damaged. I sat on the floor and picked up the foot pedal. It was hot to the touch, and the smell of burning wire was seeping out of its inside shell. Without any tools at my disposal, I couldn't inspect much further.

"Tomorrow, I'll come early with my electrical tools. I think I can fix it," I said to Masht Ghara as I stood up.

He patted me on my back, nodding. As promised, I showed up at work extra early the next day, with my gray burlap tool sack slung over my shoulder. I walked over to the storage room where the broken sewing machine was and sat on the floor next to it, hoping I would be able to fix it.

The next thing I knew, Masht Ghara was standing over me.

"Salam," I greeted him politely.

"Mohsen, what time did you have to wake up to get here so early?" he asked, as he sipped his cup of tea.

"I don't know. I think it was four or five," I said nonchalantly. I opened my bag, like a surgeon getting ready to operate on his patient, and carefully pulled out a variety of screwdrivers, a voltmeter, a pair of pliers, a box of matches, and several bits of wire. I arranged them neatly on the floor next to me. Then I unscrewed the bottom of the foot pedal. A quick glance told me everything I needed to know.

Masht Ghara peered over my shoulder. "Do you think it can be fixed?"

"Easily," I said, feeling a little prick of pride swelling up inside me. "The wires look worn down, that's all." I showed him the inside of the nearly fried controller.

He let out an "ahh" of understanding and nodded.

Masht Ghara watched in amazement as I loosened the screws inside the controller that held the wires in place, cut the burned parts using pliers, and quickly removed the insulation on the wires to expose their metal ends, before attaching them to the screws.

"*Afareen* (well done), Mohsen! How do you know all this?" he asked in amazement.

I puffed inside the foot pedal to blow off any dust that might have remained inside the device and began explaining. "Well, I have been doing electrical work for as long as I can remember," I said, while closing the machine. "I worked at the hospital repairing all kinds of equipment. After that, I started doing a lot of electrical work for neighbors and family. I guess I just learned as I went along." I looked up smiling. "This should do it, Masht Ghara."

I plugged the machine into the wall and stepped back so he could assess the machine for himself. He glanced at me in a playfully skeptical way, grabbed a piece of fabric, placed it under the needle, and pressed lightly on the foot pedal. The clack-clack of the sewing machine was no longer piercing but sounded like pleasant music to my ears.

"You really fixed it!" He laughed boisterously. He stood up and patted me on the shoulder.

I couldn't contain the huge smile that spread across my face.

Later that day, I saw Masht Ghara take Mirza Agha to the storage room to show him that I had fixed the sewing machine. Mirza Agha never acknowledged my accomplishment. I felt sad for his wife and children, who had to put up with his arrogance every single day.

By the end of the first week, I had the routine down. The deafening sound of the sewing machines didn't bother me much, and even the skin on my fingers had grown thicker, so I barely cut them anymore. Best of all, though, the workers began to realize that I was a great asset to have around. They asked me to help when something went wrong with their sewing machines or other appliances. The man who pressed the uniforms approached me to fix a dead iron a few times, and in return, he showed me how to create identical crisp and sharp creases on any piece of clothing to make it look well made.

All the workers, including Masht Ghara, treated me as if I were their son. Sometimes they even asked the cafeteria owner to give me a bowl of abgoosht and put it on their tabs. They chatted with me during lunch, while Mirza Agha continued to behave as if my existence in the factory didn't matter. Sometimes I wondered why he had offered me that position.

On Thursday, when payday arrived, the atmosphere of the factory seemed happier, with people humming popular songs as they sewed away in anticipation of getting paid. Around three o'clock, the workers formed a line in front of Mirza Agha's desk, where he sat with the company's treasurer. From the middle of the line, where I stood, I could hear the treasurer calling an employee's name, and then he would tell Mirza Agha how much money to hand out of the sack on the floor in front of his feet. I smiled each time I heard a large amount of money being called out and wondered how big my pay would be.

"Mohsen." The treasurer called my name, and I approached and held out my hand in front of Mirza Agha. Mirza Agha looked at me, then at the treasurer, then back at me. The room suddenly became quiet—so quiet I thought everyone surely could hear my heartbeat.

The treasurer didn't announce the amount of money that Mirza Agha owed me, as he had done with the rest of the workers. Instead, Mirza Agha stood up. He was only a head taller than me, but at that moment, I felt as if I were standing next to a giant. He put his hand into his pants pocket and took out a single bill. "Mohsen, I'll give you five tomans each week and save the rest for you until the end of the summer. I don't want you to spend it all at once."

I nodded without objecting, although I knew I would save the money. However, it felt good to know that Mirza Agha was looking after my best interests. I wondered if he really cared for me but didn't know how to express it.

The rest of the summer marched on in much the same way. Each day I rose early, before my family, and rode the bus through the quiet streets to the factory. I felt proud that in addition to doing my own job, I was helping other workers get theirs done by repairing their machines. Each week on payday, I got my five tomans and wondered how much money I had accumulated. The excitement of wearing the wonderful new clothes on the first day of school was indescribable.

A week before my last day at the factory, I gave Mirza Agha my notice and asked him to please have my money ready for me by the end of the week.

"Don't worry, Mohsen. I will," he said and patted my shoulder. His touch felt a little strange. I couldn't understand why he was showing me affection now when he had never done so before.

On my last day at work, I approached Mirza Agha's desk, with my heart pounding excitedly in my chest. When I reached the front, I proudly held out my hand and thought about how empty his bag of money would be after my turn had passed.

"Here are your five tomans. Next person," he said and looked away.

My mouth dropped. "*Eh?* Mirza Agha, today is my last day, remember? I should get all my money you have saved up for me."

"I'm sorry, I forgot. If I give you all the money now, I won't have enough to pay the rest of the people. Come back next week," he said, nervously rubbing his chin.

I looked behind me but saw only one other person waiting to get paid. I thought Mirza Agha had plenty of money in his bag to pay me in full, but out of courtesy, I didn't say another word.

As agreed upon, I returned at the beginning of the following week, but to my disappointment, Mirza Agha had forgotten yet again.

"You know every time I come here, it costs me one toman each way to catch the bus," I said, my voice quivering.

"Tomorrow. Mohsen, tomorrow. I promise," he said as he jotted down a reminder note to himself.

I left, feeling confident that tomorrow I would *finally* get paid. The next day and the day after, Mirza Agha did not have my money at hand.

Finally, on the third day, as I was waiting at the bus station for the blue bus to pull over, my stomach began twisting and turning in pain, and I decided not to get on. Instead, I turned back and went home, with tears rolling down my face. By now I knew it would be a waste of bus fare and my time to go to the factory to claim my money.

As I walked into the house, I wiped my tears with the back of my old patched sleeve.

Momman noticed my red eyes and sniffly nose. "Mohsen Jon, what's wrong? You look like someone whose ship full of saffron has sunk," she said, stroking my cheek.

"It's nothing," I said, flashing a fake smile.

"How come you aren't at the factory today? Did you finish your work at Mirza Agha's?"

"I gave my notice last week."

"And did he pay your money?" Her light brown eyes narrowed and focused straight into mine. I felt as if she sensed the truth but was waiting for me to respond.

"No, he didn't," I whispered, hoping she would just let it be.

"What a stupid man," she said. Her brows came together, wrinkling her forehead. "Only a crook would steal money from a child! I'll get to the bottom of this." She shook her head in disgust. "

"It's okay," I said.

"It is not okay. Don't let people treat you this way." Momman was a petite woman, a head shorter than me, but suddenly when she stood up, she seemed tall and powerful, dressed in her long, worn-out floral skirt and a pink shirt that she had sewn for herself years ago. I am sure that if Mirza Agha had been present, she would have put him in his place.

Momman picked up the telephone receiver. My parents had lent some money to one of their friends. Instead of repaying, he had given us an old black phone. She dialed her sister's number without hesitation. "I'll take care of it," she told me. "Don't worry."

My aunt promised Momman that she would talk to her husband, but I knew she couldn't do anything. Mirza Agha was a stubborn man, someone who would not listen to his wife's complaining.

A week later, on the first day of school, I shuffled into the schoolyard and let out a deep sigh, staring down at my all-too-familiar pair of scuffed up, torn, black shoes and the same worn-out suit I had worn the previous year. Tears filled my eyes. It was then that I made a promise to myself that I would never again let anyone rip me off and that I would learn to stand up for myself.

The seasons came and went, and before long, the hot and muggy summer had arrived again. One day, as I was fixing Momman's iron, my cousin Asghar came to our house. I wondered why he had shown up; he usually only came by when he needed something.

"What's going on Asghar?"

"Mirza Agha asked me to work at his factory this summer," he said as he investigated the iron I was working on.

"Oh?"

"It feels weird to work among a bunch of grown men."

"Don't worry. You'll get used to that. They're nice people," I said.

"Why don't you come with me tomorrow?" he pleaded.

I smirked but didn't say anything.

"Masht Ghara wondered why you were not coming to work this year."

"What about Mirza Agha? What did he say?" I inquired.

"I don't know. He wasn't there today."

I shook my head and said, "I worked for him last year and want to do something different this summer." I didn't want to tell Asghar that Mirza Agha ripped me off.

"Mohsen, for God's sake, come with me tomorrow."

"I can't. I have other things to do," I said, knowing very well that I had no other plans for the summer. Asghar's persistence softened my heart, however, and I finally agreed to accompany him to the factory.

Later, when I told Momman about it, she frowned and asked, "Are you certain you want to work there? Remember last year?"

I nodded.

"Well, let's hope Mirza Agha doesn't take advantage of you again." Momman could easily have said no, but as always, she wanted me to be my own person, make my own decisions, and accept responsibility for my actions.

On my first day back at the factory, I waltzed inside and shouted a friendly salam to everyone. I was overwhelmed with pride and joy when every fellow coworker greeted me jubilantly and looked sincerely eager to have me back. Beaming, I walked over to my station.

Hassan Agha approached me. "You look so grown up. How old are you now?"

"Seventeen!" I said as I bent down to pick up a uniform from a pile to de-thread. It seemed like nothing had changed in this place; even the color of the uniforms was the same as last year. As I stood up, I noticed Mirza Agha staring at me from across the room. His cold glare quickly turned my happiness into an uncomfortable chill. He nervously busied himself with opening rolls of fabrics and spreading them on his desk.

A few minutes later, I watched as Mirza walked over to where Asghar was standing. I thought he would surely pass by his station and ignore him, the way he had always treated me. Instead, to my surprise, he stopped and started chatting with him. A smile spread across his face as he placed his hand on Asghar's shoulder. My mouth dropped in disappointment as the two bursts into laughter. It was clear he didn't like me, either because my family was poor or because, unlike Asghar, I was not his blood relative.

In a way, I was happy to see that Asghar wasn't experiencing the same dilemma I had gone through with Mirza Agha the previous year. Since then, I had grown a thicker skin, and Mirza's peculiar ways didn't bother me as much, although I was still angry at the way he treated me. I felt I was conveying a wrong message to Mirza Agha that it was okay for him to steal from me.

Every day, Asghar and I took the bus together to the factory, but that was the only time we spent together. The rest of the day, Mirza Agha took diligent care of Asghar, feeding him and giving him a ride home. Although Asghar and I lived only a few blocks apart, Mirza Agha never asked me to hop on for a ride.

On Thursday, the payday, all the workers formed a line in front of Mirza Agha and his treasurer, exactly as they had the year before.

"Mohsen." The treasurer called my name.

I stepped forward and held out my hand.

Mirza Agha cleared his throat and said, "Mohsen, I'm giving you five tomans for now and keeping the rest for later, so you don't spend it all at once."

I looked at Mirza Agha with my mouth half-opened; I scratched my head and thought he must be joking with me. A small chuckle escaped my lips as he called out the next name, and I realized he was serious about not paying me again. *Did he really think I was that stupid to fall for his trick twice?* I didn't know what to do. I looked around the room, hoping someone would say something to this thief.

Then I remembered the promise I had made to myself—not to let anyone rip me off again and to stand up for myself. Suddenly, frustration and anger welled up inside me, and I addressed Mirza Agha. "No. I am not stupid. I won't leave this line until I receive all of my wages for this week."

Unexpectedly, the room became ominously quiet. The confidence with which my voice rang had surprised everyone, even me.

"After all, we *are* family," I said, staring at him.

"Family?" I heard the workers whisper to each other behind me. I could not believe this man hadn't even bothered to tell people I was his nephew. This man, this thief, was ashamed of me? He should be ashamed of himself for stealing money from a poor kid. I wondered how he would ever show his face at our house and break bread with my family again. It was right then that I decided I would never again work for Mirza Agha.

He gave me an awkward look and twisted his thick mustache as he reluctantly reached his hand inside the bag of money. "Mohsen, I only had your best interests at heart," he said as he handed me another 331 tomans.

I snatched the bills from his hand and scoffed, "*Really?* What about last year? Tell me, what happened to my pay from last summer? How many of your other workers have you ripped off?" I looked at the workers standing in the line. I wanted them to be aware that Mirza Agha wasn't an honest man and was capable of cheating any of his employees.

Mirza Agha's face turned beet red, and he appeared at a loss for words. He looked down and whispered to the treasurer to call the next guy.

I stepped aside, my anger seething. Every bone in my body hated this man.

As I was leaving, Masht Ghara stopped me at the door. "I will make sure you get paid in full each week," he pleaded, his eyes filled with remorse and shame.

"Your son isn't a trustworthy man, and I don't like to work for people like him," I said in a loud voice, hoping Mirza Agha heard my words.

"I understand, son. I am sorry." He shook his head. "You are a good boy, or should I say, man?" He patted my shoulder.

"Thank you, Masht Ghara."

I couldn't believe that a nice man like Masht Ghara could father someone like Mirza Agha. As for Asghar, he stared at the floor the whole time I was shouting at Mirza Agha, with his ears burning red in embarrassment. I'm sure he partly blamed himself for putting me in this situation in the first place. I couldn't blame Asghar for not saying anything, since Mirza Agha treated him completely different from me. I couldn't have been happier for Asghar about that. He was my cousin and a friend, and I cared for his well-being.

As I left that day, instead of taking the bus, I decided to walk home to vent the emotions churning inside me: anger, disgust, excitement—but most of all, pride because I had stood up for myself just as I had promised.

A few blocks from home, I spotted a sleek blue suit hanging in the window of a tailor's shop. I stood in front of the glass, surveying the crisp, soft fabric. A sense of longing gradually replaced the anger I had endured earlier, and I felt as if somehow I had grown taller in the last few hours. I saw myself in the glass as I lined myself up against the suit. Indeed, it looked genuinely nice on me. As I stared at my reflection, my mind wandered off, and I began thinking of ways I could save enough to wear that suit on my first day of school.

MAKING A RIFLE

AGE SEVENTEEN

I eventually learned that some curiosities are better left alone.

It was a hot, summer day; Akbar and I were walking and window-shopping on Ferdousi Street. This street was one of our hangout places too whenever we had nothing else to do. It was always crowded, because it had many interesting shops—clothing boutiques, record, appliance, and many other shops. If anyone wanted to buy anything imported from Europe or America, they visited this street.

As we wandered from one store to another, Akbar pulled me toward a hunting supply shop. In the window, they had a display of guns, rifles, and knives of all shapes and sizes. We knew about guns from books and John Wayne movies we had seen or the handles of the guns sticking out of police officers' gun belts. This was our first time seeing them close up, only one meter away from us. We had heard rich families hunted birds or deer during the winter season and we envied them—not because they were killing animals but because they had guns to hold. We found that very exciting.

"Wow. Mohsen, look at this one! The wood is so nicely polished."

We tilted our heads at different angles to see every detail of those rifles. Akbar and I were afraid to go inside the shop, because we thought the owner would throw us out due to our raggedy appearance. After a brief period of admiration, we walked away to look at other shops, but we continued to talk about the rifles and how beautiful they looked.

Half an hour later, we convinced each other to go back and take a closer look at the rifles inside the store. When we reached the shop the second time, both of our hearts were pounding from nervousness. We gave each other a quick nod before going in.

The man at the counter was tall, skinny, and very well dressed. He looked us over from head to toe.

We greeted him, "Salam Agha."

I think he felt sorry for us, since it was obvious we weren't customers, yet he let us go from one glass counter to another to look at different rifles, knives, and other hunting supplies on display.

I looked up and saw a display of hunting rifles hanging on the walls. I slowly approached the owner of the shop and pointed at the rifles behind him, "Sir, excuse me," I said. "I have a question."

"Yes?" he said indifferently.

"How much are these rifles?"

"They are about 180 to 200 tomans."

I did not show any expression, just nodded my head, and moved away, but inside I was shocked at how expensive they were.

Akbar came and stood next to me. The clerk noticed our excitement and decided to take one of the rifles out to show us. He knew we were too young and too poor to buy anything from him; plus, only people who had a valid government license were able to purchase a hunting rifle. He placed a rifle on the counter for us to look at. He didn't let us touch it.

Akbar and I were in heaven; we never imagined we would be looking at a rifle so closely. After spending such an exciting time at the shop, we thanked the clerk for the time he spent with us, said goodbye, and left.

On the way home, the image of the rifle stayed in my head. I kept thinking, *There must be a way to recreate what we saw.*

"You know what, Akbar? We can make a rifle. It might not turn out to look like store-brand ones, but it will work like one."

Akbar looked at me in disbelief and said, "What are you talking about? How could we possibly make one?"

I said, "All we need is a pipe and a wooden board." By this time, we had reached my home. Before I went in, I told Akbar to ask his sister's husband, Mr. Mohammedi, to show us how a gun worked and how to make a shell gun. Mr. Mohammedi was in the military and used to train soldiers on how to use, assemble, and disassemble guns. He was an arrogant man. I didn't care for him, but we had nobody else to consult about the rifles.

The next day, Akbar came to our house and told me that luckily Mr. Mohammedi had time to share his knowledge about guns with us on Friday, only two days away.

On that day, Akbar and I headed to his sister's house. Mr. Mohammadi opened the door.

"Salam," we greeted him.

He didn't reply and pointed for us to enter. "Let's go. I have everything ready," he said and took us to a small room. On the carpet, he had placed a notebook and a couple of colored pencils. We sat on the floor, and he started explaining about guns and how they worked. I could tell that he enjoyed showing off his knowledge; he described everything in detail by drawing pictures using the colored pencils to make it clearer for us. I was surprised he never questioned us about why we were interested in learning about guns. He just wanted to prove to us that he was a smart man. When he finished, he tore out the pages and handed them to me for future reference. He had explained everything in enough detail to give me a better understanding of how a gun operated.

Akbar and I did not stay much longer and left after he completed his explanation. We thanked him for his time and headed out. I knew exactly what to do and what to buy after our visit with him.

The next day, we went back to a gun supply shop on Ferdousi Street. Both Akbar and I approached the man behind the counter. "Salam, Agha. We are here to buy an empty shotgun shell, gun powder, over powder wad, shot wad, and a box of pellets."

He went to another room and put a spoonful of gun powder in a small bag, then he took out everything else we asked for from a large box underneath his desk. He put everything on the counter and said, "Five tomans." By the way he talked and looked at us, we knew he did not want us to be hanging around his store much.

As soon as we paid him, we thanked him and left. I took out the shotgun shell and showed it to Akbar. I pointed to the base of the shotgun shell and told him, "This is the rim, and according to Mr. Mohammedi, we have to make sure the diameter of the barrel is large enough to snuggly fit this part."

We did not stay on Ferdousi Avenue much longer; we were on a mission to find the right-sized metal pipe, the piece that was going to substitute for a barrel in our homemade rifle.

Akbar was extremely excited about our new project. He was at our house early every morning to search for the right-sized pipe. We went to all the plumbing shops in our neighborhood but had no luck. One of the shop owners told us we might find something at a scrap-metal store. We went to the one near our house where I used to sell scrap metal to help my parents with their expenses. I looked around, this place looked the same as it did many years ago. It brought back some sad memories.

When we told the man what we were looking for, he took the shotgun shell from me and went to the back of the store. I don't know how he knew where things were; his shop was filled with all kinds of metal pieces, metal appliances, metal miscellaneous items. He came back with a long metal pipe.

Akbar and I looked at each other and smiled. We asked him if he could cut it in half. He did and then he weighed the piece. "Five rials."

I gave him the money and scuttled out the door with Akbar. We wanted to make it out the door before our delight took over and we began bouncing from joy.

Later that evening, we found a wooden board in a vacant lot close to Akbar's house. Akbar and I took turns carving the wood using a knife and a hammer. Then we used sandpaper to smooth the surface so the pipe could sit on it nicely. I placed the pipe on the wooden piece and held it there, while Akbar tied the two together with electrical tape. To make our homemade rifle look cool, we painted it black and left it in a corner of our backyard to dry. Surprisingly, nobody in the family asked us what we were going to do with this one-meter pipe attached to a wooden board. I wouldn't have told the truth; I didn't want to get into trouble.

While the paint was drying, we filled the shotgun shell with gunpowder, over powder wad, and shot wad, and then inserted ten silver-color pellets through the opening at the top of the shell. We did not have a crimping tool, so we used glue to close the hole. Overall, we were happy with the way our rifle looked.

The following day was the execution day. Both Akbar and I could not wait to find out if our rifle really worked. Akbar came to our house early that day as usual. Since our house was always crowded with my siblings and Momman's students, we decided to go to his house to try the gun. I put our homemade rifle in a black cloth and put the shell in my pocket. Akbar carried a nail and a hammer.

Both Mr. Mohammedi and the owner of the rifle shop had told us that if we struck a nail at the primer with a hammer, it would act as a trigger and expel the pellets.

On the way to his house, we both were quiet; neither of us had any idea what the outcome of our project would be. I knew we had applied the principle of how a gun would work, but anything could go wrong. I felt anxious to get it over with. Nobody passing us could tell what I was carrying on my shoulder, only that it was something long wrapped in a piece of cloth.

When we reached Akbar's house, he opened the door. "Salam, salam," we said, waiting for somebody to reply. When no one answered, we knew the house was empty. Akbar wanted to ask his neighborhood friends to come and watch, but I talked him out of it. I did not want to be embarrassed if the gun did not work.

We chose the upstairs hallway facing my aunt's bedroom. We shut the door to her room, and I put the "rifle" on Akbar's shoulder, facing the lower part of the closed door. I told him to stay steady while I inserted the shotgun shell into the pipe. Then I put the nail against the primer.

"I'm going to count to three before I strike the nail. Stay steady," I said.

Akbar looked back and said, "I am ready."

My heart was pounding as I counted, "One, two, three," then I banged the nail with the hammer slightly. I heard a big boom and the rifle kicked and pushed Akbar's shoulder back, the way a real rifle would. He lost his balance and fell on the floor.

In that instant, I was confused and shocked. My face felt red. For a moment, I didn't know what to do. Akbar lay there shaking, with a petrified, scared look in his eyes.

"Are you okay? Are you okay?" I asked, pulling him up.

Akbar and I looked at each other and didn't know what to say. Neither of us thought the gun was going to work. When we collected ourselves, we noticed that the entire bottom of the door to my aunt's bedroom was gone.

"How are we going to explain this?" Akbar pointed at all the wood pieces scattered on the floor and the big hole in the door.

"Don't worry. We'll figure out an explanation," I said as I picked up the rifle from the floor. "I am so glad we didn't invite any of your friends from the neighborhood. What if the pellets had hit one of them and killed him? What if we really hurt ourselves or somebody else? How could we have explained that to anyone?" I stopped and looked at Akbar.

"What do we tell my mother?" he asked.

"We will tell her the truth. She will not believe us if we make up stories." I felt embarrassed for being such an idiot to do such a stupid thing.

While we were waiting for his mother to come home, we collected all the pellets on the floor and disassembled the rifle so we could throw it away. Then we went downstairs and waited for her to return.

When the door opened, Akbar and I both took a deep breath.

My aunt came in with two fresh breads in her hands. She went upstairs to put her chador in her room. It did not take long before we heard her scream: "Akbar! Mohsen! What happened here?"

We told her in detail what we had done.

"Khaleh, I know it was very foolish of us to do what we did." I quivered while looking down with embarrassment at my feet. "I wish I could fix the door for you."

"No, Mohsen Jon, it's fine. I am just glad nobody got hurt or died," she said, patting our heads. We were shocked that she didn't punish us.

Akbar's family could not afford to fix the door. It would have been too expensive to replace it—around one hundred tomans. Every time I went to their house, that door served as a reminder of my stupidity. Eventually, I replaced it with my own money. It was the right thing to do.

Developing Pictures

Age Seventeen

There is power in admitting what you don't know. When you do that, people are more than willing to help you with their knowledge.

As I was cleaning up my Kodak black-box camera, Akbar showed up at the house. "Oh," he said, "I didn't know you had a camera."

"One of Aghajoon's customers owed me some money for the wiring work I did for his shop. He gave me a camera instead of paying cash."

Akbar laughed and said, "How do you know it works and the guy didn't rip you off?"

"If he gave me a defective camera, I know where his shop is. Also, I am working on a project for him and will not complete it if he cheated me." I finished cleaning, stood up, and confidently said, "Let's take some pictures."

"Can I take them?" Akbar asked.

"The roll I bought has twelve black-and-white exposures, which means we can only take twelve pictures, so how about you take six and I take the other six?"

Akbar nodded as we headed out.

"We should hurry up before it gets too dark. This camera didn't come with a flash. Even if I had one, it would be too expensive to buy a new lightbulb every time I flashed it."

"Can you make one?" Akbar asked. Then he smiled and said, "Why am I even asking? You probably can."

"I have an idea of how to build one with aluminum foil, but we'd have to use the same lightbulb as in the real flash. That would still be expensive."

As we walked down the street, little kids began spotting the camera in my hand. They followed me, saying, "Mohsen, Mohsen, can you take our picture?"

Our twelve pictures ended up consisting of kids who asked us, people standing in line to get bread, a man pushing a donkey on the street, and a few of each other.

As soon as we came home, Akbar excitedly took the film out of the camera. He unrolled it and exposed it to the sun.

"What are you doing?" I shouted, snatching the film from him. I stopped myself just short of yelling and calling him names.

He looked at me puzzled. "I wanted to see the pictures."

"*The pictures?* The pictures are ruined now. We had to develop them to be able to see the pictures. Now we have to wait till I buy another roll of film to be able to take more pictures," I said, annoyed.

Akbar insisted that his friend who owned a photo shop would be able to develop those pictures.

"Unless your friend is God, he can't develop these," I replied.

Akbar took back the roll of film and walked to the photoshop near his house. I went along just for the satisfaction of proving I was right.

At the shop, Akbar handed the roll of film to his friend, Freydoon Agha, who was standing behind a counter. He looked to be in his thirties.

"What is this?" he asked, puzzled.

"We have taken some pictures and we'd like to have this film developed."

Freydoon Agha laughed so hard I could see all his upper teeth. "You have opened up the film and ruined it. Next time, don't unroll the film."

I looked at Akbar and said, "I told you so!" Then I asked Freydoon Agha, "How much do you charge to develop this kind of film?"

"About seven tomans," he said.

On the way back home, I told Akbar that seven tomans was a lot of money, and we could learn to develop pictures ourselves. It would be much cheaper.

"Mohsen, you always think you can do everything yourself for cheaper."

The next chance I had, I went to Naser Khosrow Street to buy a book on how to develop pictures. In my spare time, I read the book and looked at the pictures of different cameras and other photography accessories. As I was reading it, I wrote down the names of the chemicals we needed. The list turned out to be long. There were more than a dozen liquid chemicals. Akbar continued to visit us and kept asking about the project. I told him I had to make enough money to buy the film and other things for the project. I asked him to start collecting some glass bottles for different liquid chemicals we needed to buy.

Within a couple of weeks, I had completed as many odd jobs as I needed to be able to afford what we needed to start our project.

On the day we were going to buy all our chemicals, Akbar and I put all of our glass bottles into a cloth sack.

Seena Photography was the first shop that caught our eyes. The store was small, and to my surprise, it didn't have any chemical smell, maybe because everything was sealed tightly. There were many shelves filled with all kinds of cameras and accessories. I knew some of them from the pictures I had seen in my book, but I had no idea what some of the others were.

Immediately upon our arrival, Akbar and I lined up all twelve bottles on the counter, trying to pretend we were professionals who knew what we were doing. The owner came to the counter and asked us what we wanted.

I took out my things-to-get list and asked for each chemical clearly and confidently.

The shop owner smiled condescendingly. "What are the glass bottles for, and what are these chemicals you just named? I don't know any of them."

"This is the first time I've tried to develop pictures. I read in a book that we need these liquid chemicals," I answered, embarrassed I had to admit the truth.

He shook his head and said, "We have premade powder chemicals that you mix with water before use." He pointed at three big containers.

"This is developer, that is fixer, and the other one is stopper. These are just to develop negatives." He then walked to another section of the store and said, "These chemicals are to develop the pictures from your negatives."

Akbar and I took all the jars we had placed on the counter, while the man scoped the chemicals into brown bags for us. He placed all six bags on the counter in front of us.

Once I figured that he knew we were beginners in photography, I felt extremely comfortable asking questions about developing pictures. "Agha, how much of each do we need to add to the water?"

He realized my sincerity and gave me not only instructions on the ratio of chemicals to water for the mix but also a lot more information about developing pictures. He went over the process even better than the book I had read. "The tricky part is when you are transferring the image from the negatives onto the photo paper, because you don't see anything until you immerse the photo paper into the developer. If I were you, I would count or use a timer while exposing the paper to the developer. It's a trial-and-error process. You have to figure this part out yourself." Then he opened the cabinet under the counter. "Here, you need photo paper." He placed a thick pack of paper in front of us next to the bag of chemicals.

I told him we also needed an enlarger.

He looked at me and said, "Are you sure you can afford it? They are almost 110 tomans."

"A hundred and ten tomans? Can I see what it looks like?" I asked.

"There is one over there." He pointed.

Akbar and I walked to it. It was a large piece of equipment that reminded me of a microscope but much bigger. I looked at it carefully, trying to memorize how it was built. It looked fancy, but I thought I could make one. We returned to the counter.

"You are right. It is too expensive for us," I told him.

"An enlarger transfers the images from the negative to the photo paper, so if you don't have one, you can't complete the process. However, at this point, you can take your negatives to a photo shop, and they can convert those into a picture."

"Agha, we will figure something out," I said.

"I also added glass trays for you to use for mixing the chemicals." He pointed at those on the counter.

We paid twenty-five toman for the chemicals, the photo paper, and the trays. Then we picked up everything and headed home.

On the bus, Akbar asked me, "If we had taken our roll of film to a photo shop to be developed professionally it would have cost us less."

"You are right, but remember, we can use the chemicals many times that it will eventually pay off."

He nodded and agreed with me. After a long pause, he asked, "What are we going to do without an enlarger?"

"I understood its construction. It's quite simple to make an enlarger. All we need is a magnifying glass, a wooden box, a few pieces of white and black paper, two pieces of square glass, and a light bulb." I imagined in my head how it would look.

Akbar smiled and said, "Well, let's make one."

"Okay, but first, you know the small room at the top of the stairs in our house? I need your help to change that into a darkroom."

We spent the next couple of days building a makeshift enlarger, which we moved into the small room upstairs. Once everything was moved there, we began converting the small room into a darkroom by covering all the walls with black cotton sheets.

When everything was ready, Akbar and I walked out with the camera in my hands to take pictures. We were both unbearably excited because we were planning to develop them too. Once again, when the neighborhood people saw my camera, they wanted their pictures taken. We filled our camera roll with neighborhood kids, a woman carrying a basket of greens mixed with red radishes, Akbar pretending to be a singer, Momman sewing, and a few photos of me emulating the poses I had seen on action/ adventure movie posters.

Akbar and I didn't want to take any chances exposing the film to light, so we decided to start working at midnight. That night, we mixed each chemical: developer, fixer, stopper. We poured each one onto the glass tray for both developing the negatives and developing pictures. The room smelled like rotten eggs. It must have been due to the sulfur in some of the chemicals. I remembered reading about it in my book. We kept the trays for each process separate—one set on the right and the other on the left. We aligned them in the order we needed them: developer, fixer, stopper, and water. We hung a rope with clothespins to dry the negatives and the pictures after they were developed.

"Akbar, take out the film, but don't unroll it like you did last time." I laughed.

He pouted at my teasing as he removed the film and placed it on the counter. We also changed the lightbulb from the regular to red bulb. I made a mental note of where everything was located, because I knew once we turned on the red light, I would not be able to see clearly. I felt strangely tense, as if we were in an operating room about to operate, and I wanted to make sure we followed the procedure correctly to have satisfactory results at the end.

I looked around the room one last time and reviewed where everything was located. "Let's close the door and let's nail this black sheet around it to make sure no light is coming in." I handed Akbar one corner of the sheet, a hammer, and a bunch of nails.

Once the door was closed, everything was pitch black. It took our eyes some time to adjust to the darkness so Akbar and I could nail the sheet on the door. We used black electrical tape to make sure no light seeped in. Finally, I flipped the switch to turn on the red light. Under this light, things looked blurry. I had to use my memory to remember where everything was located. I began the process by myself since the room was small.

Akbar stood in a corner and tried to observe what I did as I talked through each step, so he would know what I was doing.

I unrolled the film and put it in the developer. It was only a brief wait before images started to appear. "Akbar, I see something appearing!" I felt so proud of myself for being able to develop pictures, with no experience, just by reading a book and talking to that shop owner.

Once I was satisfied with how the images looked, I placed the negatives in the fixer for some time and then in the stopper. The final stage was to immerse the unrolled film into the tray that contained water. After that, I hung the strip of film on the rope and held them in place with clothespins. To expedite this process, I used an electric heater to completely dry the film.

Once the negatives were dry, I placed the negative roll under the homemade enlarger to transfer one image onto the photo paper. As the shop owner had indicated, the transfer of images from the negatives onto the photo paper was very tricky. Since we didn't have a timer, I used a counting method to figure out how long I had to expose the negative to transfer the image. I counted to five and then took out the photo paper immersed in the developer. "Akbar, I don't like the way this image looks. It looks like a shadow, a ghost, and very blurry. I have to do another one, but this time I will expose it a little longer."

After three or four trials, I perfected the process and timing. At about two o'clock in the morning, Akbar and I ran downstairs screaming, "Picture, picture, picture!"

Everyone in the household woke up, at first confused, then annoyed. But as soon as they saw the picture in my hand, they shared our joy. I showed the picture to Momman. She smiled and said, "Oh, Mohsen Jon, when did you take this picture of me? I would have looked up and smiled had I known."

I loved that picture of Momman. She was sewing, but I could tell her mind was somewhere else.

A couple of days later, Akbar came to our house with his own roll of film. Apparently, his family had their own camera that they never used. "I want to develop these pictures by myself. I don't want your help." While the rest of us slept, he waited until midnight before climbing up the stairs to the darkroom with his roll of film. The next day, while we were having breakfast, he excitedly showed the pictures he had developed to me.

I smiled and told him, "These turned out great."

Developing those pictures cost us more money than having them done professionally, but learning that skill was worth a million tomans to me.

New Entertainment

I cared for her, and I worked very hard to prove it to her.

Iran was one the many daughters of our next-door neighbor, and we used to hang out together a lot—at least as many times that her parents allowed us to. Her family was quite conservative and didn't appreciate a teenage boy hanging around their young daughter all the time. My wish was that she would wait for me or that her parents would not force her into marrying someone else. I never told her I loved her but hoped that by caring for her she would figure it out.

One day, I overheard a conversation between her and some other neighborhood girls that she had never been to a movie and wished she could.

I was not allowed to take Iran to a movie, so I decided to surprise her by making a projector I could use to display still images of a movie. It would not be the same as watching one, but I thought it would be entertaining. I asked Akbar to come with me to buy supplies for it.

As we shopped, I explained my plan to him.

He knew I wanted to marry Iran someday. "I can't wait to see the outcome of our project," he said, giddily clapping his hands.

First, we stopped by the fabric shop at the corner of our alley to get two empty cylindrical fabric tubes—one large and one slightly smaller in diameter. When we arrived at the store, we waited for the shop owner, Rahman Agha, and his assistants to finish talking to his customers.

The fabric store was always a colorful sight. The shelves were stacked with rolls of beautiful pink, blue, and purple fabric. Some were solid colors, and others had flowery designs mixed with other colors. After most of the customers had finished their business and left, Rahman Agha looked at me and smiled. "What do you want, Mohsen?"

Momman was constantly in need of fabric for her sewing classes, so he knew my family fairly well. I also did some electrical wiring for him. "Do you have any empty cardboard fabric tubes six centimeters in diameter that I can have?" I asked.

He looked under the counter and found one. "Here. This is the only one I have." He handed it to me.

I examined the tube, and the diameter was perfect. "Do you have a smaller one that can fit into this one?" I looked around his shop to show him an example of the size.

"What do you want to do with it?" he asked.

I explained, "I am making a projector to show movie images to the neighbors."

I don't think he believed me but continued looking. "Give me back that tube." He pointed, then went to the back of his shop. "There," he said, as he showed me how perfectly the one tube he'd found slid into the other.

"This will work. Thank you." I took the tubes from him and handed them to Akbar as we walked out the door.

"You have to invite me to see those images," he said jokingly.

I looked back and assured him I would.

Next, we went to Mehdi Agha's shop to buy wood. He was busy pounding nails into a chair he was building. When he saw us enter, he stopped hammering.

"Salam, Mehdi Agha," I said.

"Salam, what do you want, Mohsen?" He knew me since Aghajoon's shop was across from his.

"I'd like to make a square box, one meter by one meter." I gestured the size with my hand.

He went to the corner of his shop, walking on the saw dust and wood shavings that covered its ground. He took out a panel and cut it into four equal pieces. The saw made a "yurr-yip" sound as he went back and forth on the wood. "Four tomans," he said, wiping the sweat off his face.

I gave him the money and took the four pieces of wood.

At home, Akbar busied himself with pounding nails into the wood to make it into a box, while I picked up the bigger fabric tube and made two slits, one at the top and one at the bottom, large enough for the strip of the film to go through.

"I am done," Akbar said. "What's next?"

I placed the large fabric tube on the box and drew a circle, using the tube as the circle's circumference. "Cut a hole around this circle." I searched inside my toolbox to take out the magnifying glass I had bought during one of my Naser Khosrow trips. I attached it to the end of the smaller tube.

"Are you sure this is going to work?" he asked.

"We will find out tonight. I bought two rolls of still strip images to try."

Neither of us could wait to see the results. The last thing I had to do was place a 100-watt lightbulb inside the projector next to the big hole. I took the box from Akbar and cut a small hole at the top and inverted a lightbulb inside so we could easily plug it into an outlet. Everything was set up. I placed the homemade projector on a chair, with the bigger tube sticking out toward the wall across from Iran's parents' house balcony. I moved the smaller tube back and forth inside the bigger tube to make sure it was working. Akbar and I tried to busy ourselves with other things until it got pitch dark outside to try our invention.

At nine o'clock, I took out a Dean Martin still-image strip and one with Fardeen—a famous Iranian actor. These were the only ones I could afford to buy. I asked my family to go to the backyard so I could surprise them with what they were about to see. Thankfully, everyone had been busy with their tasks inside the house throughout the day, so they had not paid much attention to what Akbar, and I were making.

"Akbar, plug in the bulb." I knew that as soon as the light hit the wall across from the projector in our pitch-black backyard, all the surrounding neighbors would stick their heads out, either by climbing the brick wall between our houses, going to their balcony, or looking out of their second-story windows to figure out what we were doing. The houses in our neighborhood were wall to wall beside each other.

Iran and her family were the first to appear on their balcony, which overlooked our backyard. They had the best view, and I had arranged my projector intentionally so she could see the images in detail.

"What are you doing?" Iran asked.

"Salam. Wait for a minute. You'll see," I said as I inserted the strip through the slits on that large tube. I felt nervous, and my hands were shaking a little. This was the first time I was using the projector and had an audience. I especially wanted to impress Iran. On the wall, there was a big blur of light, and I thought something had gone wrong, so I fiddled with the tubes, trying to focus the image on the wall. When my family started clapping, I knew the image was perfect.

"Dean Martin, Dean Martin, my favorite American actor," Iran said, jumping up and down on the balcony.

I moved the strip up to advance the still image to the next one when people stopped making comments or when someone shouted excitedly, "Go to the next one. Go to the next one."

The clapping and excitement continued for hours, which filled me with joy, especially when I heard the happiness in Iran's voice.

Everyone enjoyed watching those images on the wall. The projector became our entertainment for some summer weeks. Sometimes I invited Maheen, Iran, or some other neighborhood kids to come to our backyard to watch. They sat on the blanket Momman had placed on the ground and waited for me to project the images. They made up stories for each slide.

Over time, Iran—and even I—got bored watching those images. There was only so much imagination we had to expend on them.

One day, I noticed the projector sitting idle in the corner of a room, the fabric tubes sticking out. I remembered that Rahmaan Agha wanted to see the projector. I picked up the box with all its accessories and placed them on my homemade cart and headed to his shop.

Surprisingly, no customers were there. He was in a corner reading a newspaper.

"Salam, Rahmaan Agha."

He nodded.

"I brought it for you to see," I said.

"See what?"

"The projector. Remember when you gave me those two tubes?"

He smiled and nodded.

I walked him through the instructions, "Here, take these still image strips and show them to your family." I handed him at least twenty. Momman had told me to never provide my services free of charge and always to charge people for anything I did or gave to them. For some reason, I wanted to give Rahmaan Agha that projector to enjoy with his family.

I, on the other hand, needed to think of some other way to entertain Iran.

OUR FIRST TELEVISION

AGE EIGHTEEN

Sometimes, when you make a wish, it feels as if the universe aligns everything, so your wish comes true.

That summer passed, and school started. One day, Akbar came over to tell me that Kobra, Momman's niece, had bought a television and that it was very cool. Knowing that a TV would provide great enjoyment to Iran and also my family, I wished we could have one. I had to convince Momman to suggest to Aghajoon to get one for our household. I had to figure out how.

Iranian New Year was approaching, and I knew that would be the best time to catch Momman in a good mood. My plan was for our family to arrive at Kobra's house and get her to show off her TV. I always looked forward to Iranian New Year, since we visited all of our relatives and exchanged little gifts—mostly money—and ate a lot of food. That year was even more exciting since we would see Kobra's television.

Norooz (New Day) is the beginning of New Year in Iran. Before Norooz, which is considered the biggest celebration of the year, people clean their houses and buy new clothes for everyone in the family. Momman used her creativity to make beautiful dresses for my sisters from remnants of fabric her customers had brought—such as a pink top and flowery skirt with ruffles at the bottom.

Another major ritual is setting Haft-Seen, which involves seven specific items that start with the letter S: *sonbul* (hyacinth), *sabzeh* (greens), *senjed* (special berry), *seer* (garlic), *sekkeh* (coin), *serkeh* (vinegar), and *samanoo* (a dish made of wheat). Many other items are placed on the sofreh, depending on how fancily each household wants to arrange their haft-seen—such as a mirror, goldfish, cookies, apples. This is a tradition Iranians have kept since we were Zoroastrians. When Arabs attacked Iran in 633 AD, they forced their religion, Islam, onto Iranians.

Each item on the sofreh corresponds to something in nature. For example, greens are a symbol of birth and growth, garlic is a symbol of health and medicine, and special berry is a symbol of love.

Momman decided we would visit Kobra and her family on the third day of New Year. I convinced her we should go in the late afternoon, because I knew Kobra would have her TV on. In those days, the programs started later in the day.

On the way to Kobra's, Momman started her routine that involved giving her children a long sermon on how to behave and not to eat a lot of food. "Leave some food for others. Don't embarrass us by taking fistfuls of nuts and all the cookies," she said, as we were walking briskly to Kobra's house.

"If they don't want their guests to eat the food, why do they leave it out on the table? They would hide it," I told Momman jokingly.

All my siblings giggled, but Aghajoon frowned and said in a deep voice, "Listen to what your Momman says." He no longer hit me because I had grown up, or maybe he realized I had turned out to be a good son.

Momman continued, "You should only eat a small amount. We don't want her to think we're all starving."

But I am always starving, I thought.

When we arrived at Kobra's house, Momman gave a stern look to remind us of our conversation, before knocking at the door.

After we had greeted and wished each other a happy Norooz, Kobra invited us to join her and the rest of the family in the living room. As we were walking there, we heard a noise coming from inside.

"Kobra Jon, are there other people visiting? Do you want us to come back later?" Momman asked.

"Oh no, that is the sound of our television. We bought one not long ago."

I was more curious to inspect their TV than I originally thought I'd be, but I needed to keep my mind focused on tricking Momman. In the living room, the coffee table was decorated with a platter of oranges; a big bowl of mixed pistachios, almonds, raisins, and hazelnuts; and ornate plates of artfully arranged cookies and candies. As we entered the room, Kobra's children were sitting on the carpet and staring at an English program dubbed in Farsi. A beautiful actress named Suzanne Pleshette was talking.

All of us, including my parents, were fascinated by the television. My siblings and I sat down and watched. The entire time, Kobra kept offering us fruits, sweets, nuts, and hard candies. Surprisingly, we ate very little food; we were mesmerized by the TV program.

After a couple of hours, my parents stood up and asked us to say goodbye. My siblings and I begged them to let us stay longer, but to no avail.

On the way back home, our conversation was about how much we genuinely enjoyed the television program. Momman told Aghajoon, "Did you see how much the kids liked watching the television? We should get one for our household."

I was shocked that Momman started a conversation about buying a TV so quickly and I didn't have to plead with her to ask Aghajoon.

Unfortunately, Aghajoon did not agree with her and said there were more important things to take care of before buying something just for entertainment.

I knew we would eventually buy one, because Momman had come up with the idea herself. She had a way of getting what she wanted.

Over the next couple of weeks, we heard our parents argue over purchasing a television at least once or twice a day. Momman continued to say the kids would enjoy it, and Aghajoon kept saying we couldn't afford it.

Three or four months later, my parents found out that one of my maternal uncle's friends had left Iran for the United States and sold all his furniture, including a television, to my uncle. As soon as Momman heard her brother had a television, she was determined to get one for her family.

One school night, Aghajoon asked me to go to Takhteh Jamsheed Street with him to check out televisions. That night, Momman had a painful toothache, and her face was swollen. She had wrapped a white handkerchief around her face to cover her cheek to keep it warm and reduce the pain. It was a superstitious ritual my mom believed in.

It took us an hour or so by bus to get to our destination. At the shop, we looked at a few styles of television sets. They were much more expensive than I originally thought. After we had compared their prices, Aghajoon suggested we visit his brother, Amoo Reza. The same uncle who sold us the refrigerator. He and his family lived in the vicinity. I hadn't forgotten how he ripped us off with the refrigerator he sold us, but I felt excited that I was going to see my cousins.

When we arrived at Amoo's house, it was already nine in the evening. My cousins looked very tired, and I felt bad for them. They most likely had eaten their dinner and were ready to sleep. As in many households in our neighborhood, kids were usually fed in the early evening. However, wives waited to eat with their husbands when they arrived home from their shops later at night. My cousins could not sleep since they lived in a one-bedroom house.

My hair stood on end when Aghajoon accepted his brother's dinner invitation. I kept my mouth shut, even though I knew Momman would not like that we spent time with Aghajoon's side of the family.

By the time the brothers finished eating and talking, it was around midnight. They didn't have a phone at home, so we couldn't let our family know where we were. I felt bad for Momman and my siblings because they were probably very worried about us.

As soon as Aghajoon opened the door to our house, there was Momman, with her wrapped-up, scrunched face, angry and staring daggers at Aghajoon. "Where were you all this time? Didn't I ask you to come home early because Mohsen has school tomorrow?"

"Since we were close to my brother's place, we stopped by to visit them. They asked us to stay for dinner, so we did," Aghajoon said, while taking off his shoes. His demeanor was much more casual than Momman's.

"What? You went to your brother's house this late in the evening on a school night, and you had dinner there too? You had a lovely time with your brother while I was suffering with a toothache? If you want to watch a television, just look at my swollen face, the best picture." She removed the handkerchief and showed us her swollen face. I could tell she was in a lot of pain, because she was not able to fully open her mouth to talk.

Aghajoon tried to justify the visit to his brother's house, but it didn't help.

For the next two or three days, our household felt gloomy and sad. Momman had stopped talking to Aghajoon. I think he could not stand seeing her angry face every time she ignored him. To make her happy, he bought a television shortly after that fight. The price was about three thousand tomans, which he paid in installments of two hundred tomans per month.

They told us that they would deliver the television set the next day around four. My siblings and I took turns running to the street and back to see if the delivery truck was coming.

It was late in the evening, around seven, when our doorbell rang. I put my hand on the doorknob to open. Behind me, my siblings had lined up. They were jumping up and down and clapping their hands. We all knew the television delivery guys had arrived.

Momman showed them where to install the television. The two guys took the television out of the corrugated box, placed it close to an outlet, and plugged it in. In those days, TVs had a key to a door that concealed the screen. The delivery guys took the key and opened the console door; six or seven knobs were on one side of the screen, and the speaker was on the other. It stood on four wooden legs.

One guy pulled a knob, which turned it on. It started making a crackling sound and showed static on the screen. I could not wait to see how the images looked. One of the guys left and came back in with a large box that I assumed was the antenna. He went to the rooftop and installed it there. He threw a pink wire down, which was connected to one end of the antenna. The other end he attached to the back of the television. As soon as he did that, the picture became clear and crisp. I quietly observed everything they did, because I would be the one who would have to repair the TV if anything happened.

Before they left, they handed the key to the console to Momman, along with the manual and a one-year warranty paper.

Momman offered the delivery guys some tea and cookies, but they refused. "We have two more deliveries to make before the TV programs end for the day. The owner of the shop wants us to check the quality of the picture when we install a TV, and we can't do that if there is no broadcast."

Momman told us that she would allow us to watch television on Thursday evenings and Fridays only and not on school nights, since we had to study. Once she made that announcement, she turned off the television and locked it.

We all got mad and started pleading. "Please just let us watch it tonight!" Etty said.

As we were arguing back and forth, Aghajoon came home, excited. "Let's see how this thing works! Mohsen, turn it on. I want to make sure everything is okay."

With that, Momman silently handed me the key and went to make tea and bring Aghajoon's dinner.

I gladly opened the console and turned on the television. We all sat down and watched until Momman returned. When she came back, there was a love scene in which the woman was almost naked with a man in bed. They were kissing each other.

"What are you watching? Turn it off! *Now!*" She left the room, saying, "If I had known they showed this kind of program on TV, I would never have asked for one."

That night, we continued to watch until they played the national anthem, indicating that all the programs for the day were over. As I was locking up the television, I checked out the back of it; there was a very thick board with holes for ventilation. I looked inside the holes and saw that many vacuum tubes were still on. I really wanted to open it and explore. I thought, *Maybe later, when nobody else is in the room.*

Friday finally arrived, and I didn't have to hang out at Aghajoon's shop to help. Most of our neighbors, including Iran's family, knew we had bought a television, because they could see the antenna on our rooftop. It was a symbol of pride, especially since our household was the first in the area to own a TV. I asked all the kids in our neighborhood, including Iran and Maheen, to gather at our house to watch *Felix the Cat*. We had the best time and laughed a lot. I wished we could've had some snacks to offer to everyone in the room. It would have made the day just a little bit more fun. Nevertheless, I felt happy that I was able to spend more time with Iran.

A week or so passed, and I was still very curious about how the television worked, so one afternoon when Momman was busy with her sewing in the other room and Aghajoon was still at his shop, I decided to tinker with the TV.

I asked Etty to sit in front of the screen and help me.

"But why?" she said. "What do you want to do?"

"Just sit there and tell me what happens when I move these tubes."

"You are going to mess it up and make Momman and Aghajoon very upset."

"I know what I am doing. I just take one tube out and put it back in. I'm not going to mess it up. It's simple."

"Okay, but it won't be my fault if you break it." She sat there as I unscrewed the brown board on the back of the television. I removed it and set it aside. Then I looked inside, at all the interwoven vacuum tubes of all sizes. Each was stamped with a number and some unknown English words.

I turned the television to the news. "Are you ready, Etty?" I asked.

She nodded, and I reached down and removed one of the tubes. When I took it out, I asked, "Okay, what happened?"

"The sound is gone but the picture is there."

I took another one out and screwed the previous one back in. "How about now?"

"There is no sound and the image is smaller now."

I continued removing one tube and putting back the one I had taken out. "Okay, now what?"

"There's sound, but there isn't any picture," she said, annoyed.

As I continued removing tubes while putting others back in, I started unscrewing more tubes than I was putting back in. I got confused. My heart started pounding, and my face felt hot. I had no idea which tubes went where.

Etty kept repeating, "Oh! No picture, no sound. It is all dark now."

"I know that! Stop telling me over and over again!" I shouted.

Etty shrugged and said, "I told you not to do this. I knew it was a bad idea, and now look what happened."

I ignored her and didn't answer. I was angry and frustrated. I tried to put the tubes back in, but some of them didn't fit in the holes. I hurriedly placed the tubes in the holes; some of them didn't fit but screwed in halfway. Most of them looked crooked. I quickly screwed the board back on and told Etty, "Let's go. And don't tell anyone."

That evening after dinner, Aghajoon wanted to watch some television, so he asked one of my sisters to turn on the TV. Obviously, there was nothing. Etty and I shot a nervous glance at each other. Aghajoon got up, came close to it, and turned it off and on many times. Nothing showed up. He looked at me and said, "You know how to fix things, what's going on here?"

I looked at Aghajoon, with a poker face, and said, "Televisions aren't really my specialty. I don't know how they work."

Aghajoon finally gave up and told us he would call the service department to have it checked. "Good thing we have a warranty on this. It hasn't been a week, and it already needs to be repaired!" He sounded frustrated.

The next day, Aghajoon called a technician to check it out. In one week, my family had gotten so used to watching television that we didn't know how we had spent our free time before that.

Around six in the afternoon the next day, our doorbell rang. I opened it.

A tall man holding a briefcase asked if this was the house with a broken television.

Momman showed up shortly and said, "Mohsen Jon, show him where the television is, then go to the shop and tell your dad the repairman is here."

As usual, Aghajoon asked me to watch the shop while he went home to talk to the TV technician. It didn't take him very long to return, and I could tell from the expression on his face that things worked out. I was relieved. As much as I wanted to ask him if the TV was fixed, I held back. I would know as soon as I went home. *Why aggravate my dad unnecessarily?*

When I got back home, my siblings were watching the television. Etty and I exchanged a smile. As soon as Momman saw me, she said, "Can you believe it? He was trying to blame it on us!"

"What do you mean?" I asked coyly.

"Apparently the tubes in the back were wonky and he said someone had tampered with them, but Aghajoon told him nobody here touched it."

A couple of days passed; I could not hide the truth from Momman for long. My conscience didn't allow me. I confessed to her that I had fiddled with the television and that it was me who took out those tubes.

Momman looked at me with a smile. "Mohsen Jon, it's okay. No harm done. Next time don't hide the truth from me. Don't you feel better now that you were honest and told me what really happened?" She walked away as she patted my shoulder.

The Girl Next Door

Age Eighteen

Money talks. I learned that the hard way.

In our neighborhood, many girls were either younger or the same age as me. We used to play games together, such as catch, hide and seek, and hopscotch; sometimes we just talked.

Over time, two girls, Maheen and Iran, grew closer to each other and they confided their secrets to one another. I used to see them whisper to each other and laugh. In the beginning, all the kids in our alley felt pity for Maheen. She caught polio at a young age and could no longer walk. She had to use crutches. Over time, she proved us wrong by participating in all the plays we played. We no longer noticed her crutches as she was running from one corner to another. She did everything all the girls in the neighborhood did. In no time, she changed pity into admiration through her attitude, charm, and humor. When she grew up, she captured all our attention with her beautiful voice, her loving and kind personality, and her beautiful face.

Sometimes I invited Maheen and Iran to come to our house to watch a comedy show or an American movie dubbed in Farsi on TV. They came with all their sisters to see the programs with my sisters and me. At that time, I was the only teenage boy in the neighborhood. All the mothers who had girls wanted me to marry their daughters, but I grew to care only for Iran.

Maheen's mom always jokingly said, "Mohsen is going to be my son-in-law. He is marrying my daughter."

Maheen and I looked at each other and smiled. She knew I was really in love with her best friend, Iran, the girl next door. I had told her I was planning to marry Iran when I got a decent job and became independent.

My plan was to become a pilot right after high school. Then, I'd go to her house to get her parent's permission to marry her. I never told Iran that, but I think in her heart she knew what my intentions were.

Back then, everyone in the neighborhood had their nose in everyone's business, and rumors traveled amazingly fast. I kept hearing about the son of one nearby neighbor who was interested in Iran. He was planning to send his mother for *khastegari* (marriage proposal).

Khastegari is an old Iranian tradition wherein the females in the suitor's family—usually the mother, grandmother, and aunt—went to the girl's house to ask for her hand in marriage. During this meeting, the girl being wooed often joined the other guests; she brought cups of hot tea on a tray and a bowl full of sugar cubes for the guests, usually serving the elders first. Sometimes the relatives of the suitor asked questions while she stood in front of them, so they had more time to check her out, for example, size of her nose, the color of her eyes, her figure, and her personality, as if they were planning to buy her.

If the suitor's mother was pleased with the girl, both her personality and features, she then asked her family's permission to come back with the other relatives to move further along with the process. In the meantime, both families investigated each other, checking into the gossip and rumors of their neighbors or whoever was willing to share any information about them

Once everyone in the family had approved, the negotiations about the marriage and the wedding ceremony started—for example, the amount of the *mehrieh* (dowry), how many guests they should invite, where the marriage ceremony and reception would take place. These were all discussed and decided.

I had seen Mr. Naderii, Iran's suitor, in the past. He looked much older than her, by at least fifteen years. He was a heavy-set, mustachioed man who wore thick glasses. We never really talked; I just said hello to him out of respect, and then he acknowledged me by nodding his head. I didn't believe the rumor about his affections for Iran until I heard it from

Maheen. Even then, I did not take it too seriously and thought nothing would come of it.

I knew Iran cared for me. Though she never said it, I could see it in her eyes. I didn't ask Iran about Mr. Naderii, because I didn't think she would marry a man who was much older, was not good-looking, and had a big tummy. Iran had said many times she did not like men who were overweight.

A couple of months passed, and I noticed Mr. Naderii's mother visiting Iran's house often, each time with a box of cookies, flowers, or basket of fruit. I didn't let it bother me. Iran and I were still close. She was still coming to our house to watch TV, and I went to their house to visit with her.

One day Maheen said, "It looks like Iran is going to get married soon. Everything seems to be working based on both families' plan. They are going to finalize the agreement tonight."

What could I do? I was an eighteen-year-old boy who hadn't finished high school and didn't have a decent job. Also, my parents, especially Momman, didn't want to hear the word marriage from their children until they'd gone to college. Education was important to Momman; everything else could wait.

Usually, it took some months for both parties to settle all the wedding affairs. The groom's family had to pay for all the wedding expenses, so they wanted to make sure they knew the cost ahead of time. The only items the bride's family paid for were the groom's suit and the bride's dowry.

I had a tough time believing Iran was marrying someone else. When Maheen told me they were finalizing everything tonight, I decided to eavesdrop on their conversation. Later that evening, I marched up and down the alley outside Iran's house to find out who was going to visit her family and when they were going to be there. When I saw a couple of women in their black chadors and Mr. Naderii in a black suit knock on Iran's front door, I knew Maheen had told me the truth. My heart sank and my stomach turned. I didn't know what to do; I felt angry and heartbroken.

I knew they'd take their guests upstairs to their living room to talk about the details of the wedding. Their living room shared a wall with one of our rooms upstairs; it had a French door that opened onto a balcony overlooking their yard—the same balcony from which she had watched the still images on my makeshift projector. A high brick wall separated their backyard from ours.

On that night, I took a long wooden stick and attached a microphone to one end of it. Then I took a receiver and a couple of wires, and I connected the two together. I attached both of the wires to a battery. From the window of our room, I carefully passed the stick through the open rail in front of their balcony and let it rest there. It was dark out, so I didn't have to worry about anyone seeing this little hearing device from their living room. I put the receiver close to my ears and listened to their conversation. I could hear their voices, but the sound was muffled. I could not make out anything from the conversation.

Occasionally I heard the word mehrieh and sometimes their laughter. I didn't give up; I sat there for two hours. I kept listening to comfort myself, and also I didn't know what else to do. I began to feel a sense of loss.

The next day, I ran into Iran coming back from Aghajoon's shop. "Salam," I said, walking beside her.

She didn't acknowledge me and crossed the street.

I think she did not want to be seen with me. I had turned into a stranger to her. How could she throw away our friendship so easily? I felt very sad and confused. I didn't know what to do. I figured her parents had instructed her not to talk to men anymore. If her suitor saw her talking to me, it might make him upset and break the marriage proposal.

Most families wanted to marry off their daughter as soon as they found a suitable husband. Sometimes the girl didn't have the chance or choice to finish high school, especially if she was from a poor family. Iran's family was poor, and there were five other girls. Her parents' intentions were to marry them off to men who were financially stable.

Weeks later, I heard Momman tell Aghajoon that Iran was getting married and that she had asked Momman to make her wedding dress as soon as they bought the fabric. Iran came to our house many times to have her dress fitted. I sometimes saw her in it when I was in the backyard studying. She walked up and down the hallway in her high-heel shoes to make sure her dress flowed well. She looked ecstatic and smiled all the time. The combination of her white satin wedding gown and her fair complexion, long light brown hair, and big brown eyes made her look even more beautiful. She looked so innocent and lovely.

I was crying on the inside, but I didn't say anything to anyone. The most painful part was when Momman asked me to press Iran's wedding dress. I swallowed my tears while ironing the beautiful gown. I did my best to make her dress as beautiful as Iran was. I wished I had been born much earlier so I could have been established by the time Iran turned seventeen.

In my heart, I was hoping for a miracle to prevent the wedding from taking place. But later the following week, Iran got married, and we all attended her wedding. When Aghajoon went to Mr. Naderii to shake his hand and congratulate him, I did not follow him. I could not be happy for the man who had stolen my love from me. I sat at a table where I could see the couple, while people approached them to wish them well and happiness in life together. Iran looked very pretty in her dress and whispered things to her husband that made him laugh. I had lost Iran to a rich man.

I continued running into Iran occasionally since she lived in her mother-in-law's house, which was three doors down from ours. Most of the time, we only said hello and walked by. It felt strange that we had lost our friendship so quickly, and stranger that Iran forgot about me in such a short time, as if I never existed. Maybe the best way for her to cope with it was to pretend that it was never there.

A few months after her marriage, I saw her leaving her parent's house. She had gained a lot of weight and applied very heavy makeup, green eye shadow, and red lipstick. She was not the same skinny, innocent, young girl I knew once. She had become a grown woman overnight.

A year or so later, Iran and her husband bought their own house in a particularly nice part of town. I did not see her very much after that. Frankly, I was no longer interested in her. She was not the same person anymore.

After many years had passed, I heard that Iran had given birth to a little girl. I wished Iran and her family well.

Joining the Military

Being in the military was tough. But if I had a choice, I would do it all over again.

After finishing high school, I took the *concor* (college entrance exam). The exam questions looked quite challenging to me; I wasn't able to answer half of them simply because I didn't understand them. Halfway through the test, I gave up and randomly filled in the circles on the answer sheets.

Some weeks later, when they announced the results, I bought a Keyhan newspaper to find out if I had passed. I didn't wait to get home to search for my name. I stood on the corner of the street, where I bought the newspaper and opened the fold and nervously searched for my last name. I knew I hadn't passed but decided there was no harm in looking; maybe a miracle happened, and my random answers ended up being correct.

When I didn't see my name, I closed the newspaper. On the front page was a large picture of a chubby, nerdy-looking guy with a round, smiley face. Underneath it was a caption saying his name and that he received a perfect score in the exam. I wondered how anyone could answer all the questions correctly. I looked at his picture closely. It seemed that he was laughing at me for not passing the test. Below his name, there were smaller images of nine other kids and their names and ranks.

On the way home, I thought about my various skills. I bet none of those kids on the front page of that newspaper knew how to make an incubator, repair any machine, or fix the wiring of their houses.

When Momman found out I didn't get into any colleges, she told me to sign up for a concor preparation class at Hadaf High School, an hour away from our house by a bus. The fee was about two hundred tomans per month, which was a lot of money for my family, but it was for education, so my parents didn't hesitate to give it to me.

A good friend from high school, Davood, was taking the same class, so we studied together most of the time. Even after all the studying and prep work, the second time taking the exam was just as hard as the first time. The same thing happened: I didn't pass, which was very disappointing for everyone, especially me. I had worked hard, but the competition was stiff; there were hundreds of thousands of students and very few colleges in Iran, so the entrance rate was exceptionally low.

Momman noticed my disappointment and asked me to fix one of her sewing machines to get my mind off things. While I was disassembling it to figure out the problem, the doorbell rang. It was Davood. We greeted each other.

"Guess what?" he said.

I was too deep in self-pity to answer, so I shrugged and went to Momman's classroom to continue working on the sewing machine.

He followed me. "I went to get my concor test score. What do you think I got?"

I was not very enthusiastic to know so I just drearily muttered, "I don't know."

"Three hundred out of one thousand. I did not get even half the questions correct," he said smiling.

He wanted to make me—and probably also himself—feel better by being silly. I thought it was very kindhearted, and it did slightly relieve me.

"When do you plan to sign up for *Sepahii*?" He sat down and watched while I fixed the machine.

Sepahii was a two-year mandatory military program. For the first six months of the program, men and women went to bootcamp. There, they trained to use a gun and learned military skills in case the country went to war. Also, depending on the bootcamp they were assigned to, they were trained in *Sepah-e danesh* (teaching the villagers to read and write), *Sepah-e behduhsht* (teaching the villagers about health), or *Sepah-e tarveej va abadanii* (teaching the villagers about livestock, agriculture, and crops). Each person was stationed at a village for eighteen months to help the villagers with one of the services above.

Davood and I talked for another thirty minutes; he tried to make me laugh by telling me the latest jokes. I knew that it wasn't the end of the world, and the two years would pass quickly. At the door, we planned to go together to sign up.

After registering our names, one of the recruiters gave us a yellow piece of paper with a list of things to buy before reporting for duty. We needed a plate, a cup, utensils, and a bag, and they all had to be green. We also needed some personal items, such as toothbrushes, toothpaste, clothes, socks, and black shoe polish. At the bottom of the page were the names of some stores where we could find the items.

Davood and I both had some money with us, so we decided to make a stop at those stores to buy what we needed before heading back home. All the stores were on Char Rah e Hassan Aband Street. The entire street turned out to be military supply shops. We followed a flock of other young men with the same yellow paper into the largest store on that street.

I looked around. There were various kinds of swords, spears, and army knives behind the counter, and all types and colors of uniforms hung on the walls of the store. The store owner obviously knew we were going to join the army soon and tried to help us look for what we needed.

I found it embarrassing when people could tell I was going in for my two-year service, because it meant they knew I had failed the concor exam. A couple of days before going to bootcamp, I went to the local barber to get a buzz cut; they had told us to get one before reporting or they would give us one at the camp. I had always kept my hair short enough to not need combing, so when I went to Mr. Kianii, the local barber, he didn't have to make it much shorter. I was glad he didn't ask for an explanation, because I wasn't in the mood to give him one.

Later that evening, Momman helped me pack my green bag with my personal belongings, so I could have it ready next to my ironed blue suit. The atmosphere of our house felt gloomy, and Momman cried a lot. She had tears coming down her face while she was arranging my clothes and other items in the green bag. It didn't stop there. At night when she was sewing her customer's clothes, I saw her wipe the tears from her face.

I was sad and nervous and had butterflies in my stomach. I had never been away from home and didn't know what to expect of the army. I was the first boy in the family to join the service. My older cousin, Asghar, had not graduated from high school yet because he had to repeat some of the grades. Akbar was younger than me and was automatically exempt from the service due to being the only son and having a retired father.

Around six o'clock in the morning, Momman woke me to get ready. After having some tea, feta cheese, and bread, I put my blue suit on and picked up my green bag. I hugged and kissed my siblings and my parents.

Everyone was quiet and somber. Momman's tears kept pouring down. As I stepped outside, she had me go under the Qur'an and turn around to kiss its cover. This was an Iranian superstition meant to bestow God's protection. Aghajoon had a bowl filled with water in his hand, which he poured on the ground as I walked away toward the top of our alley— another superstition meant to ensure I would return home safely. Before I turned toward the bus station, I looked back and waved goodbye one last time. Momman kept wiping her face.

On the bus, I found a seat next to a window. When the driver and passengers looked at me, they figured that I was heading for Sepahii. It was the most likely explanation for a young man with a buzz cut, a green bag, and a nervous look. Everyone smiled at me and nodded. Some seemed to be proud of me; others sympathized with me.

I stared out the window to take my mind off my worries. The sky looked gray, and it was drizzling. The wind scattered the red, yellow, and orange leaves across the ground. The bus passed the streets where Akbar and I used to hang out together as little kids and buy things for our projects. I saw the movie theater where I climbed up a pole to see bits and pieces of John Wayne movies. I thought of the silly things I did when I was a little boy, and smiled. The time had gone by fast, and here I was, a twenty-one-year-old going away from his family to learn to be a grown man.

I reached my destination and saw Davood waiting for me at the entrance of a large field. I waved at him, and we joined the crowd of boys with buzz cuts. Occasionally, I saw a boy with long hair. Most of the kids walked around alone; there were only a few like me and Davood who knew each other.

While we were waiting to get instructions about what to do and where to go, Davood and I talked about where we wanted to be stationed, what kind of rooms we would have, and when we hoped to see our families again. Having Davood there helped calm my nerves. We were in it together.

Around eleven o'clock, the heads of the army showed up. They all had serious looks on their faces and numerous medals hanging from their uniforms. Uniformed kids our age kept saying, "Sir, yes sir," while saluting them.

One of the officers roared into a microphone, "I want you to form rows of lines, one hundred people per line!"

The crowd started moving. I looked around; it reminded me of my school assembly when we had to line up before going to our classes. Davood and I decided to stay in the same line, hoping we would end up going to the same place. Other officers walked between us and screamed, "Stupid kids, form a line!"

Rows of lines were formed, and everyone was standing up straight, with their green bag next to them. Nobody dared to say anything.

One of the high-ranking officers came around. He moved from one line to another, assigning the branch of Sepahii

"Sepahii-e danesh," he shouted, pointing at one line.

"Sepahii-e behdash." He pointed at another line.

"Sepahii-e tarveej va abadanii," he yelled, pointing at our line.

Then each branch was assigned a place for bootcamp within Tehran. Mine was stationed in Karaj, which was only two hours from our house. I had heard this branch of Sepahii was the easiest.

After being told where we would go, one of the uniformed drill sergeants came around to take our names. I wanted to say something to Davood, who was standing in front of me and probably just as excited as I was. However, I decided against it. I didn't want to get us both into trouble.

After they assigned everyone a station and a division of Sepahii, another officer screamed into the megaphone, "Each line! Get on a bus so we can head to bootcamp!" If we delayed in following their instructions, the officers started insults: "Stupid kids, stupid brats, lazy kids, move!"

Outside, many long brown military buses were waiting for us. Everyone got into their specific bus, which took them to their bootcamp. Davood and I entered ours. Unlike the city buses, these were very clean, and the upholstery on the seats was well kept and not torn. Davood and I greeted the driver and sat next to each other. The atmosphere inside was happy; everyone was talking and some of the kids in the back were telling each other jokes and laughing.

After everyone got in, the driver closed the door and headed toward Karaj. There were no officers to scream at us, and we could freely move around. A couple of kids started singing and snapping their fingers, some kids began tapping on the back of the seats in front of them to make music, and then a couple of other kids started clapping and dancing. Davood and I, along with many other kids, watched and enjoyed the performances.

We reached the camp, and the driver asked us to get off. We all put on our serious faces and walked into the camp. The camp was a large barren field surrounded with barbed wire.

Officer Ballali, as his nametag indicated, began to scream at us to make a line from tallest to shortest: "This is how you will form the line every time!"

The drill sergeant divided us into two groups of fifty, with each fifty subdivided into rows of ten. The tallest person was positioned in the front and the shortest in the back. As we did this, he continued, "This is the army. Your momma isn't here to take care of you. You have to follow our instructions exactly." He reminded me of my elementary school principal —tall, round face, with mean beady eyes.

'Behind you, there are ten units! Each unit has sixteen beds!" He divided us so that all the tall kids shared the same room, middle height another room, and so on. Davood and I were the same height, but we ended up in two different rooms. "Go find your room, put your bags there, bring your plates and utensils, and then come back to your position!"

We did as we were told; a couple of uniformed drill sergeants stood in the hallway to point us in the right direction. My room had eight bunk beds with grayish blankets and white pillows. There were no dressers, so we kept our possession in the green bags. I chose the bed next to the door. I volunteered to take the top bunk because my bunkmate was overweight. I thought the army would soon get him into shape, but unfortunately it never did. He always bought loads of extra food from the cafeteria.

Many of the richer kids had no problem buying extra food, but that's not what I wanted to spend my wages on. We made about one hundred ninety-nine tomans cash per month. Most of the time, the officers pocketed some of it for various reasons: supplies for the army, additional food, miscellaneous expenses. We all knew the government took care of military expenditures, but nobody could argue for fear of punishment.

As we all got back into position with our plates and utensils, the drill sergeant started screaming at us again: "You dummies have to be faster! This is the army, not your home!"

He began walking us around the facility. "Over there is the kitchen, where we serve breakfast from five-thirty to six, lunch from twelve to twelve-thirty, and dinner from six to six-thirty. If you're late, you have to wait till the next meal!" He smirked as if enjoying the thought of our performing tough routines on a hungry stomach. "You are dismissed to eat!"

Another drill sergeant showed us the way to the kitchen; it was a large place with many tall square tables and no chairs. On each table, I saw a roasted chicken and a large platter of white rice and bread. Ten of us gathered around each table, with our plates. A drill sergeant used a knife and a fork to divide the food among us. I was very hungry and could no longer wait.

As all of us devoured the meal, I looked around and remembered the time my uncle's family was at our house and we served them chicken, and even the bones were chewed. Except here we did not have time to chew our food, we swallowed it. We had to eat, wash our plate and spoon, take them to our room, and form a line—all in thirty minutes.

When we were back in line, the drill sergeant told us he was going to show us how to do the goose step. "Swing your legs from the hip and keep your knees locked." He demonstrated.

On TV, when the army guys marched in front of the shah of Iran for various occasions, it looked easy to perform. I quickly realized it was hard to move our legs back and forth in synchrony. It took our division one month to master it. For the remainder of that day, we practiced our goose steps in our casual clothes. Before he dismissed us to go to our room, the drill sergeant handed each of us boots and two uniforms. One was brown and looked more like a suit. We were supposed to wear it when we had visitors at the camp or went outside, to look professional. The second was green and made from cheap material. This was the one we were meant to wear at bootcamp. At night, before the lights were turned off, they told us we had to be up by five-thirty at the latest, and there would be a wake-up call.

Early in the morning, we woke up to the horrifying sound of a garbage can lid being banged against another lid. The sound was so loud and annoying that we had no choice but to wake up and get ready. The lights came on. I looked out the window, with my eyes half-open; it was still dark. I put my head back down, trying to sleep again. I could hear the commotion in our room, the sound of bags unzipping, and people running in and out of the room, going to the bathroom across from the hall to brush their teeth and shave. Many of my roommates went to the kitchen to eat breakfast before forming the line. I was not hungry, so I skipped it. When things quieted down in the room, I got up to get ready. I put on my green uniform and made it just in time to stand in my line and in my position.

One of the drill sergeants blew into a bugle, making a loud sound. Two other men marched to the flagpole, carrying the flag respectfully and delicately, as if they were holding the Holy Book. I watched them unfold the flag and raise it by attaching each of its grommets to snap hooks on the flagpole. The wind was blowing hard, and the flag was fluttering continuously, highlighting the stripes of green, white, and red. In the middle was a picture of a lion carrying a sword in his right paw, and behind it an image of the sun.

After the assembly, each unit was taken to its training. The head of each unit made up the schedule for his group. Our unit was taken to the field to run for one hour. Leaders ran alongside us screaming, "Come on soldiers, run faster!"

I looked back, and most of the guys were panting and having a hard time catching up, especially those who were overweight. Luckily, when I was seventeen years old, I had joined a local gym and was fairly in good shape, so I was able to finish the one-hour run with no problem. Even though the day was cold and windy, our faces were red and sweaty. Some people were panting and cussing when they completed the run.

Immediately after running, drill sergeants asked us to stand in position and showed us how to do the low crawl. They dropped down on the dirt field and crawled on their elbows, while the rest of their body remained on the ground. Then they stood up and yelled, "Down!"

I didn't have to look back; the loud thumping sound indicated that all one hundred men were on the ground. We all slowly dragged our bodies like caterpillars. The drill sergeants screamed, "Faster, faster! Down, down! Do not lift your head! Hey! I'm talking to you, stupid! Don't raise your head! Imagine your enemy is out there! You don't want him to see you, or he'll kill you! Do you want to die? Keep it down!"

I didn't know who he was talking to, maybe all of us. Even with all the lifting and running at the gym, this practice was hard on my body. My thighs were cramped, my arms hurt, and I heard my heart pounding hard. Sweat was pouring down from under my arm, my face, and my entire body. I was so glad that the weather was chilly. I don't think any of us could have continued this practice in the hot and humid summer days.

Occasionally, I looked up, and it seemed like the more I crawled, the farther the end zone seemed to be. By the time I made it, I was out of breath, tired, and my entire body ached. One thing was for sure: we were all relieved this part was over.

I looked around, and the front of everyone's uniform was covered with dirt, but nobody had the energy to dust it off. Around eleven o'clock, the drill sergeants screamed, "Soldiers, go to your room and get ready for lunch!"

We headed back, tired but happy that we survived the tough routines. We knew the remainder of the day was easy: lunch and then attending a class on how to assemble and disassemble guns.

One day of training completed, 1,079 more days to go.

We had one hour to get ready for lunch. Everyone was either limping or panting. The chubby guy, whose bunk was under mine, plumped down on his bed and said, "Guys, if I die, don't tell my parents it was because of practices; make up a heroic story."

Everyone was in a bad mood and pretended we didn't hear him. The sound of a whistle indicated it was time to go to the kitchen. We all took our plates and utensils and headed down to the cafeteria. We ate our lunch in a hurry and then washed our plate and spoon. When I went back to the room to put them in my green bag, one of the drill sergeants was in the room.

"Everyone! Get in here!" he ordered. When all sixteen of us had gathered, he said, "This is the army! Look at your beds, undone, blankets are all jumbled up, pillows are all in different locations! Your momma isn't here to clean up after you! It's your duty to make your bed every day, blankets tucked in, with sharp edges and the pillow on top!"

We all glanced at each other, thinking now we must wake up even earlier to do another chore before we congregated in the mornings.

"I am going to show you how to make your beds every morning! You cannot make up your own design! This isn't your home! When you finish your bed, it should look like a matchbox, everything tucked in and sharp! Everyone follow the instructions I give you, otherwise you will be punished!"

They treated us like we were little children, getting punished every time we failed to do what we were told. He approached one of the beds and quickly shoved and wrapped the blankets under the mattress snuggly and was done in a noticeably short time. Then, with a profoundly serious look, he said, "Soldiers, you do it now!"

Each of us started working on our own bed. The top bunk was harder because I had to pull and push the blanket while I was sitting on it. The ones who had lower beds stood on the floor and could easily maneuver the bedding. None of us was able to copy what our drill sergeant had done; the bed corners were curved and not the way his looked.

I was frustrated and paused to think that there must be a way to make this work, without putting so much effort into it. I came up with the idea that I could use three pieces of hardboard—two the same length as the mattress and a shorter one. Once inserted into the space between the mattress and the bed frame, I could easily make the three edges look as sharp as a knife. The corner where we put the pillow didn't matter. But would I get in trouble if I brought in hardboard pieces? I decided not to; I didn't want to be punished for something as stupid as the edges of my bedsheets.

On the way out, our drill sergeant removed his army cap and scratched his head. "When you go home, bring three pieces of hardboard to position between your mattress and bed frame so you can achieve the sharp ends."

I stared at him, puzzled. What just happened? Was he able to read my mind? Did he come up with this idea himself, or did everyone in the army do that? It was a strange coincidence. Why didn't he tell us about this trick from the beginning? Did he enjoy looking at us defeated, or did he want us to appreciate his solution more after getting frustrated while trying to make our beds?

After the assembly, our group was guided toward the classroom. It was a large room with many brown metal chairs; a blackboard on the wall; and a large picture of the shah of Iran in his elaborate white uniform, decorated with many medals and an unusual insignia on his shoulders, which I learned was unique to him as supreme commander of the armed forces.

A skinny and short man came in with a thick book. He threw it on his desk so hard that it made a big bang. We got scared and opened our eyes. He laughed sarcastically and said, "Good, now you all seem to be awake. Soldiers, pay attention to what you are taught, because there will be a written test at the end of your six months at bootcamp, and if you don't pass, you will have to retake the training."

The instructor softened his throat and said, "Today, the discussion is about machine guns"—he lifted the one he had in his hands—"and grenades and how to throw them." Then he drew an oval-shaped image on the board with a little tail at the end. "The most common are the time-delay fragmentation anti-personnel hand grenades. The primary function of this kind of grenade is to kill or injure nearby enemy troops. To ensure maximum damage, the grenade is designed to launch dozens of small metal fragments in every direction when it explodes. You want to count to ten before throwing these because if the enemy gets hold of it and throws it back at you, you are dead."

Suddenly, we heard a loud thump from the back of the room. We all ducked, including our teacher, who hid behind the desk.

One of the students in the back giggled and said, "Officer, don't worry. Nobody threw a grenade. Ali fell asleep and is on the floor."

We all burst out laughing. The teacher was the only one who was not. His face turned red, and his eyes bulged out due to anger. He stood up and yelled, "You will be punished for this! I am going to report you to your officer!"

I looked back to see who Ali was. It turned out to be my overweight bunkmate. I sympathized with him. The poor guy had no energy left after running for miles and doing the low crawl. The teacher continued his lecture for another hour, but it was very hard to concentrate after that incident.

The horrifying sound of the whistle indicated it was time to assemble. It was close to sunset, so the flag was going to be brought down and put away. In the line, all of us stood straight, listening to the national anthem, and three of the officers marched toward the pole respectfully, silent and alert. One of them lowered the flag slowly, his admiration for it visible.

Everyone was quiet and watching carefully; the only sounds we heard were the occasional wooing of the wind and the national anthem. Red and yellow clouds splashed across the sky as the sun dipped beneath the horizon. It was very calm and comforting. The three officers unhooked and folded the flag, making sure it never touched the ground. Then they marched back to their original location and waited for the guy to finish blowing the bugle. All these ceremonial procedures gave me goose bumps —an appreciation of what military crew all around the world do to defend their countries.

After dinner, we all conked out around eight, an hour before the mandatory shut-down time. I had never in my life fallen asleep that quickly.

The next day, we woke up to the same horrifying sound of two garbage can lids banging into each other. Although I had slept for almost ten hours, I was still exhausted. I had to power through the aching in my arms and thighs in order to make my bed and get ready for the day. I tried to minimize any involvement with my drill sergeant to avoid any punishments, especially not being allowed to go home on Thursdays.

I had only been at bootcamp for two days and already I missed everything about my family. Before leaving the room, I noticed Ali's bed was already made and he was not there. Had he already woken up and left? Again, I skipped breakfast and made it just in time for the assembly.

After the sunrise flag-raising ceremony, the sound of the whistle indicated it was time to break into our units for the next event. "Soldiers, we are going to warm up with running today!" one of the drill sergeants said, heading toward the barren field.

We followed him. I caught up with Ali on my second lap, while he was still in his first one. He was having a hard time running; he couldn't even bend his knees. "Come on, Ali! The practices should make you stronger, not weaker. You were running faster yesterday."

"That's because yesterday I didn't have all this pain. Today, I do," he mumbled. He was a funny guy, and I was beginning to like him. He had an answer to justify every one of his actions. It never occurred to him that maybe his size and weight had something to do with his being slow.

I smiled and passed him. My legs hurt, but I did my best to tune out the pain and finish the run as quickly as I could. That way, I would be able to relax a bit before everyone else caught up.

At the end of the line, I waited as sweat poured from every pore in my body; my uniform was soaking wet. Every now and then, the cold wind blew on my sweat and gave me a gentle shiver.

Ali and a couple other guys were the last to finish.

The drill sergeant whistled and shouted the moment the last guys were done, "Next, we are going to do *kalagh par*! Squat down, put your palms behind your head, and jump like this," he said, hopping.

Ali was standing next to me. "God, kill me and rid me of my misery," he said while trying to bend his knees. I am sure it must have been hard for him to perform this routine.

We continued this exercise for about one hour; our unit was practically dead by the time we finished. The second day of training was much harder than the first because of our cramped and sore muscles. The sound of the whistle indicated we were done and should get ready for lunch. Same as yesterday, everyone headed to the room to get their plates and utensils before going to the kitchen. Ali and I walked together.

"You know, Mohsen, if I knew the army was going to be so hard, I would have studied harder to go to college."

I looked at him and agreed. "By the way, what happened yesterday? What was your punishment?"

"Don't ask. It'll make me cry," he said. I respected his wish, and we continued walking quietly. I don't know what made him decide to tell me. "I was a guard from 3 a.m. until 6 a.m. That was my penalty," he said, as we entered the kitchen.

"What is that? What did you have to do?" I asked, surprised.

"Oh, nothing, I woke up, made my bed, went to the hallway, and released the first-shift guy, who was walking up and down the hallway. I took over. He went to bed, while I carefully guarded our unit so we wouldn't be attacked by the enemies." He laughed sarcastically. "Yes, enemies. Who are they? I have no clue!"

"Well, this is the army, and you have to do what they tell you to do," I said, handing my plate to the drill sergeant to get my food.

"We had to exchange passwords when the shift changed, for what reason, I don't know," Ali said, shrugging. "Do you think I can last here?" he continued, as we walked to a table to eat our food together. "Mohsen, what are we supposed to be eating?" he asked, swallowing his food.

"*Loobia polo*" (green beans and rice).

"I don't see any green beans, and besides, this thing has no taste or flavor."

"What do you expect? This is the army and not your home. Your momma isn't here to cook for you," I said, trying to imitate one of the officers.

"Yes, sir," Ali said, playing along.

We both laughed. After we finished, we went to our room to put the washed plates and spoons back in our green bags. Around the same time, the whistle sounded. Everyone went outside and formed a line, waiting to find out what our next assignment was.

"Soldiers, go to the classroom," one of the drill sergeants barked.

We sat down in the same seats as the previous day, except this time Ali sat next to me.

"Mohsen, I will die if I have to stay up tonight being a guard again. Please quietly wake me up if I happen to doze off."

The instructor came in with an M16 rifle in one hand and handouts in the other. We looked excitedly at him and his beautiful gun.

Ali looked at me and said, "Don't worry, this is going to be interesting, so I'm going to be alert."

I smiled and said, "I think all of us are."

The instructor held up the rifle. "Class, we are going to talk about the M16 today—how to safely handle it, assemble it, and disassemble it. You, hand these out." He pointed to one of the soldiers in the front row.

When I looked at the rifle, it took me back to my childhood memories and the time Akbar and I tried to make a rifle.

"This is an M16 semi-automatic rifle, but it's all together. Now, how do you take it apart to clean it?" he said, holding up the rifle.

It was a magnificent gun; I hadn't seen anything like it before. Iran bought all its military supplies from the United States—airplanes, weapons, military communication equipment, etc. Iran had a great relationship with the U.S. during the shah's rule.

The instructor resembled Mr. Mohammadi, Akbar's brother-in-law, who taught us how a gun worked. He had a similar husky build, short curly hair, and a pompous attitude. Even his round, acne-scarred brown face, and beady eyes reminded me of Mr. Mohammadi.

He cleared his throat to get our attention. "Next week, each of you soldiers will receive one of these guns and will be responsible for keeping it clean. To do that, you have to disassemble it, wipe down the pieces, and then reassemble the unit," he lectured, while taking the rifle apart. "Press the spring clip and release the barrel band, then remove the upper-hand guard and the barrel. Next remove the trigger housing pin and the trigger housing. Remove the recoil spring and guide it out of the face of the receiver and remove the operating rod. Finally, there's the bolt to remove, and then you have a fully stripped M16," he said.

That was fast, I thought. It might have taken him less than a minute to do all this.

"I and some of the other army folks can do this blindfolded," he said arrogantly.

Ali and I looked at each other, amazed.

"Next I am going to reassemble it blindfolded." He covered his eyes and skillfully put everything back together, while telling us the names of each part he was picking up. At the end, he lifted the gun, all in one piece. "If I had bullets, this gun could be used to shoot."

The rest of the time, the instructor talked about gun safety and how we were responsible for what we did with our guns. "Never point it at any of your fellow army men, even if you're sure it's not loaded," he said with a frown. Then he continued with a brief description of how to shoot an M16.

I wished they had given us each a gun to practice with while he was demonstrating; it would have been easier to follow. When the sound of the whistle blew, he dismissed us. We stood up to leave the room. It was almost sunset and time to lower the flag.

The second day was over, and we had all made it. I couldn't wait for the third day to begin. The quicker these days passed, the faster we arrived at Thursday, when we could go home. I was filled with joy.

The rest of that week followed a similar routine. We practiced goose steps, running, and crawls in the morning, followed by our meal, then a class in the afternoon regarding various military topics. They taught us about guns, types of bullets, military equipment, diseases we might catch in a war zone, and how to hide ourselves during the day and at night.

Finally, Thursday arrived. The bootcamp had a different feeling to it. All the young recruits were exceptionally cheerful, and nothing bothered us anymore. Every time we left the site to go home, we made a line. The officers came around to check our uniforms for cleanliness and flawlessness; no tears or missing buttons were allowed. Our boots had to be polished and shining. We had to look crisp when we went out.

Everyone from our unit went home because we were all from Tehran. Most of the kids took the bus, but some rich kids had cars to transport them back and forth. Sometimes, these kids gave the officers a ride, and in return, the officers occasionally gave them a day off.

Every week, two men out of all of us had to stay behind. They were *pasdar* (guards). I don't know what their job was, but I think it might have been guarding the surroundings, making sure everything stayed secure. During their shift, each guard had to march up and down the hallway to make sure nobody came in. Guard duty had three different shifts: nine to midnight, midnight to three, and three till six in the morning. Each guard woke the other one up before his shift was over.

Going home the first week was an unbelievably happy occasion. We left the facility early in the morning. Before they released us, the drill sergeants gave us instructions: "I want you to sew an elastic band at the bottom of your pants so you can tuck them into your boots. I also want to see your names sewed on the pocket of your tops."

We took our green bags, boots, hat, and uniform and headed toward the same brown bus. The bus was filled with laughter, singing, dancing, and clapping. Davood sat next to me and whispered, "These kids are *alakii khosh*" (happy for nothing).

I sort of agreed with him but didn't make any comment.

While we were riding the bumpy road, Davood turned to me and said, "Today I realized how much I want to go to college. I am going to study extremely hard as soon as I get out of the service to pass the concor exam."

I wished the same thing but didn't say anything to Davood. Instead, I promised myself that as soon as I left Sepahii, I would hit the books to be able to enter the college of my choice. The army had already taught us both that if we didn't get a college degree, we were going to have a hard life.

I eventually reached my house and rang the doorbell. Momman opened the door, screamed my name, and hugged me when she saw me.

While we were having lunch, I talked about bootcamp. "I am stationed at Karaj and will be able to come home every Thursday and leave on Friday around 2 p.m.," I said, chewing on a piece of bread.

Momman kept repeating, "Thanks be to God, thanks be to God. You are so close to us, only two hours away."

Later in the afternoon, all my siblings came home from school; they were glad to see me. My young sisters climbed all over me, while my twelve-year-old brother, Saeed, grabbed hold of my uniform and put it on. It looked way too big on him.

He kept asking, "Where is your gun?"

I looked at him, smiled, and said, "They haven't given me a gun yet."

His disappointment only briefly stopped him in his tracks, before he went back to marching up and down the room in my large new boots. He kept tripping, but he didn't give up.

During dinner, my parents asked me how things were at bootcamp. I explained what we did and informed them not to worry if some Thursdays I didn't come home. I didn't explain that it might be because I was being punished.

The next day, I slept till ten, which was very unusual for me. Momman realized I was very tired, so she didn't let any of my younger siblings wake me up. The atmosphere had turned gloomy by noon. Everyone could sense my approaching departure.

I told Momman I needed to insert an elastic band at the bottom of my uniform pants, per army instructions. I put on my uniform so she could mark my pants and sew the band. She knelt to fold them in, then she looked up and asked, "Mohsen Jon, is this good?" she said in a trembling voice and teary eyes.

I could not say anything and only nodded my head to say it was fine. I was afraid I might cry if I opened my mouth.

While Momman was sewing the elastic band on, I stitched my name tag on the left pocket of my uniform. We both listened to the *Golhayeh Rangarang* program on the radio. The classical music fit our dispirited mood. Momman sniffled while she guided my pants under the sewing machine. She fought back the tears as well as she could, but I could hear her. I knew everyone would eventually adapt to my schedule. Until then, we were going to have to suffer through it.

The time for my departure arrived. I hugged and kissed everyone before I headed out. I assured everyone, including myself, that before long I would be back.

I crossed the street and noticed my reflection in the storefront window. I hated seeing myself in my uniform. It reminded me I had failed the college entrance exam and was a loser. On the way to the army bus, I ran into some people whom I had done electrical work for. I tried to avoid their stares by looking in another direction. I didn't want them to find out I hadn't passed the exam.

Unfortunately, one of them recognized and stopped me. "You look good in that uniform. I didn't know you were in Sepahii."

I smiled and said, "I just signed up and am stationed in Karaj."

"That's good, which branch?" he asked.

"*Tarveej va abadanii,*" I answered, looking at my watch to pretend I was late. "I'm sorry, I'm late for my bus. Goodbye."

I didn't wait for them to respond, and crossed the street, walking between motorcycles and cars. I knew what I did was considered very rude, but I wasn't in the mood to talk about Sepahii.

At the station, many kids were waiting for the bus to arrive. The atmosphere in the bus was sad, and nobody spoke. We busied ourselves by looking outside or placing our heads on the back of our seats, trying to take a nap.

When we arrived at camp, the kitchen was open for dinner, but I didn't go. I had no appetite. Around nine o'clock, the lights were turned off, a sign that it was time to sleep. We all lay down in our beds. I knew everyone remained awake for at least an hour or so, but nobody said anything. We were all thinking similar thoughts: *Will I be able to follow instructions this week? Will I be able to avoid getting any punishments?* Gradually, my eyes got heavy, and I fell asleep.

Life at bootcamp dragged on for six months. We had to constantly obey all the rules or be severely punished. We could not say anything to our officers for fear of being penalized and not being able to go home— the worst punishment. Many times, I felt they were pushing us to our limits just to see what we could stand. The condescending comments never ceased either. Many times, I wanted to speak up, but I bit my tongue.

However, there was one time I could not hold back any longer. The day felt very cold, our teeth were chattering, my entire face was numb, and I am sure everyone else's was too. On that day, officer Ballali said, "Hey wimps, you need to work harder and faster."

I said, "Sir, we are very cold, and you keep telling us to work faster, and that we are bunch of sissy soldiers. But I can tell you are cold too, because you put your hands inside your jacket pockets to keep warm."

He bulged his eyes at me, surprised that I dared to insult him in front of all my fellow unit mates and drill sergeants. He walked away and didn't say anything. To this date, I don't know what came over me. I knew I was going to get in serious trouble, but I was sick and tired of constantly being called names like "stupid," "idiot," and "spoiled."

For someone who thrived on being creative and working on a variety of projects, this place had nothing to offer me. The next day, my punishment started. Suddenly, I was ridiculed more than anyone else in my unit. The drill sergeants constantly picked on me: "Solider, how long have you practiced goose-stepping?"—pointing at me—"You are not following the instructions; you're messing it up completely!"

I knew then that I was in trouble.

BULLSEYE

AGE TWENTY-ONE

I cheated the first time, but the second time I mastered the art.

One afternoon, one of the drill sergeants said, "Today, you will receive a gun, which you are responsible for. Every day, you will retrieve it in the morning and turn it back in at the end of the day. You are to carry this gun with you at all times. This gun is glued to you even during your exercises."

I looked around the room to see the expression on my teammates' faces. Nobody looked thrilled. I thought, *Some of these guys are so small that they have a demanding time carrying themselves, let alone a big gun hanging from their shoulders.* It was not as though any of us were weak, but none of us was the kind of man who enjoyed carrying around a heavy gun. The drill sergeants called our names and gave us the number of our assigned guns: "Mohsen Fashandi, #225; Ali Fazli, #226," and so on until everyone had a gun. We headed toward the armory, where they kept all the M16s. A drill sergeant was standing at the door watching the soldiers going in and out. Rows of shiny guns were mounted on the walls, with a number above each gun. The same number was written on the handle.

The scene reminded me of the time Akbar and I discovered the gun shop on Ferdousi Street, and he encouraged me to enter the shop even though our clothes were torn and shabby looking. The only difference was that this time I was neither eager nor excited to touch the guns—maybe because everything was forced on us, and I didn't really have a choice in the matter. I searched for my assigned number and found it easily. I picked up the gun and was surprised that it was much lighter than I had expected

—maybe three kilos. I ran outside while carrying the gun to join the rest of my unit in the field.

Once everyone had arrived in line with their gun, the group drill sergeant showed us how to clean, disassemble, and reassemble the gun. This was a repeat of what the instructor had shown us on the second or third day at the camp, except this time it was hands-on. Some of us got it after the first demonstration, but for others, it took some practice.

Every morning, we checked out our guns and formed a line to start our routine while the gun hung from our shoulders. It was exceedingly difficult to go through training with this piece of metal hanging from our shoulders. The constant shouting and whistleblowing reminded us that we had no choice but to obey the orders.

"Soldiers, you need to work harder! Wimps! What would you do if this were a war zone?"

Ali, who was crawling next to me, mumbled under his breath, "If this were a war, we would've already died by now and been set free."

During the winter, the snow made our training even harder; the ground was slippery, and performing the low crawl was torture. The front of our uniforms got wet and muddy while we slithered.

When the drill sergeant dismissed us at the end of the day, each team headed back to their group dorm after checking in their guns. I looked around to check out the other men. We were all cold, muddy, and exhausted. In our rooms, we took turns hanging our uniforms to dry. It felt exceptionally good to change clothes and get into our dry, warm long johns.

Exactly one month later, right after the flag-raising ceremony, the drill sergeant from every corner screamed, "Soldiers, get into the bus! We plan to practice shooting M16s!"

They had told us about this event, but I didn't think it was going to happen so quickly. As I sat down on the bus, with my gun between my legs, I took the opportunity to take a quick nap. The nightmarish sound of the whistle jolted me out of my slumber as we approached our destination.

We were in a vast, barren field encircled with barbed wire. Black-and-white target stands were placed on the ground. The freezing air smacked me right in the face. I started shivering and exhaling wispy clouds with every breath.

"Everyone, pick up a helmet and put it on, we pair you up with another solider, and lie on the ground! Whoever is shooting should be on the right, and the shooter's assistant should be on the left! Before you lie down on the ground, decide who wants to be the shooter first! Then position yourself."

The sergeant paired me with Mustafa, who like me, was of smaller stature. We decided that I'd be the shooter first. Fifty paired-up soldiers were waiting patiently for the drill sergeant's order to start shooting the target in front of them—thirty-two meters away. I adjusted my gun and waited for one of the drill sergeants to hand me the ammunition.

While we were waiting, the drill sergeant shouted, "When you are done shooting, place your gun on your right-hand side! You can't stand up under any circumstance! Even if you are dying, you have to be in this position! If something goes wrong with your gun or if you have a question, raise your left hand and one of us will approach you to answer it!"

During the practice, one of the drill sergeants told us that some years ago, he had to kill one of the soldiers because he stood up in the middle of the exercise. He thought the soldier was going to start firing at other people, so he shot him in front of everyone.

As I was lying there, something in my pants pocket started to bother me. Earlier that day, I had borrowed a pencil from Ali to write a note; instead of returning it, I put it in my pants pocket. I felt extremely uncomfortable but didn't have any choice but to leave it there until we were permitted to move. The snow beneath us was starting to melt into my uniform, soaking and freezing me to the bone. I'm sure it was the same for the rest of my unit. My teeth were chattering, and the pencil in my pants was starting to dig into my thigh.

Finally, the drill sergeants came around and handed the bullets to the shooters' assistants. "Don't load them until we tell you," they screamed.

Each drill sergeant was responsible for ten soldiers, and they all looked extremely nervous, especially after passing out the ammunition. I assumed they were worried that one of us might go berserk and start firing at everyone. Nobody in my unit looked crazy, but there were some kids who jokingly made comments like "Just shoot me and set me free."

"Pass the ammunition to the shooter and let them load!" the drill sergeant hollered as they were walking around in between us to monitor the activities.

I pressed the release button on the gun. The magazine popped out. I heard the clicks all around me of everyone loading their gun at the same time. Nobody could talk except the drill sergeants and the officers.

When everyone's gun was loaded, the drill sergeants blew their whistles and shouted, "Stay in your position and on the count of three, start firing... one... two... three... fire!"

When I pulled the trigger, the gun made a deafening noise, and the shell came out of the side of the gun and fell to the ground near me. I had to hold onto the gun firmly so the shot wouldn't recoil against my shoulder every time I fired. I was concentrating so hard that I didn't know what was happening around me. I kept thinking, *Where are the bullets going? Am I hitting the target?*

After a while, all the shooting stopped, and everything quieted down. I couldn't wait to find out how well I did.

"I hope I can do this," Mustafa said, before the drill sergeant's booming voice interrupted him.

"Shooters! Stand up and go to your target to find out how well you did! We will come around to give you a score!"

As I hesitantly approached my target, I discovered that I had only made four hits at the edges. It turned out that my aim was terrible, and the sergeants were either going to mock me, punish me, or both.

While I was waiting for the drill sergeant to approach me, I suddenly remembered that I had a pencil in my pocket. My mind formulated an idea, and I took out the pencil. Carefully, I looked around to see if anyone was watching me. The coast was clear, so I quickly poked a few holes in the target's bullseye to make it appear I had hit it perfectly three times. I darted my head around as I put my pencil back in my pocket. Everyone was busy, and nobody seemed to have noticed my misdeed.

What I did was not daring or brave, but I did it because I figured it was not going to hurt anyone. If I had gotten caught, I would have been in a lot of trouble, I am sure. I stood next to the target and waited for the drill sergeant to evaluate my shooting and give me a score. Once he approached me, my heart started pounding, and I made a quick prayer.

He looked at the target and said, "Good aim."

I just stood there, chest out and straight. "*Sepas sarkar*" (thank you, sir), I said. I touched the pencil in my pocket and, in my mind, thanked God.

Before I lay in my position next to Mustafa on the ground, I took out the pencil from my pocket and set it next to me. "Your turn, Mustafa," I said happily.

He looked at me. Tears were running down his cheeks. "Please, can you shoot instead of me? I have a wife and a two-year-old daughter. I don't want to die."

During practice, the drill sergeant had informed us that sometimes the bullet gets jammed in the barrel and explodes—causing both the shooter and the people around him to die. I think Mustafa was concerned that might happen to him, and maybe he had heard other horror stories. I had never seen a grown man cry and didn't know how to react to it. The only thing I could do was agree to shoot for him. I told him since our heads were down and we're the same height and stature, nobody would realize if we switched places.

"I am going to look around. When I say *go*, you crawl over me to change positions," I whispered.

While the drill sergeant was occupied with ordering, screaming, and whistling, I timed the switch. "Go!" I told him.

He went over me so quickly that it surprised me. It was like he had done it dozens of times. We moved around a little bit to get into the perfect position. We kept our heads down to not be recognized. I noticed the drill sergeants started tensing up again and getting nervous since shooting was about to start again.

The same instructions as the first round were repeated. "Under no circumstance are you to stand up or we will have to shoot you down! Place your gun on the right-hand side when you are done shooting! If you have any questions, raise your left hand!"

I had learned what to expect, so the second time, my experience was completely different. The gun didn't recoil against my shoulder as hard as the first time, nor did the loud noise bother me as much. When we were told to inspect the target, I told Mustafa to go because they knew my face from the first round.

I curiously watched Mustafa as he approached, wondering how well I did this time. The drill sergeant showed up next to him and evaluated the target. I saw that they exchanged a few words.

Then Mustafa ran back and shook my hands. He cheered, "You hit the target eight times, four times right in the bullseye!"

I had done better for Mustafa than for myself! Even counting the three pencil bullseyes, I had hit the target only seven times.

Around four o'clock, we headed back to bootcamp. I was hungry and tired but happy the day was over. Mustafa and I never spoke about what we did that day, but we nodded to each other whenever our eyes met.

THE VILLAGE

AGE TWENTY-TWO

Life in the village was simple. God's will was supreme, and the villagers were content with what He granted them.

The best part of bootcamp was the time they took us to the farm, which was within walking distance. This area was a vast field with all kinds of animals. There were cows, bulls, chickens, roosters, ducks, sheep, and goats all roaming around. Luckily, it was wintertime, so the place didn't stink.

The instructor showed us how to check the animals' health. He grabbed a sheep, bent down, opened its mouth, and looked inside, "Check for thrush in here, teeth should not be broken, and the gums should not be swollen. Animals don't eat if they have pain inside their mouth." He let go of the sheep and pointed at a cow. "If a female is in heat, she will secrete mucus from her vagina, make noises, and you'll see them curl their lips and raise their heads. When we find out the animal is in heat, we bring in the strongest and biggest male to mate with her." The instructor pointed at a couple of large bulls grazing.

The instructors also taught us about plant diseases and their treatments.

I tried to retain as much of the information he was conveying as possible. They had told us that the top soldiers take priority, choosing their province of choice for the second part of their Sepahii. I wanted to be one of them so I could select a place close to Tehran to be able to visit my family on a regular basis.

One week before the completion of our six-month bootcamp, the atmosphere in the camp drastically shifted. The drill sergeants started letting us sleep in, there were no more practices in the mornings, no goose steps, and no afternoon classes.

The day of our departure finally arrived. We were done with bootcamp. The drill sergeant announced our scores. These were an accumulation of how well we did in our practices and the grades we received on the quizzes. The scores were posted on a board from highest to lowest.

I walked to the board, certain my name would be at the top. I started at the top but didn't see it; it was not in the middle either. I was beginning to think they had forgotten about me. I was still scanning the board up and down when I saw Mohsen Fashandi at the very bottom of the list. That's when I figured out Officer Ballali's true punishment for disrespecting him. This was how he demonstrated his power over me.

The drill sergeants escorted us in groups of fifty, starting with the top scorers, to select the villages where they wanted to go. I noticed that most were not diligent students; they were the rich kids who gave rides to the officers on Thursdays. That's when I realized that sometimes in life, it is all about who you know and not how hard you work.

I was in the last group of fifty, and Mashhad was the only place available, so I had no choice. In a way, it worked out nicely for me because Etty attended Mashhad University.

Before we left bootcamp to go home, Officer Ballali shook everyone's hands, talked to each person, and handed him one thousand toman cash as he moved to the next person. This was the money the government gave us to cover our travel expenses to get to our designated villages. When he reached me, he quickly gave the money without shaking my hand, looking at me, or speaking to me. He didn't even give me the chance to apologize —not that I would have; I was seething under my composed exterior.

As I stepped into the green bus to take me home, I looked back to take another look at the wide barren field and all the memories that would remain with me for the rest of my life. The army had trained me to be more responsible, tolerant, and quicker. I hated to admit it at the time, but the army turned me into a man. Davood stepped onto the bus, shook my hand, and sat next to me. He told me that he was stationed in Isfahan, a fourteen-hour drive from Mashhad. It was obvious I wouldn't be able to visit him, so I promised to catch up with him whenever I was in Tehran.

Ali came in shortly after and told me he chose Mazandaran. Ali was much closer to Tehran than either Davood or me. He could visit his family more often. As hard as I tried not to let it bother me, it did. I had worked harder, but he had the better assignment.

I had two weeks to prepare for my trip to Ferdous, a village in Mashhad. Every day, I shopped for different items I thought I would need: stuff for personal hygiene, some clothing, and a large suitcase. We couldn't afford to travel, so we didn't have a suitcase at home.

The night before my departure to Mashhad, the house was very quiet. Everyone knew I wouldn't be able to come home every Thursday anymore. I wouldn't be able to call home since the village most likely didn't have a phone. My only way of staying in touch with everyone was to write letters. On my day of departure, I wore my regular clothes—a shirt and a pair of slacks—and said goodbye to my family. I hated saying goodbye. The word seemed so final, so separating . . . Though I knew it was only for a short time, the word made me feel even more distant.

I had butterflies in my stomach and tried ridiculously hard not to cry. I picked up my suitcase filled with personal belongings and headed out before my sadness had a chance to burst out of me. Momman asked me to go under the Qur'an and turn around to kiss its cover to be protected by God. Aghajoon had a bowl filled with water in his hand, which he poured on the ground as I walked away. I couldn't look back and wave. I was already crying and on the verge of losing all control over my emotions.

It took twelve hours to get to my destination by bus. The next day, I went to the Department of Agriculture in Mashhad. There, I ran into Naser, whom I trained with during bootcamp. On our last day in bootcamp, he mentioned to me that he was very happy to be stationed in Mashhad. He and his family used to live there, and some distant relatives still resided in parts of the city. After talking to some of the men at the desk, he approached me and shook my hand.

"I'm glad to see you here," I said, putting my things down.

"Don't get excited yet. They still don't know where they're going to station me."

Puzzled, I asked him what he meant. He whispered, "Well, things are not very organized. When I came here, they told me they didn't know where to send me. They are waiting to figure out what to do with me. In the meantime, they've given me a room. I am sure it will be the same with you. Here, let's go find out about your situation," he said and tugged at my sleeve to follow him.

As Naser had predicted, they had no idea where to send me either. They told me to share a room with Naser until they assign me to a village. As we were heading out, one of the men at the desk said, "By the way, it's mandatory to have your uniform on at all times."

I looked at the tall and chubby Naser and noticed he was also wearing civilian clothes. I didn't mind putting on the army clothes here; nobody knew me in Mashhad, so I didn't have to explain to anyone the reason I was wearing it. I accompanied Naser to his place, a couple of blocks away —a small room with two beds, just enough space to move around without running into each other. In the hallway was one bathroom that we shared with ten other men. They also were waiting to be stationed in a village somewhere in Mashhad.

"Is there a restaurant close by? I have not eaten all day!" I said, as I changed into my uniform.

Naser took me to a small place; the food arrived soon after we ordered it. The waiter brought two platters of rice topped with saffron, two skewers of kabab, and barbecue tomatoes on the side. Naser ordered two glasses of doogh.

My mouth was watering, I couldn't wait any longer. I ate everything, down to the last grain of rice on my plate. The food was delicious, and it filled me up. Naser and I sat there and talked about memories from bootcamp. I told him how Officer Ballali had punished me by giving me the lowest score in our group. "I studied all the time and followed instructions. Yes, I made a mistake and stood up to him, but he should have been a bigger man and forgiven me. I think that would have taught me a better lesson than taking revenge."

Naser didn't say anything at first; he just nodded in agreement. After a short silence, he said, "I don't think we will be going anywhere for at least a few days. Do you want me to show you around Mashhad? How about we visit the Imam Reza shrine. Whoever comes here for the first time has to pay respects to him."

The idea sounded fine to me, so the following day, we took the bus to the shrine of Imam Reza. We got on without paying any fee. I whispered to Naser, "The guy didn't ask for the fare."

"If you have an army uniform on, you don't pay," he said.

It reminded me of the times when Akbar and I came up with all kinds of plans to trick the bus driver.

I looked out the window. Beautiful white and pink azaleas and tall green plants were everywhere. The city was beautiful and immaculate. I hadn't seen plantings on any of the Tehran streets I used to go to. The tall golden dome of Imam Reza shrine appeared in the distance, and I knew we were getting closer.

At the entrance door, I looked at the beauty of the shrine. The walls were covered with intricate square and octangular designs made with blue, white, and yellow tiles. I had been to shrines in Tehran, but none were this magnificent; beautiful verses from the Qur'an were written in between the tiles.

Inside, many arch-shaped doors led to where the imam was buried. White and gray pigeons were cooing while pecking on the ground to eat the seeds some visitors threw for them. In the middle of the courtyard, the sound of water was very soothing and serene. Naser and I joined the other people at the fountain, rolled up our sleeves, and performed *wudu* (a ritual of washing one's hands, face, and feet before praying or reciting the Qur'an). Women did the same thing, but in another section, away from the presence of men. Before entering the courtyard of Imam Reza, women who were in miniskirts or other secular clothing covered themselves with black chadors because Islam forbids males from looking at female hair or other body parts, unless the man and woman are related.

We took off our boots and gave them to a bearded old man behind a counter and received a number.

"Watch your wallet, there are many pickpockets here," Naser warned me.

We went into one of the many hallways leading to the shrine; Naser told me there were eight entrance doors because Imam Reza was the eighth successor after the Prophet Mohammad. The sweet aroma of rosewater filled the area. It felt good to walk in my socks on the beautiful marble floor. The ceiling, with its many elegant crystal chandeliers, was decorated with fine small mirrors and tiles.

"Naser, this place is spotless. How can a public place be so clean?"

"Every night, dozens of workers come in to sweep, dust, and polish this area," he said. In every corner, men were on the floor reciting the Qur'an, praying with their lips, while moving their rosary beads one by one. Some had their hands up, pleading to God; others were crying and wiping their tears. Everyone was in their own world.

Around the grave was a *zarih* (grilled lattice structure) coated with gold and silver and beautifully decorated hand carvings. Naser and I joined many other visitors and went around it, touching each small opening of the grill, putting our foreheads there, and kissing the metal out of respect. Some people tied a green piece of thread or a lock onto the grill, leaving it there until the imam granted their wish. Men and women threw coins, tomans bills, or wish letters through the openings of the grill. A lot of money was collected; I am sure some of it was used to pay for the maintenance of the shrine. I put my head on the grill and closed my eyes. I asked God to keep my family healthy and help me pass the college entrance test to enter a university after I finished my Sepahii duty.

At the end of our visit, we stepped backward, careful not to run into anyone. When we reached the door, we bowed with respect and left.

"Mohsen, you are very lucky. If you came here on Fridays or any other holy day, there would be so many visitors that you can't even touch the silver grill."

We spent the rest of the day walking around Mashhad, eating food, and having a pleasant time. For the next couple of days, our routine was to check with the office about our status, and after they informed us that there was still no news regarding our assignments, Naser continued to show me around town. He turned into my tour guide in Mashhad and did a great job.

Finally, after almost a week, we were told that Naser was going to Neyshahpour, and I was going to Ferdous. They gave both of us the address of the Department of Agriculture. We gathered our belongings, hugged, and wished each other good luck. I thanked Naser for showing me around. I never saw him again after that day.

I took the bus and headed to Ferdous, a small city about 340 kilometers south of Mashhad. While I was in bootcamp, I had heard on the radio that two consecutive earthquakes had occurred in two villages close to one another. The first, measuring about 7.3 on the Richter scale, happened in Dasht e Bayaz; a day later, an aftershock measuring 6.4 hit Ferdous. The report said the quake had destroyed about 175 villages, killing close to twelve thousand people. The shah of Iran, the queen, and the prime minister visited the area many times to try to comfort the victims and provide aid to their families.

When I got on the bus, I sat in the front seat to talk to the driver. The bus was in even worse shape than the one I rode coming to Mashhad. The seats were torn; some of the windows were cracked; and it smelled like combination of body odor, cigarette smoke, and mold. Most of the passengers were bearded men in black turbans; they had come to Mashhad to visit the shrine of Imam Reza to pray. Others were there with their wives and children.

I was extremely nervous and afraid of how things would work out in the new location; I didn't know anyone in Ferdous. The driver was concentrating on the road, so I decided to relax. I put my head back and closed my eyes. Everyone on the bus was quiet, and I easily sank into sleep. I was in a half-asleep daze when the driver announced, "We are in Ferdous." I shook myself awake and got off.

Immediately, I noticed the ruins of clay buildings everywhere. People had set up tents to live in until their homes were fixed. It seemed that not much had been done in the way of repairs. While walking, I peeked into one of the tents, out of curiosity. The ground was covered with flattened cardboard boxes, pillows, and blankets. In the corner, there was a lantern and a small heater to warm up the place and cook.

When I reached the Department of Agriculture, it was like night and day. The building looked as though it hadn't been damaged at all by the earthquake.

I approached a man at the desk. "Salam, I come from Mashhad. They told me to contact you to be stationed at Ferdous," I said, placing my belongings on the floor.

He got up and left without saying anything. Shortly after, he came back with another man. He was in his mid-thirties, with a mustache and a receding hairline.

"This is Aghayeh Mohandes" (Mr. Engineer), the first man said.

We shook hands. "I am Mohsen Fashandi and they told me you need someone in Ferdous."

Mr. Engineer scratched his head, looked at the other man, and said, "Frankly, we don't need anyone here, but let me see what I can do for you. Where are you from?"

"Tehran," I said.

"There are some others from Tehran here. Let me take you to them until I figure out what to do with you."

Mr. Engineer had a car and a chauffeur. I picked up my suitcases and followed him outside. On the way to meet the others, I saw more destruction from the earthquake. I stayed with two soldiers for a couple of days, until I was assigned to Arask, a nearby village. The following day, those soldiers gave me a ride to the village; Mr. Engineer followed us in his car.

When we arrived, I noticed the houses were flat-roofed and made of clay. We parked and walked the remainder of the way to the house of Hussein Partovii, the village teacher, who was originally from Ferdous. I was to stay with him until I could rent my own place. It started pouring hard, and the pleasant aroma of first rain filled the area.

The village looked like a maze; one alley led to another, reminding me of when I went to the bazaar to buy shoe supplies for Aghajoon. I couldn't figure out how anyone found their way around, especially since the houses all looked the same. Caravans of camels with loads of dried branches on their back walked by, with their owner guiding them. Mesmerized, I stood there and watched them pass by me. The sound of slow and rhythmic bells tied around the camels' necks reminded me of some of Omar Khayyam's famous poems. "This is so beautiful," I said to Mr. Engineer.

He shook his head and laughed. He continued with his walk. I guess he was used to seeing scenes like this. A couple of times, I had to move aside to let the local people riding on their donkeys pass.

"Is there any power here?" I asked.

"There is no plumbing or power here."

"No plumbing or power?" I emphasized.

I found myself wishing I were back at bootcamp. The training was difficult, but at least we had clean water and electricity.

We reached Hussein Partovii's place. He welcomed us and shook our hands. His place was painted white and had a cheap rug on the floor, a lantern, and a heater. Next to it were well-used copper pots and pans. The aroma of rice and gheymeh, mixed with tomato sauce and yellow peas, blanketed his entire room. He had made a delicious meal and asked us to stay.

After lunch, Mr. Engineer and the other two soldiers returned to their offices in Ferdous. Hussein and I walked toward the house of the *kadkhoda* (village chief). On the way, he showed me the different facilities. "This is the public bath," he said. "It's open to men on Thursdays and Fridays and to women on Wednesdays. The rest of the time, it's closed." He pointed at a small clay structure. "And this is the Bank of Saderat. You can do all your banking here."

I looked at the small place and wondered how they operated with no electricity. The post office was the most interesting of all: it was a grocery store with all kinds of items—potatoes, onions, dried legumes, flour, sugar, and other things. On the counter, I saw a metal box with a slot to drop in letters. The old, bearded merchant went to town once a week to bring in more supplies; at that time, he took the mail with him.

At the door of the kadkhoda's house, Hussein paused for a minute to tell me that a bus went to Mashhad every other day if I ever needed to go there. We knocked and went in. The kadkhoda was performing his afternoon namaz. The tall, bearded man watched us from the corner of his eyes, while reciting verses of the Qur'an under his lips.

We took off our shoes and left them at the door. It felt very uncomfortable to sit on the bumpy ground with flimsy carpets; it reminded me of our floor when I was growing up. A small smile crept into the corners of my mouth with these memories of home, while waiting for the kadkhoda to finish his prayer. I looked around; his place was simple, just like Hussein's. The bedding was organized in one corner, pots and pans in another; there was a portable kerosene heater to cook and warm up the place. A little hole in the wall brought in some light.

When the kadkhoda had finished, he closed his prayer rug and joined us. Out of respect, Hussein and I stood up.

"Sit down, sit down," he said, shaking our hands.

Hussein pointed at me. "This is Mohsen, and he is stationed here for Sepah-e-tarveej. Right now, he is staying with me, but he would like to have his own place. Do you know anyone who wants to rent their place to him?"

"I don't know anyone, but I'll ask around. I will also let Mullah Yusef spread the word around in the masjid."

The kadkhoda left the room and came back with three cups of tea on a silver tray and three small slices of sweet bread, made probably by his wife; it tasted unbelievably delicious. Occasionally, I looked at Hussein to translate what the kadkhoda was asking me. I was getting used to their dialect but still had a hard time with some phrases and words.

I stayed with Hussein for a couple of days, before being approached by a man who had heard from the mullah that I was looking for a place to rent. I didn't care what it looked like; I took my bag and followed him. I was happy I could finally settle down in my own house.

The wooden door made a squeaky noise when he opened it; a musty aroma filled the dark room. He told me the rent was fifteen tomans a month and left me to myself.

I told Hussein about my new place; he helped me set things up. I was excited to be on my own and have some privacy. I bought a small oil heater and a lantern, and Hussein lent me a few things: a fold-up bed, a pot, a pan, a plate, a couple of utensils, and teacups. I was set to begin my life in this tiny village called Arask and to assist the villagers with their agricultural and livestock challenges.

Soon, all the farmers in the village knew I had come to help them with their crops. They called me Aghayeh Sepahii (Mr. Sepahii).

From my place, it took five minutes to walk to the farm where the village people had acres of cotton and Persian melons planted. In the beginning, I got lost a lot in the maze of the village and was sometimes unable to find my own place. Once, I had to be escorted by a little boy. I had been walking around in circles for what seemed like an eternity. I passed the boy four times before he spoke up: "Mr. Sepahii, are you lost?"

I nodded, too ashamed to say any words.

He took me through the maze back to my home. It was embarrassing for a grown man who was a soldier to be escorted by a little boy back to his own place.

As the months passed, I began to feel I wasn't making a difference. The farmers did their own thing and seemed to know the crops better than I did. I was so excited when one of the farmers knocked at my door to ask for help. He took me to where they had planted the melons to explain the problem.

"Mr. Sepahii, do you see these white spots on the stem?" he asked, pointing at Persian melon crops as he continued. "Well, we don't know what we are doing to cause this. Can you do something to save these plants?"

I was happy that, somehow, I had gained enough of their trust for them to seek my knowledge. I bent down and touched the white powder. It felt dry, and I could easily smear it on my fingers. After taking some samples of the dirt and the white material, I sent it to Mr. Engineer at the Department of Agriculture in Ferdous to help me figure out what it was. Once I knew the name, I could help them treat the disease.

I took the samples to the local grocery store to mail to Ferdous. I waited for a couple of weeks, but there was no response. Every day, the farmers asked me, "Mr. Sepahii, any news?"

I felt bad because I knew the farmers needed to resolve the problem soon before they lost all their crops. I decided to investigate it myself and come up with a solution. I could no longer wait. I examined how the farmers watered their plants and noticed that a lot of water went onto the stems and the leaves. They got wet and stayed wet for some time, causing mildew to grow. I helped the framers change their watering system so the water went directly to the roots and no longer splashed on any other part of the melons.

Some weeks later, one of the farmers brought me the sweetest melon I had ever tasted as a token of appreciation. After that incident, the entire village greeted me and invited me to their houses for tea and homemade sweet bread. Their gesture made me very happy, and I felt accepted into their community. They seemed to respect me, and I felt I was finally making a difference.

Later, I found out that the Department of Agriculture had received my letter but never bothered to correspond. They didn't care what happened to the farmers' crops, which made me angry and frustrated. They only wanted to collect their paychecks and not do any work, something I could not understand. I had always made my best effort to make a good change, and I figured they should as well. I told Hussein about it.

He shook his head and said, "It's too bad. That is why the villagers don't get excited when a new Sepahii shows up. They know that nothing changes, and everything stays the same."

Days went by, and I gradually got used to the village's customs and traditions. In the early morning, I woke up, had a quick breakfast, and headed to the farm to check things out and answer any questions they had, to the best of my knowledge. I tried to help the villagers as much as I could, but I had limited resources. I didn't have access to any tools, and the transportation was awful. A bus left once every two days to Ferdous, where the Department of Agriculture was. If I left the village, I could not come back for at least two days. I had to stay in a motel or arrange to stay with another Sepahii. It was too complicated, and none of the expenses were reimbursed by the government.

There was no planning or coordination in the government either, which made things worse and upset me more. Once, I wanted to show the villagers how to use fertilizer to increase the production of their crops and help the plants stay healthy. I wrote to Mr. Engineer to send me a couple of bags of fertilizer; I didn't get them until months later, when it was too late to use.

In the fall, the Department of Agriculture in Ferdous sent a crew to vaccinate the animals. Their visit was abrupt and unannounced. They stopped by my house and said, "Mohsen, let the farmers know we are here to inoculate their animals."

I scratched my head and angrily said, "Most of them have taken their sheep to the fields to graze, and I'm not sure when they're coming back. Why don't you give us notice? That way I can let the mullahs inform the farmers of your arrival when they attend mosque for their daily prayers." I didn't have to tell them that; they knew the routine of the villagers. They didn't care about anything except their own pocketbooks. Every time these men left Ferdous to go to the villages, they received three or four times their wages as a bonus.

To make matters worse, some farmers performed an *estekhareh* (a way of consulting the Qur'an) to find out if God wanted them to do certain things. They asked God what to do, put their forehead on the book, and opened it. On the top right side of some Qur'ans, the word *good* or *bad* was written. Based on that, people made decisions about getting married; buying a house; doing business; or in this case, vaccinating their animals for various diseases.

One time, a farmer came to me and said, "Mr. Sepahii, I asked God if I should vaccinate my herd of sheep, opened the Holy Book, and it said, 'bad,' so I am not going to do it."

I was devastated. What God doesn't want His creatures to have a healthy life? I could not do anything; those were the man's animals, and it was his decision.

A few days later, the same man knocked at my door, crying, "Mr. Sepahii, all of my sheep are dead. They were fine last night."

I really wished that I had the heart to tell him, "Go and talk to your God about misinforming you." I held my tongue, though, after seeing him so badly hurt.

While serving at that village, I realized this entire program was messed up; everyone was looking after their own pocketbook and trying to work as little as possible. I thought about writing to someone to tell them how corrupt everything was, but I knew it would not get anywhere.

Someone would probably destroy my letter before delivering it to a higher-up.

At night, due to no electricity and no other means of entertainment, the villagers got together at each other's houses to have tea and homemade sweets. They referred to these gatherings as *cheraghanii* (celebrations of light). Sometimes, they invited me to join them. We had a fantastic time together; we told jokes, recited poems of famous poets by heart, and someone sang local songs while others clapped.

Some nights, the moon brightened the entire village, as if it were daytime. Other nights, the clear sky looked amazingly glorious; there were so many bright and shining stars twinkling like diamonds glued onto black velvet. It was, perhaps, the most beautiful thing I had ever seen, up to that moment. The stars were so close that I sometimes thought I could reach out and grab them. On a few very special nights, there were meteor showers. On those nights, I found a place to sit on the ground and watched the heavenly show as long as it lasted. It was magnificent to behold . . . I often wish to see such nights again.

On Thursday nights, the day before the Iranian weekend, a few of the other soldiers in Sepahii who were stationed in nearby villages visited me. They used to hide bottles of vodka in their bags. I didn't drink, but I watched them ingest more and more until they passed out.

I never figured out what was so much fun about consuming so much alcohol. They were so drunk that they didn't know where they were or what they were doing. I made them throw away all the bottles from my house before my helper, Abbas, showed up. It was against Islam to drink, and I didn't want to leave a bad impression with the villagers.

Abbas was a fourteen-year-old boy who helped me with daily household chores. He washed dishes, brought me water from the well, and cleaned my clothes for a small wage. He showed up at my door one day and asked if I needed an assistant. "Please, Mr. Sepahii, I will do everything for you for only one toman." He told me he was looking for a way to make money to help his family.

One day I asked Abbas to bring me my chemistry book from pile of books I had on the floor. I tried to study for concor exam whenever I had time. "Mr. Sepahii which one is it?" I looked at him puzzled and said,

"The one which says chemistry on the cover." He told me that he couldn't read or write.

I felt bad that such a smart guy could not have any education. I asked my friend Hussein to lend me a few books so I could teach Abbas. Over time, he learned to read like an elementary student, which made me happy.

I think his mother, Nargis Khanoom, appreciated what I had done for her son. Sometimes she gave him food to bring to me. Everything she made was as delicious as my mother's cooking. Occasionally, I ran into her, either when I was going to the farm or coming back from it. We just nodded and acknowledged each other's presence. For a woman who had four children, she was very thin. Every time she saw me, she rearranged her chador to offer me a glance of her face. I never thought much of that gesture, especially since I honestly was not into married women.

Sometimes her husband invited me to their house for tea and *kolocheh* (sweet bread). He was much older than she was and always frowned and complained about different things. "This tea is too cold, get me another one. Why do the kids make so much noise? Bring Mr. Sepahii some sweets."

I was surprised that she obeyed him all the time with no fuss. "Yes, Agha, yes, Agha."

Some days, I ran into Hussein, and we chatted at his door about this and that or the challenges we had encountered that day.

The young girls in their late teens who passed by flirted with us with their eyes or the way they greeted us. "Oh, Salam, Mr. Sepahii," they said, giggling.

Hussein and I looked at each other and smiled. "She likes you, Mohsen. Why don't you see her dad to ask for her hand in marriage?"

"Are you kidding? I'm not ready to get married, and my mom would kill me if I brought home a girl. Education takes priority."

We both laughed and continued with our discussion.

One late afternoon, Nargis Khanoom and Abbas brought me a plate of rice topped with saffron and meat. "Mohsen Agha, I made this for you. I hope you like it." She placed the food on the floor. Then she turned to her son and said, "Abbas, go home. I have to talk to Mr. Sepahii."

I was surprised to hear that; it was very unusual for a female to be alone with a male, especially in a small, religious village. What did she want to tell me? Maybe she wanted to ask me about her son's work and if I was happy with him. Maybe she wanted to thank me for teaching him to read and write. While I was engrossed in my thoughts, I noticed that she had removed her chador, exposing her black wavy hair. Immediately after that, she took off her clothes, dropping everything on the floor, an action I had not seen coming.

I was shocked and speechless. My eyes bulged out, my face felt hot, and my heart started pounding. I looked at her naked body, flat stomach, plump breasts, dark nipples, and hairy private parts. I had never seen a naked woman in person. I think I honestly felt a little afraid. I had no idea what caused her to do such a thing.

I sat there and looked at her looking at me. She was probably waiting for me to make a move, but I was frozen. I don't remember how long she waited, before she bent down to put her clothes back on, one by one. Finally, she put her chador on and left without saying anything. I probably had disappointed her by not touching her and making her feel desirable.

I was confused and numb. I could not figure out what had made her decide to do this. *Did she think that city men do these kinds of things all the time? Was she in love with me? Did she think I was in love with her? Did I say or do anything to promote this behavior?*

After she banged the door shut on her way out, I came back to my senses and decided not to make a big deal out of what had happened. I ate the delicious food Nargis Khanoom had brought. I noticed that the portion was larger than what she usually gave me. She probably expected to eat it with me afterward.

The following day, I ran into Hussein, I told him about the incident. "You know Nargis Khanoom, Abbas's mother? She came to my house and got naked," I said laughing out loud.

Hussein looked at me baffled. "What do you mean?"

"She took off her clothes in front of me. I have a hard time believing it myself, but I know it happened."

"So, did you do it?"

"I didn't know what to do or how to do it."

"You are so naive. She has four children; she knows what to do. You should have left it up to her. You should have told her you don't know what to do." Hussein continued, "Next time, you let her do all the work."

"I hope there is no next time, because she doesn't excite me. I really don't want to be with a woman who has a husband and children."

Nargis Khanoom and I pretended that nothing had happened between us when her husband invited me for tea and sweets to their house. I knew I had done the right thing by not taking advantage of that situation.

Life went on in Arask, and I made a lot of friends there. The farmers liked me and knew I wanted to help them, although in most cases, they knew how to fix their own challenges. A month before my duty was completed, I received a letter from the army to report to the Mashhad office to obtain my completion card. That letter released a giant sigh of relief from me. I was so close to being back in Tehran.

A couple of days before my departure, I said my farewell to all the farmers and their families. Some farmers gave me sweet bread to take to Tehran to share with my family. I wished Abbas and his parents my best.

Abbas brought me a small carpet. "Mr. Sepahii, my mom made it herself and wants you to have it," he said, as he handed it to me. The design was exceptionally beautiful—a woman pouring tea into a cup.

I thanked Hussein for being a great friend and for always keeping me in good spirits. We shook hands and hugged. I never saw him again.

The next day, I walked to the bus station to report to the office to receive the documents that showed I had completed my two-year mandatory army service. On the bus, I placed my head on the back of my seat and looked out the window to see farmers using primitive tools to grow their crops and livestock. I felt sorry that the people working in the government didn't care for these farmers.

I closed my eyes and readied myself for the next chapter in my life; I was certain that it would be the greatest and most exciting yet.

GOING TO AMERICA

AGE TWENTY-THREE

One time, my grandmother told me that our destiny is written on our foreheads and God has plans for us to meet certain people in life. I wondered if God wanted me to meet people who lived far away from my home . . . and if so, where?

About a month after I completed my mandatory service, I took the college entrance test, and so did my younger sister, Motty. This was Motty's second time taking the test. I am sure she was more prepared than I was. Every time I visited home from Arask, she was studying till four in the morning without taking a break. Sometimes she skipped her meals and wouldn't bathe for months. I used to tease her about her body odor.

She just rolled her eyes and continued with her studies, determined to pass the exam to get into medical school.

On the day of the test, Motty and I left the house together around seven o'clock in the morning. Momman made us go under the Qur'an for good luck. "I wish you both best of luck and hope you pass the exam with the highest marks," she said, holding up the Holy Book.

I don't know about Motty, but I was nervous. I was not at all sure what I would do if I didn't pass the test this time.

When we reached Tehran University, everyone was waiting for the doors to open. Some of the students were reviewing their notes, which made me more worried. I had gone over my notes and books only when I had a chance, maybe two or three hours a day in the village. All subjects—math, physics, chemistry, literature, and natural science—were hard for me. It had already been two years since I received my high school diploma. Except for math, I had forgotten everything I had learned.

The moderators started the exam at exactly eight in the morning. "Open the booklets in front of you and start your test."

I nervously answered the multiple-choice questions; I worked fast and didn't waste too much time analyzing them. I marked the box and moved on to the next one. I knew the answers to some but guessed most of them.

After three hours, the examiners made us put down our pencils and said, "Stop, stop. The test is over. Close your booklet and put it on the right-hand side for one of us to pick up."

I hurriedly marked two or three boxes randomly, before following their instructions. I looked around the room, trying to figure out what everyone thought of the test. Some had a big smile, some looked sad, and others were relieved that the test was over. I knew I had not done well. Like the previous times, I had guessed many of the answers.

Outside, I stood at a corner, waiting for Motty. She looked stressed and pale when she joined me.

"I could not find my seat, and when I did, the test had already begun. I started ten minutes late," she said, crying.

I felt bad for her and tried to calm her down. "It's okay. I am sure you'll get into a good school. If not in Tehran, another school nearby."

She looked at me and said, "Do you think? I didn't get a chance to answer two or three pages."

I nodded to reassure her.

About a month passed, and the day that would determine my destiny arrived. I was worried all day long; it would be a miracle if my name were listed on the paper. Aghajoon came home with the Kayhan newspaper, all excited, probably thinking both of his kids had passed the exam. "Here, Mohsen." He handed it to me, and I took it from him nervously. I was afraid my past would repeat itself.

Again, on the front page, there was a picture of a nerdy-looking guy with his name printed underneath. The guy received a perfect score. I smiled and mumbled, "Another goofy-looking guy. How come the smart ones look different from the rest of us?"

There were smaller pictures of other kids, probably who made it to the second or third rank, but I was not interested in them. I wanted to find out if our names were there. I went to the room where Motty was.

She gave me an anxious look and said, "Oh, God, let us be here."

I spread the paper on the floor and opened it to the page where the names were announced in alphabetical order. The two of us hunched over the paper and looked under the letter F.

Motty screamed, "There is my name, I am accepted at Ferdousii University, the same school Etty is going to!!" She was laughing and screaming, "I got in. I got—" Then suddenly she became quiet as she realized my name was not there.

Concerned, she looked at me. I was sad and disappointed, for I had failed the exam once again, but I tried not to show it. I smiled at Motty and said, "I told you, you shouldn't be worried. I knew you would get into a good school."

By now, everyone in the family knew my sister had passed the test, and I didn't. Etty was a freshman at Ferdousii University. My parents were happy that both their daughters would be going to the same college and keeping each other company.

Momman saw me sitting in a corner, hopeless. She joined me and said, "Don't worry. We'll figure something out for you."

I smiled. I didn't know what other options I had. I wanted to get into a college, but what else was there besides retaking the test, and what if I never was able to pass it? I was never good at multiple-choice tests. I preferred essay-type exams, where you answer the question to the best of your knowledge. No playing with the words; a slight modification would make the answer right or wrong.

In the evening, Aghajoon brought some pastry to celebrate my sister's admittance into a good school. She deserved it; she worked extremely hard for it.

The next day, in the evening, I joined Momman in her classroom. "Mohsen, what do you want to do?" she asked me, threading a needle.

"What if I don't pass the test ever? Plus, I have to wait one more year to take it."

"I know, it's too bad they don't offer it more than once a year . . . Well, you can't stop at your high school diploma. You have to continue and get into a college."

"I know," I said, aggravated.

Momman looked at her distraught son, while tying a knot at the end of the thread and getting ready to hem a pair of black pants. She stopped, looked at me, and blurted out, "How about you go abroad? Find out where you can go!"

I don't know how the word *abroad* came to her mind. None of our relatives had gone outside of Iran to study. I looked at Momman in disbelief. We were not rich. There were seven kids in my family, two daughters already in college with their own expenses, tuition, room, and board. I thought, *How can I go anywhere outside of Iran? The cost is horrendous for airfare, college fees, and living expenses.*

I laughed and could not believe what I heard. I questioned, "*Abroad*? Like where?"

"I don't know. Research it. We won't know until you get the facts and the requirements."

For the next two days, Momman kept asking me if I had found any information. By then, I knew she was serious about her suggestion, and I started checking into my options. Some of my friends had applied to colleges in India, and I thought that could be one of my choices too.

I told Momman about my idea. "Remember Kareem? I found out he is going to India to attend a college there. The tuition is not high, and because the country is near Iran, the airfare is not expensive."

Momman shook her head in disagreement and said, "India, why India? I've heard it's a very poor country and people die of many diseases. Find a better country. How about America? One of Aghajoon's customer's sons went there and really likes it. The schools are exceptionally good, and you'll learn a lot."

America, to most Iranians, was a fantasy land, a place out of reach—beautiful, organized, powerful, prominent, and influential. The majority of people wanted to go there, either to study or visit.

"*America*?!" I laughed. "It is awfully expensive to go there. Every dollar is at least seven times our currency. That means one hundred tomans is only about fourteen dollars. We can't afford it. I'm not your only child. Etty is a college student and Motty will be joining her in a couple of months. You also have four other kids."

"Okay, okay. At least look into it. Don't be concerned about the money, let us worry about that."

I thought Momman was a big dreamer; going to America was out of the question. I knew education was important to her. She had made it known to her children.

I remembered a story she told me one day while I was helping her in the classroom. I was fifteen or sixteen years old, and I was ironing one of her client's outfits. We were chatting about different topics, and I don't know why Momman started talking about her childhood. She said she wanted to become a lawyer.

"Mohsen, I was the only one in my household who loved going to school, and I never missed a day. Nobody else was as dedicated. Your uncle went to night school when he was forty years old because he needed to be able to read contracts and add and subtract in the new business he had established."

I looked up, puzzled. *Had my uncle not been able to go to school until later in life?* He was my favorite male relative and highly intelligent.

"Yes, back then, nobody was interested in studying. People sent their boys to work to bring in money and help the family financially. The girls got married at the age of twelve or thirteen, as soon as they had a prosperous suitor, regardless of his age. Your aunt was only twelve years old when she married twenty-five-year-old Mirza Agha."

Every time I heard his name, it reminded me of the summer I worked for him at his uniform factory. He never paid my wages. I wondered how he felt ripping off a young boy. I didn't care for that man at all.

"When Aghajoon came to ask for my hand, I told my mother I would like to continue my studies and go to college. She looked at me and said that by the time I finish school, I would be an old woman. Is twenty-one old? I don't know."

I could tell Momman was broken-hearted for not being allowed to continue her studies and wanted to give her children what she was deprived of—a higher education.

Her voice brought me back to the room. "Let me know what the requirements are for attending a school in America."

I knew there was no way out of this. Once Momman decided on something, it had to be done. I went to the Office of Education to find out what I needed to do, although I knew financially it was impossible for me to leave for America. I was inquiring about it only because of Momman.

Later, at home, I gave her a full report. "I found out that I need a statement from the bank showing twelve thousand dollars in my parents' account. Apparently, many Iranian students who went to America didn't have enough money, so they ended up becoming beggars or homeless. This fund would be proof I have sufficient money for at least a year."

I thought as soon as Momman heard this requirement, she would want me to look at less expensive countries, maybe even India. I was shocked when she said, "That's not a problem, Mohsen, apply as soon as you can."

I didn't know where the money was coming from, but I did what Momman asked me to do, with the hope that I would attend a college somewhere. The next day, I took copies of my translated high school transcript and went back to the Office of Education to get information about American schools. They had many catalogs with lists of American colleges and universities. Each column had the name; location of the school; tuition; and other prerequisites, such as grade-point average or whether TOEFL (Test of English as a Foreign Language) was needed.

I made a list of four or five colleges with the least expensive nonresidential tuition and with conditions I could meet. With the help of one of the employees there, Mr. Ziaii, I filled out application forms for West Virginia Institute of Technology in Montgomery; Marshall University in Huntington, Ohio; and a couple of other schools. We mailed the forms, along with a copy of my grades. I waited for their replies.

I still could not believe I was applying for colleges in America. The places I had chosen required a six-month preparatory English as a second language (ESL) class. Mr. Ziaii recommended an institute in West Baden, Indiana. "Many Iranians go there; you won't feel homesick, and they can help you," he said.

I applied there too. A month passed. Every time the postman knocked at our door, my heart sank. I was anxiously waiting for a reply from any of those colleges.

One afternoon, in the late summer, I was fixing one of Momman's sewing machines when she came into the room, holding an envelope in her hand. I got excited and left everything.

"Mohsen, I think this came from America. It has foreign words written all over it." She handed it to me.

I could not believe it; I didn't think any of the schools would respond. I opened the envelope and started reading. I looked up, smiling; it was an acceptance letter from West Virginia Institute of Technology in Montgomery, West Virginia. I had gotten into their electrical engineering program. A multi-page I-20 form was included.

"So, what does it say?" Momman asked.

I told her that I got in and had to take the I-20 form with me to the American consulate to apply for my student visa.

I went to Aghajoon's shop and shared with him the great news. Later, he came home with a box of pastries.

Etty was coming home later in the week to spend time with us and help Motty prepare to go to Mashhad with her. They had decided to become roommates. I still couldn't believe it: I was going to receive my engineering degree from an American school! It was surreal.

In a couple of weeks, I got my passport. The process was simple, especially since I had completed the two-year mandatory army services. During all this, my ESL school acceptance letter arrived too. Everything was falling into place. The only thing I needed was a statement from the bank for twelve thousand dollars.

One afternoon, when I came home, I walked into the room while Momman was talking on the phone with her brother. She waved her hand for me to sit down. "I need the money to send Mohsen to America. Yes, Duhduhsh," she paused for a moment and then continued, "We applied for a loan from Saderat Bank. I will pay you back as soon as we receive it."

I had conflicting feelings about going to America—happy that I would finally get my higher education and sad because my parents had to go into debt to send me there. Every time I brought up the subject of funds—and lack of it—Momman didn't want to hear it.

My uncle continued to question Momman about her decision to send me to America. She kept saying, "Duhduhsh, I am sure we want to do this. If you don't want to lend me the money, just say so. I will get it elsewhere."

At the end, it seemed he had agreed to give her the money, because Momman was thanking him and said, "Put the cash in an envelope. Mohsen will come to pick it up tomorrow morning." She thanked him once more before hanging up the phone.

With the money I had saved up from my Sepahii time, my parent's savings, and my uncle's loan, we were able to put about twelve thousand dollars in the bank under my name; it was equivalent to eighty-four thousand tomans. That was a large amount of money for my parents. Their monthly income was about one thousand tomans—about one hundred fifty American dollars.

After gathering all my documents—the I-20, passport, bank statement, translated high school transcript, and acceptance letter from the ESL school—I went to the American embassy on Takhteh Jamsheed Street.

I received a number from a man at the door and waited for somebody to call it. I was nervous and had no idea what to expect.

An Iranian man called my number: "77."

I straightened up my gray suit and blue tie and walked up to his window. A middle-aged African American man was standing next to him and carefully listening to our conversation. I think he understood Farsi.

I handed my documents to the Iranian man.

"Why are you going to West Virginia?" he asked, reading the letter of acceptance.

"I am going there to study electrical engineering."

"Do you belong to any organizational group here?"

"No."

"Are you planning to join any organizational group when you go to America?"

"No."

The man looked at me from behind his glasses, checking me out. Probably he wanted to figure out what type of person I was—troublemaker, studious, etc. He handed my documents to the Black man, who put a stamp on my passport and returned my documents to me. "Good luck in America," he said in English.

"Thank you," I replied in English. I smiled and could not believe that the process of getting a visa was so simple. I was going to America, the land all Iranians dream of. The land of opportunities, the land where John Wayne was from, the land where all the people were beautiful, with big blue eyes and blond hair. The land where everyone had movie-star figures, slim and tall. The land where people were kind, and everything was organized and orderly. The land where food was plentiful, and there were no hungry people on the streets. The land where everyone was rich, and money was everywhere. That is at least what we Iranians imagined America would be like.

On the way home, I kept opening my passport to check the student visa stamp on it and make sure I was not dreaming.

Everyone at home was happy to hear the great news, especially Momman. Her eyes were shining, probably because she didn't have to worry about her son not going to college. With Etty back at home, we spent a lot of time together. They were planning to go to Mashhad soon; the new semester would start shortly. I was planning to leave two days after they left, as I had to go to West Badan first to attend the ESL school, and after completing it, move to Montgomery.

I was really scared and nervous about going abroad. I was only twenty-three years old, and the only time I had left Tehran was when I went to Arask. It was far, but I was still in Iran. I thought, *God, how am I going to survive in a country where I don't know anyone, and people speak a different language? What if I get lost or am confused and don't take the correct connecting flight?* I had never traveled by plane.

I was beginning to have a change of heart; I no longer was eager to go. The day Etty and Motty left was a sad day for me. I accompanied them to the train station. On the way, they were talking mostly about their school. I tried to look calm on the outside; on the inside, I was like a volcano ready to burst into tears. When they got on the train, we hugged and kissed each other. I had no idea when I would see them again, since I would be going to the USA. All three of us started crying and hugged once more. I loved them very much, especially Etty. We were very close. She truly was my buddy, and we went through so much together in life.

The atmosphere of our house began to be sad; everyone was quiet, and Momman cried a lot. It was like the time I was going to bootcamp, with the same uncertainty and same fears. I cried unnoticeably every time I remembered I would be leaving my family soon. I packed my bags, putting in the things I bought from the bazaar: dental hygiene supplies, soap, socks, underwear, shirts, and pants. We thought it would be less expensive to get things in Iran, plus I would not be familiar with how things were in America and where to shop. This way, my parents would be more relaxed knowing I had the things I needed with me.

The night before my departure, I said goodbye to my uncles, aunts, Madarjoon, the neighbors, and all the shops around Aghajoon's shop. Everyone cried and asked me to write them a letter as soon as I got settled. I could not believe I was going away, and I didn't know when I would see them again.

My flight was at seven in the morning. Momman set the alarm for four, giving me ample time to get ready. At night, I looked around the room, wondering when I would be able to return home. While I was wiping my tears, I prayed to God that the alarm would not go off, so I would miss my flight. With that hope, my eyes got heavy, and I fell asleep.

"Mohsen, Mohsen, wake up wake, up. You have to get ready to go."

I had knots in my stomach and my heart was heavy. I was angry at God for not answering my prayer and letting the alarm go off. I had no choice but to prepare to leave my family, my neighborhood, and my country. I had asked Momman not to wake anyone up, because I didn't have the guts to say goodbye. But they woke up anyway from the noise Aghajoon and I made going up and down the stairs, carrying my two suitcases to the front door.

I hugged and kissed my sleepy younger sisters and brother one by one. "Study hard and take care of yourself" I said, trying not to shed any tears. I hated saying farewell to my family. My heart sank and my stomach felt queasy. Saying goodbye to Momman was the most difficult; she was my mom, but I felt we had grown up together. After all, our age difference was only seventeen years. She was my confidante, my rock, and everything else a child would want in life.

"Momman, I will write as soon as I get there." My voice was trembling. I tried to be calm and show that I was okay, but it was the saddest day of my life, sadder than losing Banu or losing Majeed.

Momman asked me to go under the Holy Book, and she prayed to God to protect me.

We took a taxi to the airport. Aghajoon accompanied me. I looked out the window and tried to remember the streets that carried all my childhood memories, such as the days I thought of something to make and hopped on a bus with Akbar to buy the material for it—developing pictures, building an incubator, and making a rifle. I reminisced about my early years, even though they were times of hardship, hunger, many tears, and sadness.

At the airport, Aghajoon and I hugged each other.

"Mohsen, take care of yourself. Write us as soon as you get there. Focus on your studies," he said.

I only nodded in agreement for fear I might start crying if I spoke. I headed toward the plane worried, sad, and nervous. I stepped on the first stair. I looked back and waved goodbye to Aghajoon.

Who would've imagined the poor, hungry boy with torn clothes and cracked hands would one day go to America to attend college and become successful?

ABOUT MOHSEN FASHANDI

 Mohsen obtained his electrical engineering degree from West Virginia Tech and worked as a manufacturing supervisor in various US companies for many years. Shortly after he came to the United States, his first sister, Etty, joined him and earned her doctorate degree in biochemistry and nutrition.

Mohsen and Etty encouraged our parents to send all their children abroad for higher education. That is exactly what Momman and Aghajoon did. By the end of 1978, six out of their seven children had come to the United States. Motty, Mohsen's second sister, never came to America. She obtained her doctorate degree in pharmacy and started her business and family in Iran. Mohsen never saw Motty again after he left Iran, only had phone conversations with her. Mohsen's parents moved to the United States and became citizens. Momman passed away at the age of eighty-seven. Currently, Aghajoon is ninety-six. We lost Etty to cancer when she was fifty-nine. Mohsen suffered from the loss of Etty, who was not only his first sister but also his buddy throughout childhood. They experienced a lot of hardship together.

Nobar Khanoom, the midwife, guessed correctly: Momman gave birth to eight children. Majeed passed away when he was nine months old.

Sara Fashandi, the author of this book, was born after Majeed, making her the sixth child in the family.

Mohsen retired from working in the corporate sector and began investing in real estate. Currently, he manages his properties. Mohsen is married, with two beautiful children and a lovely granddaughter. He lives in Chicago.

ACKNOWLEDGMENTS

Thank you to my brother, Mohsen, who trusted me with writing his stories. I had to contact him a million times to clarify the technical details of some of his projects—with him assuming everyone knows about electricity and how it works. Fourteen years in writing this book was worth every minute, as those moments spent over the phone and in person brought us much closer and made us bond even more.

Thank you to my sister Farah, who motived Mohsen and me to re-polish these stories during the Covid pandemic.

Thank you to my sister Minoo for helping me with the dates these events took place. I don't know how you remember them from so many years ago, but I'm grateful for your intact memory.

Thank you to my brother Saeed, who lent me the key to his home, so I could have a nice place to escape to for some quiet time and to be able to focus on polishing the stories.

Thank you to the Saturday Memoir classes and all the great feedback and comments provided about the stories by Dr. Linda Joy Myers, Dr. Jacqueline Doyle, Kara Levine, Lilah Fox, Jerry Alexander, Maura Sutter, Dr. Etty Fashandi, and Dr. Azadeh Tabazadeh.

Thank you to Momman and Aghajoon and all my six siblings, whom I adore and love. You all helped me be the person I am today.

Thank you to my niece, Michelle Fashandi, my nephews, Armon Jalali and Alex Fashandi, who read the stories and provided feedback

Thank you to Ed Levy, who edited the manuscript. I could not have done this without you.

Thank you to Jude Berman, who copyedited the manuscript. I am grateful to you.

Thank you to my son for your support during this journey.

And finally, thank you, God, for placing these great people in my path to experience life in such beautiful and meaningful ways.

CPSIA information can be obtained
at www.ICGtesting.com
Printed in the USA
BVHW092026260722
643032BV00012B/359

9 781737 581468